MECHANICS-
MERCANTILE
LIBRARY.
Arthur F Mathews '06

HOW THE GOVERNMENT GOT IN YOUR BACKYARD

HOW THE GOVERNMENT GOT IN YOUR BACKYARD

Superweeds, Frankenfoods, Lawn Wars, and the (Nonpartisan) Truth About Environmental Policies

JEFF GILLMAN ☆ ERIC HEBERLIG

Timber Press
Portland ☆ London

Published in 2011 by Timber Press, Inc.

The Haseltine Building
133 S.W. Second Avenue, Suite 450
Portland, Oregon 97204-3527
www.timberpress.com

2 The Quadrant
135 Salusbury Road
London NW6 6RJ
www.timberpress.co.uk

Printed in The United States of America

Library of Congress Cataloging-in-Publication Data

Gillman, Jeff, 1969–
How the government got in your backyard : superweeds, frankenfoods, lawn wars, and the (nonpartisan) truth about environmental policies / Jeff Gillman and Eric Heberlig. — 1st ed.
p. cm.
Includes bibliographical references and index.
ISBN 978-1-60469-001-9
1. Environmental policy—Political aspects—United States. 2. Agriculture and state—United States. 3. Agriculture and politics—United States. 4. Science and state—United States. I. Heberlig, Eric S., 1970– II. Title.
GE180.G54 2011
363.7'05610973—dc22

2010028452

A catalog record for this book is also available from the British Library.

For Suzanne,
Catherine, and Clare
—Jeff

★★★

For Tracy, Colin,
Mena, and Ellie
—Eric

★★★

Contents

Acknowledgments 9

Introduction 11

1: Science, Political Science, and the Science of Politics 20

2: Organic Food: Safer, Friendlier, Better? 34

3: Pesticides: How Dangerous Is Dangerous? 56

4: Fertilizers: Good for the Crops, Bad for the Water? 81

5: Alternative Energy: Is Ethanol Overrated? 98

6: Genetic Engineering: A Time Bomb Waiting to Explode? 114

7: Plant Patents: Protecting Plants or Profiteering? 134

8: Invasive Plants: Kill the Aliens? 150

9: Legal and Illegal Plants: Why Are the Bad Guys Bad? 169

10: Local Restrictions: Is Your Backyard Really Yours? 184

11: Global Warming: Natural or Man-made? 196

12: Conclusions: Balancing Nature and Politics 217

Notes 220

Bibliography 228

Index 245

***

Acknowledgments

WRITING A BOOK takes a lot of effort, even when the work is split between two authors. First we would like to thank our families for allowing us the time to work on this project. Evenings and weekends were all too frequently divided between them and chapter revisions. We need to thank Jay Schaefer for taking this book apart and helping us rebuild it into something better, and Peggy Flanagan for catching errors and cleaning the text up so that it reads smoothly. We would also like to thank the fine people at Timber Press for taking a chance on a book that's a little bit different from what they're used to, particularly Juree Sondker and Neal Maillet. Jeff is indebted, as always, to Chad Giblin for helping run things while he was busy writing, and also to Eric Watkins, Tom Michaels, Gary Johnson, Alan Smith, and especially Esther McGinnis for their insights into various bits of science used for this book. Eric relied upon Chase Woodall for research assistance.

★★★

Introduction

IN A CORNER of Atlanta, a factory quietly relieves itself. Columns of gray smoke billow from its overfull belly, creating the only mark in an otherwise clear blue sky. The population below accepts the factory as a necessary evil. Some people even like the factory, thankful that it provides so many jobs. Some just ignore it. But there is more to the smokestack than meets the eye.

At the top of the tower sits a small box. Invisible to anyone below, the box constantly monitors the tower, day and night, rain or shine. This box tells the people in the factory what comes out of the tower. This box costs a great deal of money to install. It costs a great deal of money to monitor. It will cost a great deal to replace when it breaks, and it will, eventually, break.

The people who run this factory don't want this box in their tower. It slows them down, catches their mistakes, impedes their progress, and costs them time and money. But most of us outside of the factory are happy that the box is there. We like to know that the factory keeps tabs on the waste that exits the tower—waste that could cause acid rain and global warming, potentially devastating our environment and ruining our health. We like to know that if something is wrong the factory will shut down. We like to think that this makes our lives better. But does it?

In Iowa, stalks of corn grow tall in a field that stretches as far as the eye can see. A farmer sighs and smiles, happy that his plants are strong and prices are good. He didn't have to spray for insects at all this year, thanks to the seed he planted, which contained new genes that scientists have introduced into the corn, and for which the farmer paid extra money. The fact that he used this corn also means that he won't be able to save any seed from the corn he grew this year to replant next year. He is confident that having the cure to what were once devastating insect problems is worth it. But is this farmer's cure worse than the problem it solves?

In a suburb of Charlotte, North Carolina, a young mother walks into a supermarket intent on purchasing some vegetables for dinner. Her eyes scan to the right and to the left while she picks up a bag to hold the tomatoes she has selected. And then she stops and puts them back. There, just down the aisle, is a bin labeled USDA Organic. She goes over and selects some fine-looking produce, happy that she has avoided exposing her children to carcinogenic pesticides. But has she?

In a Philadelphia suburb, a man enters a nice two-story home and closes the door tightly behind him. He greets his wife, takes out the garbage, and checks the messages on his answering machine. Hearing nothing of consequence, he continues his evening ritual. Entering the basement, he is enveloped by a bright light emanating from a far corner. Walking down the steps he notes how splendidly his crop is growing. There is a constant hum as water and nutrients are pumped into and out of horizontally oriented tubs set against a far wall. Hanging from the ceiling above the tubs is a row of high-intensity lights providing the energy for the crop whose roots dwell in a nutrient solution while its leaves reach for this artificial sun. Only a weed could prosper so well on this herbal equivalent of life support; and weed is exactly what's growing here, forced into this dungeon because the outside world doesn't want it around. But is the world singling out this plant unfairly?

For almost 250 years, our government has been involved in making laws that govern the way we live. These laws are intended to make our lives better, our society richer, and our planet safer. Many of these laws are consistent with common sense: don't kill anybody and don't take property that doesn't belong to you. But some are a little kooky: in Pennsylvania it's illegal to sing in the bathtub, and in New Hampshire you can't sell the clothes you're currently wearing to pay off a gambling debt. With some laws it's immediately obvious that they will have a positive impact, but with others it takes years to discover what their impact will be. Indeed, even after a law's consequences have been realized some people may still argue whether the law had a negative or a positive effect on our society (do Pennsylvanians benefit or suffer from their lack of bathtub singing?). Governmental policies that deal with our environment almost invariably fall into the latter category. It is the government that requires towers to have apparatus for measuring emissions. It is the government that certifies food as organic. It is the government that restricts the growth and sale of genetically modified plants. And it is the government that restricts growing certain plants at all. Are these policies helpful or harmful to our society and environment? There is no single answer, and that, in a nutshell, is what this book is about.

As the government conducts its business, righting our environmental wrongs and helping the economy in the process, something is often lost in the mix: how all these changes affect us, the citizens. This is a shame, because when it comes right down to it, it's our backyards, lawns, gardens, and even dinners that are at the center of the environmental debate. Something as obscure as how plant patent laws are written and interpreted can affect whether you're eating genetically modified corn tonight. If the government restricts pesticide use, it's going to be your backyard that is covered with dandelions. If you live in a neighborhood with restrictions on what constitutes an acceptable lawn, you could go to jail for letting yours die. There is no escaping governmental control. If we don't appreciate and understand where this control comes from, then we're not going to be able to do anything about it.

Discussing Politics

They say that there are two things you should never discuss: one is religion, and the other is politics. We beg to differ. We have made our livings as a political scientist and a plant scientist, and these are the realms where we are most comfortable. And within these realms we see misunderstanding and paranoia drive governmental policy toward our environment. This is wrong. Policy needs to be driven by something stronger: facts, and consideration for all sides involved, not just the self-interest of an individual, a company, or even an environmental group.

A person's politics are, fundamentally, their opinions and thoughts about governmental policy. It is not only appropriate, but also necessary for us to enter into discussions about politics to understand the reasons why policy is made and how policy can affect us and the world around us. So many books are written that promote a political agenda without appreciating the arguments from the other side. This is not one of them. If you like your opinions and don't think that appreciating the other side of an argument is important, then we encourage you to put this book down right now, because it wasn't written for you. This is a book for uniters, not dividers. It's for those of you who want to understand the other side of the argument even though you may not be able to agree with it.

Your political leanings are driven by your values. If you value "naturally grown" foods, then you may cheer when a judge stops the use of alfalfa that is genetically modified so that it can't be killed by the herbicide Roundup. On the other hand, if you are a farmer who grows alfalfa, then you probably value higher yields and lower costs of production, so you may well find yourself on the other side of this argument. Likewise, if you value food that hasn't been treated with synthetic pesticides, then you may have been pleased when the government passed a set of rules that dictated what may and may not be used by producers if they are going to sell food as USDA Certified Organic. But if you think that the government's rules that proclaim a food to be organic do little to promote sustainable, local production of agriculture, you would probably be less enthused about government certification. Or perhaps you don't care. The silent majority comes into play in almost all policymaking because politicians try their hardest to anticipate what will motivate this large and silent group to act (or more precisely, to vote). Most people don't know enough to care or don't care enough to know about many of the policies being made. They just go with the flow. This book is intended for people who want to make educated decisions about where they stand on the environmental policy questions that confront our government today and in the foreseeable future. Making these decisions based on facts that are, admittedly, imperfect isn't easy to do, but for citizens of a civilized society, it is a necessity.

This is a book for uniters, not dividers. It's for those of you who want to understand the other side of the argument even though you may not be able to agree with it.

Polarized Politics

Unease in talking about politics (or religion) is usually due to a person's desire to stay on good terms with friends, neighbors, co-workers, family members, or anyone else with whom the person regularly interacts. Politics is contentious and sometimes downright divisive. In fact, there's good reason to believe that discussing environmental issues has become more difficult for Americans over the past decade because environmental issues have increasingly become a source of division between the Democratic and Republican parties and thus between our associates who align themselves with a different party than we do.

Gallup public opinion polls clearly show how our environmental opinions increasingly reflect our political party affiliation. In 1998, Democrats and Republicans were equally likely to believe that global warming had already had an effect on the environment. By 2009, however, 76 percent of Democrats thought that it had, while Republicans were actually somewhat less likely to think so than they had been a decade earlier (41 percent in 2009 to 46 percent in 1998). Similarly, in 1998, Republicans were only slightly more likely than Democrats (34 percent to 23 percent, a difference of 11 points) to think that the media was exaggerating global warming; by 2009, the difference was 41 points (59 percent of Republicans to 18 percent of Democrats). Where there had once been a mix of pro-environment and pro-development voters in both parties, now pro-environment voters have largely shifted to the Democratic Party and pro-development voters have shifted toward the Republican Party.

This polarization of public opinion on environmental issues has a direct consequence for politicians. If Democratic and Republican voters are dividing sharply on environmental issues, Democratic and Republican politicians need to appeal to very different groups of voters to win nomination for office in party primaries. In Democratic Party primaries, candidates in most areas of the country certainly want to be seen as "green" and to have the endorsements of environmental groups. In Republican primaries, being "green" can be a liability, as the conservative activists and the business and development activists are quite suspicious of the claims of environmentalists and fearful of the costs that government environmental regulations impose. Given our primary system of elections, politicians will polarize in ways similar to the voters.

Back in the "good old days" of greater bipartisan cooperation on the environment, President Theodore Roosevelt, a Republican, led the charge to protect wild lands from development by creating national parks and monuments. The Environmental Protection Agency was created in 1970, during Richard Nixon's Republican administration, with a strong push from a Democratic Congress. Republican President George H. W. Bush and a Democratic Congress cooperated to pass the 1990 Clean Air Act. But cooperation between the two parties on environmental issues has ebbed dramatically. From 1970 to 1998, the voting records of Democrats were on average only 20 points more pro-environment than those of Republicans on a 100-point voting scale (100 = solidly pro-environment; 0 = pro-pollution), according to the League of Conservation Voters. From 1998 to 2005, however, the 20- point gap became a 70-point gulf. The Democrats consistently attempt to appeal to liberal "green" voters who participate in the Democratic primaries, while the Republicans consistently attempt to appeal to conservative, pro-development voters who vote in Republican primaries.

These trends on the environment mirror a broader ideological sorting of the parties, with Democrats consistently voting liberal and Republicans consistently voting conservative. It's true that in practice the need to serve one's constituents can, and often does, trump ideological purism. Although a Democratic senator may be opposed to, say, excessive greenhouse gases as a rule, that same senator would like to minimize the economic impact of a law limiting their production on businesses in his or her state. Similarly, although a Republican senator may be infatuated with the idea of letting businesses make their own decisions about handling their toxic wastes, that same senator will aggressively seek government funding to help pay for the cleanup of a spill in their home state. Still, it's apparent that it's harder for Democrats and Republicans in Congress to cooperate in making environmental laws because they increasingly see the world very differently and are responding to very different constituencies.

Polarization on the environment is not just a matter of party politics. It's also based on the fact that the mix of environmental issues that we face has changed. Early environmental laws focused on broad goals that were highly popular—saving scenic places and cleaning the air and water—rather than the means or the costs of achieving them. Today, the problems seem much more complex. If we have difficulty understanding global climate patterns, how can we predict with confidence the ecological and economic effects of our efforts to control them? Genetically modified organisms seem pretty safe at the moment, and they reduce the use of dangerous pesticides, but will we ultimately find that they are "Frankenfoods" that damage human or ecological health? Today's environmental issues practically define the word *uncertainty*, which makes decisions hard for those who live in the political world where one wrong move can lose an election.

The result of these changes in American politics is that there are fewer environmental laws being passed by Congress. Political scientists Christopher Klyza and David Sousa (2008) report that only two out of forty-five major environmental laws were passed between 1991 and 2006: the California Desert Protection Act (1994) and the Food Quality Protection Act (1996). In contrast, twenty-three major environmental laws passed between 1964 and 1980. The other twenty laws were passed prior to 1964. Although the writers of the U.S. Constitution wanted to make it hard to pass new laws—to discourage people from using the power of government to benefit themselves at the expense of their neighbors—the way politics is practiced today takes the Founders' desire for slow motion to extreme lengths.

Rating Policies: The Left and the Right

To quantify the differences between the liberals and the conservatives, we've created a rating system. For each policy alternative we put forward, we explain which side is likely to favor or disfavor the policy and why, and then we rate their position. The more stars the policy receives (up to five), the more strongly that alternative is favored by that ideological camp:

★★★★★ **Ideal policy**
★★★★ **Highly favorable**
★★★ **It's acceptable**
★★ **Dislike it**
★ **NO**

In general, left-wing environmental policies favor strict government regulation of business. This preference is based on the assumption that businesses are only motivated by short-term profits, and will always seek to get out of their civic responsibility to keep the environment clean and its inhabitants (including us) safe if it costs them more money. Businesses cannot be trusted to act responsibly, so government must tell them what to do and how to do it, and must monitor them closely to make sure they comply. Left-wingers are more likely to adhere to the precautionary principle, which states that we should err on the side of protecting the environment even when incontrovertible cause-and-effect evidence that something damages the environment doesn't exist. They are also more willing to take economically costly actions to restrict potentially harmful practices even if it hasn't been proven that these practices cause detriment, and despite the economic effects that restricting these practices will have on our American businesses. They tend to favor regulation by the federal government based on the belief that state and local governments don't have the power or the backbone to take on their own major employers (but they'll make an exception when state regulations are tougher than federal regulations). While left-wingers favor active government intervention in the economy, they generally believe government should "butt out" of decisions regarding personal freedoms that don't affect one's neighbors. They tend to be more tolerant than right-wingers of marijuana use, for example, and less tolerant of homeowners' associations whose rules promote conformity and property values more than public health and safety.

Right-wing environmental policies tend to favor inaction, especially when it is unclear whether a particular activity causes damage. When they do favor action they tend to trust the businesses or individuals to do the right thing, believing that the same environmental goals can be achieved at less cost if the government stays out of it and allows businesses some flexibility. They prefer cooperative arrangements in which businesses decide for themselves what the most effective and economically efficient methods would be for them to meet environmental goals. Generally, right-wingers prefer state and local government action to federal government action, but they are willing to accept national standards if they are less costly to business than trying to meet the differing requirements imposed by fifty different states. Although right-wingers want government to leave us alone when we act as consumers or business people, they are happy to have government assertively promote "community standards." In some cases, this is literal, as when a homeowners' association board imposes their standards on an entire neighborhood. In other cases, community standards are essentially interchangeable with so-called traditional moral values. For example, right-wingers tend to favor the government restricting people's ability to grow or use marijuana, or have homosexual relationships.

In terms of the costs of protecting and cleaning up the environment, both left-wingers and right-wingers are willing to accept some government incentives. Right-wingers tend to favor tax breaks; left-wingers prefer direct subsidies.

With such different sets of beliefs on environmental issues, Democrats and Republicans just don't find that much common ground on which to compromise. The sad fact is that rather than addressing our national problems, the goal is often denying the other side any political victory. And even after we get beyond these partisan problems we are still left with the obstacles that the authors of the Constitution purposely put in our way to make policy change difficult: a long legislative process requiring the passage of laws by two chambers representing different constituencies (entire states vs. small districts), the presidential veto, and the courts.

How to Use This Book

Over the next two hundred and fifty pages or so we're going to take you on a tour of what, exactly, the government has done and could do about our environment. The first chapter lays out the landscape by explaining why and how politicians and other participants in the policy-making process use and misuse scientific information. The ten chapters that follow look at some of the most important issues facing our environment today. Each chapter focuses on a separate issue, setting out the essential scientific information, governmental policies, policy options (with the left-wing and right-wing ratings), and the bottom line (our own analysis). We don't provide the ultimate answers—we don't tell you to stop driving cars or to start growing marijuana—but we do evaluate and separate the data, policies, and rhetoric, giving a better, clearer basis for you to decide what the government should do about marijuana, carbon dioxide, biofuels, and everything else that affects this beautiful blue and green sphere on which we live.

CHAPTER 1

★★★

Science, Political Science, and the Science of Politics

AL GORE PROCLAIMS it an "inconvenient truth" that the planet is warming, that humans are causing it, and that the result will cause catastrophic human and environmental suffering. What's your immediate reaction? Did you say, "Darn right," or did you roll your eyes and exhale loudly in exasperation?

Sarah Palin counters that global warming is due to "natural, cyclical environmental trends." What's your immediate reaction? Did you say, "You betcha" or "Thank God someone has some common sense," or did you roll your eyes and start to snicker?

For better or worse, this contrast between Al Gore and Sarah Palin illustrates the kind of exposure many Americans have to the science of climate change. All too often, our view of science is obtained through the opinions of partisan politicians or political commentators in the media. Our evaluation of the science and the related policies has little to do, therefore, with the actual science or the actual content of the policies, but a lot to do with whether we like the politics of the person who makes the statement. If we don't like Democrats generally or Al Gore specifically, global warming must be a big hoax intended to allow big government to gain control over our lives. And the scientists who say it's real are obviously liberal ivory-tower elitists who have no common sense or clue about how the real world works. If tree-hugging, Birkenstock-wearing, latte-sipping, Volvo-driving yuppies are for it, *real* Americans must oppose it. And fortunately other *real* Americans are just like us.

On the flip side, if we don't like Republicans generally or Sarah Palin specifically, we conclude that global warming skeptics are ignorant or too ideologically rigid to face the facts. And the scientists who are skeptical of global warming have been bought off by the oil companies or other corporations that fund their research. If gun-totin',

Bible thumpin', pickup drivin' rednecks are for it, *real* Americans must oppose it. And fortunately other *real* Americans are just like us.

As we saw in the introduction, the politics of the environment has become increasingly polarized. It's not surprising that we rely on our parties and our ideologies to evaluate the merits of public policy. It's a bit more disturbing that, increasingly, we seem to be incapable of agreeing on the underlying facts and we come to see any science-based assertions made by the other side as a distortion or downright abuse of the scientific process.

These concerns raise the question of how science is used and misused in politics. Throughout this book, we'll confront some issues (such as global warming) in which discussion of the science has been swept up in the larger, ideological tug-of-war between the parties and their supporters. In other areas (such as alternative energy and biotechnology), however, we'll see that ideological lines are less clear—or perhaps the electoral stakes are lower—so that the science gets greater consideration on its own merits.

Our government implements policies that are, on the surface, based on protecting you, the environment, and your garden. Sometimes these policies are based on good science, and sometimes they aren't. When you take the time to really look at the various issues, it is easy to find yourself stunned at how casually science is accepted or rejected depending upon the whims of policymakers. Politicians frequently use scientific results out of context or give the results meaning out of proportion to what was intended by the scientists who conducted the research. The media reports any research that it thinks will draw the public eye regardless of its merits, and often scientists themselves are guilty of overinterpreting their own data. All of these factors sway public opinion, which, in turn, alters the actions of those who govern our country.

How Do Policymakers Use Scientific Information?

Political scientist William Browne described politics as "a combination of intellectual argument and emotional hell-raising." And to most of us, emotional hell-raising does seem to be the dominant method of operation on Capitol Hill, with most decisions apparently resulting from party stances rather than reliable evidence. Politicians tend to cast their votes based on what their constituents care about. Making people happy is what gets them elected, not following good science. Since most politicians generally follow the party line on the most important issues, voters usually know what they are getting when they elect a representative. But for less prominent issues, it's a bit of a different story.

Most of us are so wrapped up in our pet projects that we don't know very much about the many issues that our policymakers deal with. What's more, we probably don't even care that much about many of them. (Regional dairy compacts, anyone?) It's probable that the politicians who represent us won't have a strong ideological or personal preference to guide their decisions regarding these obscure issues, either. This is where members of interest groups who do care and who can effectively communicate their beliefs can have a profound effect. The politician calculates: "If these people can act on this issue now, they might also act based on this issue in the next election and vote for or against me based on what I do. If helping them doesn't offend any other important group of constituents, it is easier to give them what they want."

But we don't want our politicians to just accept what an interest group says. We also want what we think of as intellectual argument to be a substantial part of the decision. We want policies that science has shown to be effective, not just those that are popular with the public or pleasing to a politician's political allies. We expect public officials to incorporate the results of scientific analyses into their policies. And they do, though there are circumstances under which sci-

MEMBERS of Congress and their staffs operate in a largely oral culture where people are more important than documents. They may not formally use research but they talk to experts and hear about the results of research through testimony at congressional hearings. Politicians like narratives or stories that connect problems, solutions, and real people's lives. Fitting research into a nice story is important in helping the politician make sense of it and be persuaded by it. It also helps them explain to constituents how and why they voted or took other actions to support or oppose the policy. A marginally talented scientist who can tell a good story about his or her research is much more useful than a brilliant scientist who cannot.

entific information is more likely to be incorporated into policy. Unfortunately, there are also incentives for misusing or abusing science in the political process.

The first hurdle to using scientific research as an aid to policymaking will be immediately obvious if you've ever read an article in an academic or professional scientific journal. Scientific publications are nearly (or entirely!) unreadable to nonspecialists because they include so much jargon and so many specialized terms. The incentive for promotion and acclaim in academia—publishing cutting-edge research in specialized professional journals—works against producing research that is accessible to the public and, more importantly, to policymakers. Furthermore, science prizes results that apply across space, time, and conditions. Politicians represent small areas, like states or districts, for a few years. They are more concerned with knowing how policies will affect their constituents now than with understanding the grand, unifying laws of the universe.

Getting to the Truth

The tallest hurdle, however, is that scientific evidence can be contested or modified with future study, and so does not offer *the truth.* In other words, science doesn't banish uncertainty. Rather, it often makes us more uncertain and raises more questions. For example, if a study shows us that people who eat organic food are healthier than those who do not, is it because organic food is healthier than conventionally produced food or because health-conscious consumers, who make other healthy lifestyle choices, are more likely to buy it? And even if we can "control" our experiment for the lifestyles of those who are eating organic versus nonorganic food, are the benefits we see the result of reduced pesticide use, organic farmers using different fertilizers than other farmers, or some other factor that we haven't even thought of? We might also ask whether the researchers measured the health of the people in the study with a reasonable parameter. Should health be measured by visits to the hospital? Cancer rate? Blood pressure?

Despite what people who support one or the other side of a policy usually believe, that policy will, almost invariably, be made without the benefit of indisputable science.

Additionally, studies using different techniques, or carried out under different conditions, produce different results. If dogs treated with a pesticide develop cancer, and mice treated with the same pesticide don't, then will that pesticide cause cancer in humans? Sometimes the best science we have available just can't give us the clear picture that we need. Despite what people who support one or the other side of a policy usually believe, that policy will, almost invariably, be made without the benefit of indisputable science.

Environmental science is also one of the most difficult sciences to interpret because it is not a single discipline but rather a conglomeration of many fields, including biology, chemistry, epidemiology, engineering, planning, and economics. Each specialty has its own preferred methods, its own approaches to evaluating evidence and policies, and in many respects, its own worldview. For example, experimental biologists and epidemiologists have approaches that often create very different perspectives on environmental policy. For experimental biologists to conclude that a chemical is toxic to humans they would want to produce evidence from controlled experiments on animals and perhaps human tissues that showed not only that the

ENVIRONMENTAL policies do not have a jurisdictional home in Congress any more than they have a disciplinary home in academia. Fourteen of twenty-two House committees have some environmental responsibility, along with eleven Senate committees. In addition, there are seventy committees and subcommittees in the House and Senate that deal with some aspect of water policy alone! It is only fair to mention that these committees tend to represent the perspectives (dare we say biases) of the major constituencies they represent. The Agriculture committees tend to support the interests of farmers and agribusiness and their perspective on tobacco, for instance, while the Health subcommittee of the Energy and Commerce Committee opposes this perspective. The consequence is that many hands are involved in deciding most environmental policy questions; building coalitions across committees with so many conflicting perspectives is often a long and arduous process. Furthermore, representatives who are looking to their colleagues for expert advice, for better or worse, may not get a consistent scientific perspective.

chemical was toxic, but also what it specifically does to the animal. By contrast, an epidemiologist would examine the amount of chemical in neighborhood water supplies (for example) and correlate it with the number of people in those neighborhoods who were ill. Showing a relationship between the amount of chemical and the amount of illness would be sufficient for them to conclude that the chemical was dangerous. They wouldn't undertake controlled experiments to discover the mechanism causing the illness before concluding that a public health risk existed. When faced with the choice of how to regulate potentially toxic chemicals, policymakers would be hearing from both the experimental biologists and the epidemiologists, and would have to sort through their potentially different research results, standards of risk, and policy recommendations.

Even when scientists agree on methodology and interpretation of the evidence, they can still disagree on how strong the evidence of harm needs to be to require government action. Should the standard be a "reasonable anticipation of harm" or a "conclusive proof of harm"? For which population should the standard apply—the average member of the public, those most sensitive to potential harm (children, the elderly), or those most likely to be exposed to the chemical (usually those who work with it)? Choosing the lower threshold might mean that the government takes costly action that doesn't protect human health, because the chemical really wasn't dangerous at the levels humans are exposed to it. Choosing the higher threshold might mean that people die or are seriously injured because we weren't sufficiently cautious. Similarly, policymakers need to decide which side bears the burden of proof. Does the government (or the critics of a chemical) have to prove that a specific chemical is unsafe before it bans it, or does the manufacturer have to prove it is safe to keep it from being banned? Science can complicate policymaking by showing the need for additional information, rather than producing quick, straightforward answers to the problem.

Even when conflicting data isn't an issue, science often takes a long time to come up with good answers. Scientific results do not necessarily appear when they would be most useful to policymakers, or in response to social crises when the political demand for solutions is highest. Scientific projections into the future are often based on events of the past. If an event hasn't occurred yet, then projections into the future could be wildly inaccurate. But politicians are interested in understanding the effects of a policy before the policy goes into effect. Science does not operate on the same timetable as politics, which is centered around elections, crises, and those rare "windows of opportunity" when public opinion, interest group allies, and the politicians in power are all in alignment on an issue.

The Clean Air Act of 1970 is one of the best examples of how our government's enthusiasm to please its citizens can outstrip the ability of science to provide definitive answers. The 1960s were a time of environmental realization in the United States. Acid rain was beginning to be studied, Rachel Carson's book *Silent Spring* was published, and J. I. Rodale's magazine *Organic Gardening* was hitting its stride. People were recognizing that what we do can profoundly affect the environment in which we live. In response, Congress passed, and President Richard Nixon signed into law, the Clean Air Act of 1970, which was really a revision of the 1967 Air Quality Act, which had failed to have the desired impact. The Clean Air Act was like a sledgehammer. It required a 90 percent reduction in automobile emissions over a period of only a few years. A wonderful idea, but the lawmakers didn't take into account the technology of the time and how rapidly it could be adapted to automobiles. By 1974, it became obvious that the technology couldn't handle this law, so the timeline and standards were changed. It wasn't until 1981 that cars met the guidelines set forth by the amended Clean Air Act.

The standards that the Environmental Protection Agency (EPA) set for airborne particulates after the passage of the Clean Air Act were based on the best available science of the 1970s, but twenty-five years after this act was passed, the EPA concluded that the original standards were based on insufficient data. Sometimes, even when it seems that all of the research points to a clear answer, there's still more work to be done.

As with the Clean Air Act's projections of what could be done to curb automobile emissions, scientific projections can be simply wrong, or, as is more often the case, they can be widely divergent. In these situations, science can quickly become a political weapon, with both sides brandishing studies to support preexisting positions and discredit their opponents. When this happens, we would all hope that the sides would agree that more or different information was necessary. Unfortunately, that's usually the exception rather than the rule. More frequently, scientific disagreements reinforce political conflict.

★★★

Scientific questions in public policy are never simply about science—they are about economics, too. Within the United States there are a number of groups who would welcome the banning of pesticides from our yards based on the perception that they cause chronic diseases, such as cancer. But the science behind the claims that these poisons cause cancer is fuzzy at best. While it's true that certain studies have shown that 2,4-D (the most frequently used herbicide on turf in the United States, which targets weeds such as dandelion and ground ivy) may be related to cancer in dogs and even humans, other studies have not supported these findings. So why should we do away with this valuable chemical that keeps our yards weed free for mere pennies a square foot? It's much cheaper than hiring someone to pull the weeds.

Likewise, the ability of carbon dioxide to cause global warming is in dispute. Though research seems to strongly support its role in global warming, there is no doubt that the earth cycles through climatic changes, and it is within the realm of possibility that the current warming in various places on the earth has something to do with these natural variations rather than with carbon dioxide levels. Because of the size and complexity of the earth, it is impossible to build another one—never mind ten or twelve—to test these various theories to see which one is correct. So why should we limit the industries and cars that expel carbon dioxide when we don't even know with certainty that this gas is causing the problem?

While these scientific disagreements are certainly significant, the most important limitation of science is that it can't set priorities or address trade-offs. Priorities and trade-offs are value judgments. Science's goal is accuracy. At best, science can determine what is likely to happen if certain policy changes are made. It cannot determine whether the policy is good or bad, or whether the costs of the policy are worth it. It can't determine whether resources would be better spent doing something else, or whether implementing and enforcing a policy is even feasible. But these factors are at least as important as scientific accuracy in determining whether anything can get done politically.

The Political Abuse of Scientific Information

The limitations of scientific information make it easy for political activists to misuse or distort it. Political advocates try to win—by passing a particular policy, electing a particular candidate—and information is a means to an end. Advocates for a particular position are tempted to cherry-pick evidence that supports their goals, regardless of its quality. This leads to the hyping of results from poorly conducted or inappropriate studies. Some people call this bad science, and some people call it smart politics.

In the upcoming chapters we will discuss policies that are arguably based on bad science. Regardless of your feelings regarding the banning of marijuana, for example, it is hard to substantiate things that were said during congressional hearings on the subject in 1937, when Harry J. Anslinger, called the father of the drug war, claimed, “You smoke a joint and you are likely to kill your brother.” Such statements reverberated with the public because of the lack of familiarity with this drug at that time. Marijuana was outlawed out of fear that it was, according to Anslinger, “the most violence-causing drug in the history of mankind,” rather than because of any true scientific knowledge that it caused violence.

Drugs are far from the only things that our government controls without the benefit of rock-solid science. Science does not support the concept that allowing your yard to become a meadow causes it to become a significant fire hazard, to raise another topic we’ll discuss later. Nonetheless, that is what was argued by the city of New Berlin, Wisconsin, when they attempted to force one of their residents to comply with a law requiring a tidy lawn.

One of the greatest misuses of science within the political arena comes from something called the “sound science” movement. This movement started with the tobacco companies, who argued that links between smoking tobacco and lung cancer (and other health maladies) were not sufficiently proven. Their strategy was to avoid government regulation by using a public relations campaign to magnify the public’s and policymakers’ uncertainty about the scientific links between tobacco use and health. Other business interests have subsequently picked up on the strategy to delay or avoid government regulation. Because science can never provide complete certainty, those who demand it are establishing unattainable standards for government regulation.

Scientists who play by the rules of the scientific method and the norms of professionalism within their fields can feel a great deal of frustration when they believe their opponents are not similarly constrained, but instead distort scientific results for their own selfish ends. Scientists who become involved in policy debates face the temptation to fight fire with fire, or at least to allow the political concerns of developing the right public relations message to become the priority. Emails hacked from Great Britain's University of East Anglia Climate Research Unit in 2009 gave political ammunition to global warming critics. The emails contained suggestions that the scientists were bolstering their claims of climate change by cherry-picking the evidence that they were releasing to the public. Although scientific supporters of climate change argued that the emails were about the public relations aspects of science and did not call into question the underlying science or evidence of climate change (a perspective supported by subsequent investigations into the scientists' actions), the incident highlights the ease with which the credibility of science can be damaged in the public's eye.

Who Is Providing the Information?

The number of sources of information available to political participants today makes it very easy to find the information one wants—and to ignore anything that is inconvenient. Popular sources of information for the Washington elite are think tanks (also known as policy institutes) composed of groups of like-minded people who collect information to support or refute certain policies. These organizations, usually based in Washington, D.C., do things such as write policy analyses that are timely and accessible to policymakers. While it's true that many of them attempt to do high-quality, scientific work, other think tanks are derisively called Beltway bandits because they attempt to provide the veneer of scientific credibility to research that promotes particular ideological perspectives or preordained policy objectives. Politicians who are looking for facts to support their preexisting conclusions will often use information from these Beltway bandits to explain their actions (or lack of action) to constituents back home who can't easily evaluate the quality of the analysis or the credibility of the source.

If scientific information is to be available to policymakers, then someone has to produce it. Usually this requires financial resources to run a lab and pay the lab workers. This raises concerns in terms of the ability an industry has to produce its own analyses to verify the safety of its products or to fund researchers who use methods or have track records of producing results that are favorable to the industry's perspective. Politicians can play this game too by funding (or blocking funding) for research they think will promote the policy outcomes they want (or don't want). Political scientist Christopher Bosso, for example, documented that rural lawmakers on the House Committee on Agriculture blocked funding for research on the effects of pesticides on wildlife for many years during the 1950s and 1960s. Similarly, the National Highway Traffic Safety Administration withheld information from Congress and the public on the safety risks of using communications technologies like cell phones in cars from 2003 to 2009 because they feared that Congress would react negatively. Strategically controlling scientific information may help advocates win, but it doesn't ensure that effective policy is being made.

Politicians also frequently obtain expert policy information from lobbyists. Lobbyists are people whose profession it is to gather information on their client's public policy interests, gain access to government officials, and explain why proposed policies would be good or bad (based on their client's interests). Some lobbyists work for a corporation (such as Dow Chemical) or an interest group (such as the Sierra Club) and are experts on the issue on which they are lobbying. Other lobbyists work for law and lobbying firms and have clients on many different issues. Many have formerly worked for the government and they have influential contacts within Congress and agencies with whom outside individuals and groups will pay to communicate. The lobbyist's job is to promote the policies desired by their clients.

The lobbyist's main value to public officials is the ability to provide information that will help the officials solve policy problems and simultaneously keep their constituents happy. If an official doesn't trust the information or the credibility of the lobbyist, the lobbyist is not going to be influential. The hardest part of the lobbyist's job is gaining access—getting to meet with public officials or getting their phone calls returned—and politicians won't waste their time on those they don't think are credible. Lobbying is not a one-shot event; it is about building relationships over time so that public officials will use your information when your issues are being debated. So there is substantial incentive to tell the truth. Unfortunately, lobbyists, like everyone else, perceive and retain information selectively, and when scientific results differ to begin with, lobbyists are going to highlight the facts that support their client's interests.

Policymakers know that the information from lobbyists is biased, so you might think that they would view it rather skeptically. In actuality, however, this bias actually makes it more useful to policymakers. One reason that lobbyists are effective, and, indeed, why they are hired, is that they can provide both substantive information (how a policy will work) and political information (how constituents who are members of an organization will react) to politicians in a single source. Lobbyists can tell politicians which constituents are affected, how they are affected, and how much they care. This information indicates to politicians whether it is worth their time and effort to *do something* with that information to please their constituents or other potential supporters, such as campaign volunteers or donors.

Lobbyists can also provide information—including information based on scientific research—to public officials in a way that is much more user friendly than scientists can. Lobbyists will translate information into tiny, easily digested bites that make it readable for busy officials, emphasizing substance and policy implications more than painful research briefs. Whenever possible, lobbyists will break the information down to the level of states or congressional districts so that representatives can understand the direct implications for their constituents who will be casting votes in upcoming elections. Lobbyists are good at following up and making themselves readily available to discuss and answer questions about the material.

While lobbyists have an incentive to preserve their reputations and their access to public officials, the public relations campaigns run by interest groups are not as tightly constrained. To get the public's attention, they are more likely to cherry-pick, exaggerate, and sensationalize evidence in their advertising. Such advertising commonly arrives to attack a candidate during an election campaign (and the courts have mostly shielded campaign advertising from slander or libel penalties to preserve robust free speech and the accountability of elected officials) and politicians often feel compelled to act based on information that they know is distorted, misleading, or just plain wrong.

Where's the Public?

Though we've emphasized the role of lobbyists in providing information to public officials, normal citizens can provide expertise too. Whatever our occupation, we know what we do better than a lobbyist, and therefore have credibility with public officials in discussing how policies will affect us. Politicians obviously have an incentive to listen respectfully to policy information provided by people who will decide whether or not to vote for them. Knowing this, lobbyists often bring constituents to Washington to talk to representatives on behalf of an organization. The advantage that lobbyists usually have over citizen experts is that they are consistently monitoring what government is doing, so they can time their actions for maximum effect.

Intensity—not just information—matters a lot in politics. Remember the observation at the beginning of this chapter that politics is "a combination of intellectual argument and emotional hell-raising." Those who feel intensely about environmental issues have a reason to join (or form) groups, seek evidence to promote their intellectual arguments in scientific journals or at conferences (or fund research for someone to conduct a study), and pay lobbyists to put scientific information in front of policymakers. As a consequence, some viewpoints are more advantaged than others in the policy process.

For better or worse, most of the public does not feel very intensely about the environment. Sure, there's a "passive consensus" among the public for environmentalism. Everybody's for the environment, but few are committed to doing something about it. We want to protect the environment, but we want to do lots of other things as well. The environment ends up losing because it can't compete with our concern about our jobs, education, and homeland security. Rarely do environmental issues rank high on the public's list of top concerns: Gallup polls find only about 2 percent of the public ranking the environment as "the most important issue" facing the country. And rarely does political action of any sort rank high on many people's to-do list, even on behalf of their most cherished causes. While people who join environmental interest groups are likely to pay close attention to the issues that these groups support, the average citizen tends to be pretty passive until there's an environmental crisis that grabs media attention. The Love Canal, Three Mile Island, the Exxon Valdez, extremely hot summers, *E. coli* or *Salmonella* outbreaks, and high gas prices are all environmental events that mobilize the public. BP's 2010 Deep Horizon oil spill in the Gulf of Mexico captured public attention but failed to generate public support for energy legislation because the public blamed BP's errors for the disaster. And long-term trends, like global climate change over the past hundred years, are much less likely to capture people's attention.

In contrast, businesses have some practical political advantages over a largely unorganized public. They are already organized and can use their existing internal communications structures to mobilize management, employees, and shareholders (and potentially, suppliers and customers) for political action. Their talent, expertise, and money are used daily to achieve financial goals, and can easily be turned to communication with politicians when politics might affect business. They can use their existing resources to hire outside lobbyists, lawyers, public relations professionals, or others who can help them communicate their point of view to public officials and to the public. Politicians are likely to make themselves accessible when high-status employers in their district say they have information relevant to policy debates. Citizen's groups, by contrast, first have to organize, attract sources of financial support, and hire staff before they can regularly gain access to policymakers.

Our system works to the benefit of those who want to block change, regardless of who the protector of the status quo might be.

Businesses compete with each other for market share, however, and often have different agendas. The genesis of many local pollution laws, for example, was business leaders deciding that their city needed to clean up its image to attract new investments. Companies that manufacture green technologies will lobby on the side of environmentalists for laws that encourage (or force) other businesses to use green technologies. Despite the powerful image of corporate interests, business often loses in politics because consumer, labor, and/or environmental groups mobilize against them or because other businesses have differing views of sound public policy. Our system works to the benefit of those who want to block change, regardless of who the protector of the status quo might be.

Conclusion

Politics is about making tough choices that require a difficult balancing of competing interests, and science can't tell us when the right balance has been achieved. Politics is about making value judgments. Value judgments are outside the realm of science. Sure, science may help policymakers understand that if you do X, the result will be Y, but policymakers are still left having to decide whether Y is a desirable outcome and whether it is worth the necessary costs to attain it.

CHAPTER 2

★★★

Organic Food: Safer, Friendlier, Better?

UNITED STATES LAW includes 340 words devoted to the definition of *ketchup* (along with its aliases, *catsup* and *catchup*). The law then continues for an additional 194 words specifying how to label ketchup, before spending 482 words regulating its appropriate thickness. And you thought you knew ketchup!

Most of us are quite familiar and comfortable with our understanding of ketchup (both the condiment and the word for it). When we go to the grocery store to get another bottle, we have a pretty good idea about what we're purchasing—allowing, of course, for slight variations in taste and thickness. More importantly, we are confident that the ketchup we'll be eating is safe for us and for our kids.

Generally, we don't doubt that the food we buy is what it says it is, and that it is safe and (relatively) healthy for us to eat. We don't think about what it takes to produce that food at consistent levels of quality and safety. We have no interest in watching ketchup or sausage or other processed foods being made, and we're not aware or concerned that it takes 1016 words in government policy to regulate ketchup. Unless there is some well-publicized outbreak of a food-borne disease or toxin, the role of government policy is almost an invisible backdrop: we know the government is doing something to keep us safe, but it is out of sight and, hence, out of mind.

Some people, however, are concerned about the practices that our government allows in the production of our nation's food. They worry that our conventional food system is not as safe as our government tells us it is. Organic food is their solution.

Since the 1940s, various groups have warned us that our agricultural systems are bad for the environment and unhealthy for us. They point out that the pesticides and fertilizers that farmers are allowed to use today produce unhealthy and even dangerous food compared with what our ancestors ate. As more people have become concerned that we're poisoning ourselves with chemicals used on the foods we eat, the organic movement has grown.

Organic approaches are meant to grow and process foods using natural methods that promote ecological balance and avoid the use of synthetic fertilizers, insecticides, herbicides, and other growth aids. Instead, organic farmers might use techniques such as planting rows closer together to increase shade, making it difficult for understory weeds to grow; rotating crops frequently and in combinations that help subsequent crops yield more abundantly; planting cover crops as habitat for beneficial insects that eat pests; releasing beneficial insects such as ladybugs or lacewings; or spraying organic chemicals instead of synthetic ones. For livestock, the organic approach does not allow the use of growth hormones or antibiotics. The animals must have access to the outdoors and be fed food that was itself organically produced.

More broadly, *organic* is a philosophical approach to farming centered on doing what is perceived as the right thing for the environment and human health. Unfortunately, sometimes the fervor for this philosophical ideal outstrips the ability of organic methodologies to deliver on their promises.

For many consumers, organically grown food has become the ideal. Buying organic products gives them the ability to live out their commitment to healthy and environmentally sustainable lifestyles. Organic products have moved from niche health food stores to retail grocery chains over the past decade because we are willing to pay extra for them. In turn, as organics have demonstrated their economic viability, more farmers have turned to organic approaches out of both philosophical commitment and the higher prices they can demand. The U.S. Department of Agriculture (USDA) estimates that sales of organic foods rose from $6 billion in 2000 to $23 billion in 2009 and the annual rate of market growth since 1990 has remained steady at around 20 percent.

Since organic products sell for more and earn farmers more money, there was an incentive during the 1980s and 1990s to label more and more items as organic, regardless of how the food was actually produced and processed. During that time, reputable agencies would certify a food as organic, but these agencies were not uniform in their requirements. Different agencies had different lists of acceptable fertilizers and pesticides, so an organic label from one agency would not necessarily mean the same thing as an organic label from another. This created a demand for a standardized definition of *organic*, and a process to certify which products met that definition. The result—a USDA-backed organic label—is intended to assure consumers that they are, in fact, buying foods grown without synthetic chemicals and to protect those farmers who use the more-costly organic methods from conventional producers who might attempt to invade their market niche under the cover of misleading labeling.

The Science

The concept of organic as it is now generally understood was first introduced by Sir Albert Howard, an English scientist, in the first half of the twentieth century. He proposed using recycled organic materials, namely composted plants and animal poop, as the primary source of fertility for agricultural ground, rather than using what he called synthetic manures. He found support in the United States from J. I. Rodale, who aggressively promoted this idea of organic farming and gardening during the 1940s, 1950s, and 1960s, and who is perhaps the person most responsible for our awareness of the term *organic*. Over time, the meaning of organic has shifted somewhat. While it started out as a term that meant preserving the soil through recycling organic materials, the publication of *Silent Spring* by Rachel Carson in 1962 did wonders to promote the idea of organic agriculture with an emphasis on reducing the use of synthetic pesticides.

Today, crops that are grown organically—according to the guidelines set forth by the USDA—are supposed to be produced in such a way that they are safer and healthier for us and for the environment than foods produced through more conventional means, which usually involve synthetic fertilizers and pesticides. The government, however, does not actually claim that these foods are safer and healthier. Ultimately, we are left to our own devices to determine whether organic foods really are better. Though there have been—and will continue to be—changes in the requirements needed for a farm to produce any sort of food with the "USDA Organic" label, the basic tenet of organic production is that, with a few exceptions, only natural inputs can be used on an organic crop.

Fertilizers and Pesticides

The first thing that the typical consumer thinks of when thinking about organic foods is healthy, wholesome fruit harvested from a pristine country setting and grown without the use of pesticides or synthetic fertilizers. Indeed, many of the fertilizers used for organic production are renewable resources and are therefore healthier for the environment than synthetic fertilizers. Synthetics are based on nonrenewable natural gas (the hydrogen from which reacts with nitrogen from the air to make most synthetic nitrogen fertilizers) and coal (which drives the reaction between the natural gas and air). Organic does not mean no pesticides, however. Organic producers are technically required to try to use cultural methods to control pests whenever possible, but they do have the freedom to use pesticides, as long as these pesticides are allowed by the organic standards list created by the USDA. Many of these pesticides are considered safer than conventional pesticides, especially since some of the most toxic natural pesticides—sabadilla, rotenone, sodium fluoroaluminate, and tobacco (nicotine)—are gone from the organic grower's arsenal because companies have voluntarily withdrawn these products from shelves or because the USDA has banned their use on organic crops.

Unfortunately, not all organic practices are created equal, and organic growers still have a few nasty chemicals available to them. Copper sulfate, a fungicide, and pyrethrum, an insecticide, are both potentially dangerous chemicals for humans and for many beneficial organisms. After years of use, copper sulfate can build up in the soil to such an extent that it becomes toxic to certain plants. Pyrethrum is very toxic to good insects, such as honeybees and lady beetles.

For fruits or vegetables that require a lot of pesticides under normal growing conditions, growing them organically may be even more harmful to the environment than conventional systems.

In addition, organic pesticides tend to protect plants for a shorter period of time and are often less effective than their synthetic counterparts, so they need to be reapplied more frequently. For fruits or vegetables that require a lot of pesticides under normal growing conditions, growing them organically may be even more harmful to the environment than conventional systems. Apples, particularly those produced in the eastern states, are a prime example of a crop that needs to be sprayed frequently to control damaging diseases and insects. Organic apples often receive more pesticide applications than conventionally grown ones, potentially leading to a greater environmental effect.

Organic food is not tested for organic pesticide residues, so it could contain these toxins at some level. Theoretically, many organic pesticides break down quickly in the environment, but in the few cases where tests have been conducted on organic foods, residues of organic pesticides have been found. And residues of synthetic pesticides on organic produce, though usually lower than on conventionally grown produce, are far from rare, with as much as a quarter of produce samples testing positive for these chemicals. Though this research was conducted before USDA standards were implemented in 2002, we see no reason why the adoption of these standards would significantly alter this percentage.

Like organic pesticides, organic fertilizers may also pose problems. Some of the fertilizers used by organic growers are mined, which means they are not sustainable. The most notorious of these include guano and rock phosphate. Guano is aged manure that comes from either seabirds or bats. Guano from seabirds living in Peru was once our primary source of nitrogen; unfortunately, this resource disappeared over time because of overuse. Today, the use of bat guano from caves similarly threatens the flora and fauna that live in this excrement where it is mined (Jamaica, among other places). Also, because bat caves filled with guano aren't located in every neighborhood, there is an excellent possibility that the guano you purchase has traveled quite a distance, using a great deal of fossil fuel. Rock phosphate is extracted from strip mines (in Florida and elsewhere) in a process that is very damaging to the local environment. As with bat guano, a significant amount of fossil fuel is needed to transport rock phosphate to the farms that use it.

Even renewable organic fertilizers can be problematic. One of the cornerstones of organic growing since the days of Sir Albert Howard has been the use of composted manures as fertilizer to enrich the soil. While these manures shouldn't contain any dangerous bacteria if they are properly composted according to the National Organic Program's standards, there is the possibility that they will not be properly composted, which could be dangerous. *E. coli* can live for twenty-one months in uncomposted manure, and surveys of farms utilizing organic rather than inorganic fertilizers had 9.7 percent of their produce test positive for *E. coli* as compared to 1.9 percent of produce from farms using only nutrients from nonorganic sources. In 2006, there was a huge recall of spinach that was potentially infected with a deadly strain of *E. coli*. Organic spinach was part of this recall. Three people died, and 276 people were reported ill. In 2009, there was a *Salmonella* outbreak from peanuts and peanut-related products that originated at processing plants in Georgia, leaving at least eight people dead and hundreds, perhaps thousands, sickened. These processing plants were certified organic. While it turned out that the foods that caused the sickness were not organic, in both of these cases organic foods were recalled. The organic label did not guarantee that the food was safe. Technically, organic certification has nothing to do with food safety, despite what many consumers infer.

Nutrient Content of Organic Foods

Those who favor current government regulation of organically produced foods emphasize that these foods tend to be higher in nutrients than their conventionally produced counterparts. There is some evidence to support that, particularly as it relates to vitamin C, which tends to be higher in organically produced foods, and to nitrates, which tend to be lower. Studies show that organically grown fruits and vegetables may have higher levels of antioxidants. Because organic producers usually can't keep their produce as spotless as their conventional counterparts, the produce may have more damage. Damage signals the plant to defend itself with various defensive chemicals, which often include antioxidants. Consider that the next time you avoid a slightly blemished peach or pear.

As with produce, the government makes no claim that there is any difference between organic and conventional milk and meat.

But even those studies that show that there may be differences in the healthful chemicals in organically produced crops point out that this difference is not consistent, and there are just as many articles showing that growing a food organically does not provide any health benefits. In fact, differences in the nutritional content of foods are often related more to the cultivars of the plants grown and the soils in which they grew than to whether or not they are grown organically. Regardless of whether your 'Golden Delicious' apple is organic or not, it won't have the same amount of vitamin C as a 'Calville Blanc d'Hiver' or a 'Sturmer' apple.

As with produce, the government makes no claim that there is any difference between organic and conventional milk and meat. Science, too, doesn't seem to be able to tell much difference between the organically and synthetically produced product, and differences in livestock breed have as much or more to do with the nutritional value of the food than whether the food was produced organically. What this all boils down to is that it is absolutely impossible to tell whether any given piece of organic meat, fruit, or bread is more nutrient rich than one produced using conventional methods.

Organic Livestock

For livestock, the elimination of the use of growth hormones and the drastic reduction in the use of antibiotics, as well as access to an outdoor environment, are the primary reasons why organically produced products are perceived as better than conventional. (Antibiotics can only be used on organic farms when an animal is sick, and even then the animal must be taken out of production for a given period of time.) The use of rBST, the growth hormone given to dairy cows to increase milk production, has been shown to significantly increase health problems in cattle. Additionally, the use of rBST increases the production of another hormone, IGF-1, which is then found in milk at higher levels than in milk from untreated cows, and which may be associated with some human cancers. The FDA, however, cites research that shows that rBST does not cause levels of IGF-1 to increase above normal, and that this hormone—like insulin, to which it is very similar—is digested if it finds its way to the stomach (which is why insulin needs to be injected rather than taken orally). Still, this is an area of legitimate concern.

Government Policy

Congress first passed legislation on issues specifically related to organic farming in the 1990 Organic Foods Production Act (OFPA). This act created the National Organic Program (NOP) within the U.S. Department of Agriculture and assigned it the responsibility of creating federal standards for the labeling of organic foods. The act also created the National Organic Standards Board (NOSB), which then developed an official list of materials that can and cannot be used if a product is to qualify for USDA organic certification. These standards went into effect in 2002 and dictate that the use of synthetic pesticides, irradiation, or sewage-sludge-based fertilizers is not allowed in organically produced crops. Animals used to produce organic meats and other products must be fed organic feeds, be raised without antibiotics or growth hormones, and be given access to the outdoors. The standards cover farming methods for almost every type of farm product—fresh fruits and vegetables, grains, eggs, poultry, beef, dairy, cotton, wool, oils, flowers, and so on. Even the use of animal waste and compost as fertilizers is covered. One thing that the National Organic Program does not do is guarantee any superior health benefits from the product—contrary to the hopeful wishes and expectations of most consumers.

According to the National Organic Program, a label with the words "100 percent organic" is reserved for organically produced ingredients and processing aids. Products labeled "organic" must have at least 95 percent organically produced ingredients. Either "organic" or "100 percent organic" products may use the USDA Organic seal in their packaging and advertising. Products that contain at least 70 percent organic ingredients may be labeled as "made with organic ingredients" and can list up to three principal organic ingredients but cannot use the official seal. Products that contain less than 70 percent organic ingredients may specially identify any organic ingredients but may not use the term *organic* anywhere in the main display area of the packaging. While the use of the word *organic* is tightly prescribed, other descriptions such as "no drugs or growth hormones used," "free range," or "sustainably harvested" are not similarly regulated. Use them at will! Miscreants who knowingly sell or label a product as organic when it has not, in fact, been produced and handled according to the standards of the National Organic Program are subject to fines of up to $11,000 and may be kicked out of the program for five years.

Some farmers who are committed to the organic philosophy are aggravated by the paperwork, intrusive inspections, and general costs that adhering to government regulations imposes on small farming operations, and so choose to avoid government certification. They can't use the USDA Organic seal or describe their products as organic, but they can use descriptions such as "chemical free" or "sustainably grown." As long as consumers are convinced and buy their product, the farmer gains the price premium of organic products without paying the costs of government certification that their organic competitors pay. So, for some farmers, there is an economic incentive *not* to comply with government rules. (And, let's face it, how many of us uncomplainingly prefer to follow government or corporate rules when we can achieve the same objectives in a more straightforward, hassle-free way?) The farmer, however, does end up limiting his or her market, because government certification is, practically speaking, a requirement when selling to organic farm cooperatives, restaurants, and international markets.

Cheating and the Consequences

For those who think that these standards ensure that certification is a guarantee of organic wholesomeness, the bad news is that the government rarely imposes fines or revokes organic certification. Even when violations of organic standards are called to the attention of the USDA, it often takes years for anything to happen. A dairy in California was brought to the attention of the USDA in 2005 for violating organic standards (their cows didn't have access to pastures, among other issues), but it wasn't until 2007 that its ability to sell organic milk was suspended. In another instance, in 2007 a supplier of organic milk to major retailers like Wal-Mart and Trader Joe's received a letter from the USDA telling it to clean up its act or risk losing certification. Complaints had been filed against the company for two years, but two years after receiving the letter it was still selling organic milk despite the fact that additional complaints had been received about their production practices. While it certainly seems as though the government is willing to let things slide for quite a while before it decides to act, on a day-to-day basis, it really isn't the government, per se, that is making the decisions. That authority goes to another entity.

In the case in which the California dairy lost its certification, it wasn't the USDA that was responsible for checking up on possible violations, it was that dairy's organic certifier, Quality Assurance International. After the National Organic Standards were developed, the involvement of the federal government in their enforcement would best be described as indirect (though the government can change the standards). State and professional organizations certify producers and handlers who meet the federal organic standards. The

USDA does not directly deal with producers and handlers, but it accredits and monitors the state and professional organizations that do the certifying. (As we will see in the chapter on fertilizers, state and local governments have historically had primary legal authority over land and water use, and the federal government commonly relies on them to enforce federal environmental laws. In many instances, including organics, such an arrangement undermines vigorous enforcement of the law.)

When a producer or handler applies for organic certification, the state or private agent makes an on-site visit to evaluate compliance with National Organic Program standards. The applicant must document the substances applied to the land for the past three years, and develop an Organic System Plan (OSP). The OSP describes the practices and substances to be used in producing the crop, the monitoring procedures and record-keeping systems to provide evidence that the plan is being implemented effectively, and a system for preventing organic products from mixing with nonorganic products or from coming into contact with prohibited substances during handling and processing. After certification, the agent returns for annual reviews to ensure that standards are maintained. A lot depends on the honesty of the applicant and the attention to detail of the certifier. A lot also depends on who else is watching and whether they send any complaints to the USDA. In both the cases mentioned above, Cornucopia Institute, a Wisconsin group, notified the USDA of the problems. Without this notification, who knows how long the problems would have continued? Even with notification, the problems continued for a long time.

Various certifiers can also set different standards. Despite the work of the USDA to provide a standardized definition of what is and isn't an acceptable organic practice, certifiers may have requirements that are more strict than those set by the USDA, though they cannot have standards that are more lenient.

Although we hope that organic farmers stay true to their promises, it would be relatively easy for an organic farmer to apply a synthetic pesticide or fertilizer now and again and not be caught. Farmers aren't the only ones who might allow synthetics to find their way into an organic system, however. The producers of supposedly organic fertilizers and even organic certification agencies have also been known to fudge things. In 2009, a producer that provided almost half of the organic fertilizer to the state of California was raided to see whether it was placing synthetic fertilizers (which they apparently had on hand) into their fish fertilizer products. A year earlier, another company had been found to be amending its organic fertilizers with synthetic additives, possibly for as long as seven years.

In 2006, the USDA revoked the license of a certification agency owned by an agrichemical business that had approved organic farms that were openly using chemicals. While the USDA had the relevant information in its enforcement files, it did not remove the certifier or the farms from the program until the *Dallas Morning News*—using the information in the USDA files—ran a story. Laws that rely on whistleblowers, the media, or public interest groups to embarrass the government into enforcing them are not models of effectiveness.

Many enforcement problems came to a head in 2010 when the inspector general of the Department of Agriculture issued an audit critical of the National Organic Program. The NOP responded by requiring certification agents to spot-check for pesticide residues on organically labeled produce more frequently, to check organic labels in stores and expose any bogusly labeled products, and to conduct unannounced inspections of organic producers and processors.

The Political Dynamics

The first time that the word *organic* was used in a legal context was in Oregon state law in 1974, and the first law actually defining the term was passed in California in 1980. In 1989 a report by the Center for Science in the Public Interest listed sixteen states with laws that regulated the labeling of produce as organic. These state laws were the primary source of organic legislation for a long time before for the federal government took any action.

In the mid-1980s, the organic industry was concerned about nonorganic farmers cashing in on the popularity of the organic label and thus stealing their market share by offering cheaper, chemically enhanced products. The organics industry attempted to develop an internal consensus about production and certification standards, but it never happened.

Meanwhile, consumers were increasingly concerned about the use of chemicals in their foods. The 1989 Alar scare (see the pesticides chapter) caused consumers to flock to organic foods to avoid those foods supposedly tainted by dangerous chemicals. Consumer groups wanted to ensure the integrity of products that were sold under the organic label, since fraudulently labeled foods were waiting to take advantage of spooked consumers.

The organics industry turned to Congress in 1990 to resolve its standards and labeling issues, which led to the Organic Foods Production Act (OFPA). The industry believed that federal standards would be positive for them in several ways. Most importantly, a federal seal of approval would promote consumers' confidence in the quality of organic products. Additionally, one federal standard would be less confusing to consumers than the many different state and private standards that were being used at the time. For example, California required that conventional methods not be used on a field for only one year before the field could be certified as organic. Other states required a three-year transition period. It wasn't clear whether a product certified in California should be sold as organic in states with the more stringent standards. A national standard would also help the industry gain access to lucrative international organic markets.

Despite the united support from the organics industry, consumer groups, and the executive branch, the OFPA faced substantial skepticism from representatives on the Committee on Agriculture in the House of Representatives, the committee with responsibility for legislation on the production of food. Problems occurred because many members of the committee had long-standing relationships with major agricultural producers in their districts and thus represented the concerns of large-scale, conventional farmers. Committee members were wary of attacks on conventional farmers by environmental groups and were worried about the additional expenses that organic methods might impose upon producers, particularly livestock producers. Organic methods seemed to strike many members of Congress as countercultural. As Texas Democrat Charlie Stenholm put it, "We are being asked to believe that our method of production agriculture is faulty. I'm not prepared to do that."

The House Committee on Agriculture ultimately passed a watered-down farm bill in which such phrases as "sustainable agriculture" and "family farms" were made vague enough that both organic and conventional, mass-production farmers could claim that the bill neither promoted nor penalized chemical-intensive agriculture. The final bill also deleted funding for research on organic farming. The provisions of the OFPA were attached by amendment on the floor of the House, effectively circumventing the ability of the committee to prevent them from being passed. The law as passed allowed farmers to seek organic certification voluntarily, so that only those farmers who wanted certification would have to change their farming practices, while conventional farmers would not be affected by the new organic rules. The organics industry and consumer groups got together to facilitate speedy consideration of the OFPA by Congress, but its passage did not solve many of the conflicts that were present within the organics industry. Instead, it pushed these concerns onto the agencies that the OFPA created.

The USDA Takes Charge

The Organic Foods Production Act established the National Organic Standards Board to advise the USDA in developing appropriate criteria for identifying foods as organic. Congress created the NOSB primarily because of the fear that the USDA would be too closely allied with conventional farmers, and required that it be composed of farmers, processors, retailers, representatives of environmental organizations, and a scientist. While building consensus from all of the

POLITICS does not end once a law is passed. The end of one stage of the political process is usually just the beginning of the next stage. After a bill is passed, the executive branch is responsible for developing the detailed rules to implement the law. While the public rarely pays attention to the importance of the executive branch in this phase of policymaking, interest groups do. And so, even after a bill is signed by the president, these groups continue their attempts to influence policy. Agencies are required to publish draft regulations and allow a period of public comment. Interest groups mobilize their members to send the agency comments that are intended to influence the final regulations. Groups that lose in Congress try to weaken the regulations or to shift the costs onto someone else. Groups that win in Congress try to offset the influence of their opponents and to protect their interpretation of the language of the law. The OFPA is a classic case of these dynamics playing out—to the detriment of anyone who wanted the government to act quickly to implement the law's intent.

affected players may sound like a wonderful idea, in practice there are often long arguments between people with different perspectives and priorities. The NOSB took two years to get organized and three years to develop proposed organic standards. The USDA took another three years to review the proposal and issue preliminary rules. In sum, the first public draft of the rules appeared *eight years* after Congress ordered them to be developed.

When the standards were being developed, everyone wanted to be heard. From farmers to chemical manufacturers to backyard gardeners, people felt that their opinions were important and deserved to be incorporated. Those who didn't believe in the quality of organic food didn't go away despite the new legislation. If anything, they became more aggressive. Known as a think tank by some and a Beltway bandit by others, the Hudson Institute published a book in 1995 titled *Saving the Planet with Pesticides and Plastic,* which deconstructed the work of such organic pioneers as Rachel Carson. This book, among other efforts by those who questioned the value of organic production, led to a first draft of organic rules that upset many people.

The preliminary rules presented by the USDA were very sympathetic to conventional farmers. They allowed genetically modified crops, sewage sludge fertilizer, and food irradiation—practices that the NOSB would have banned from organic farming if left to their own devices. The organics industry mobilized its farmers and consumers in opposition to the proposed rules, and environmental groups mobilized their members as well. The USDA received 280,000 mostly negative comments from the public, forcing a revision. The final standards did ban genetically modified crops, sewage sludge fertilizer, and food irradiation, to the satisfaction of most in the organics industry. The regulations were approved in 2000 and were implemented in 2002—a dozen years after Congress passed the Organic Foods Production Act.

War Within the Organic Industry

The organics industry itself is composed of many participants with a variety of goals that are not necessarily consistent. These goals range from producing nutritious food in an environmentally sensitive way, to protecting small farms, to promoting locally grown foodstuffs, to supporting alternative food production and distribution networks (like farmer's markets and health food stores), to promoting social justice, all the way to changing the philosophy and operations of modern farmers and food retailers. As the original organic standards were being worked out, the purists and the change advocates often found themselves at odds. Organic purists wanted regulations that would promote small farms, whole foods, and local distribution. Change advocates and entrepreneurs wanted to maximize the number of organic consumers—and thus the number of organic farms—and sought regulations that would promote rapid growth of the industry. A particular point of dispute between these factions was the use of synthetic processing aids and whether these would count as ingredients toward the 95 percent or 70 percent thresholds for qualifying for the "organic" and "made with organic ingredients" labels. There was also dispute over whether food contact substances, such as chlorine used to clean food preparation equipment, would count as synthetic ingredients. Purists wanted any synthetic aids counted; change advocates did not, arguing that without those substances, it would be virtually impossible to mass-produce organic foods for retail sales to the ordinary consumer. For purists, mass production of organics itself was a contradictory idea, and using synthetics violated the spirit and probably the entire concept of organic production.

Change advocates basically won in the USDA rules, which allow the NOP to grant exemptions for specific synthetic chemicals to be used in processing without affecting the product's labeling if they are essential to making the product, do not substitute for an organic product, and do not negatively affect the environment or the healthfulness of the product. The purist faction was not satisfied with this rule and challenged it in court. In 2005, a federal appellate court sided with the purists, requiring that the USDA revise its rules and report back in one year. The ruling ordered products that failed to meet the new standards to be removed from the market within two years. The court's directive raised the specter that many organic products would have to be reformulated or relabeled and posed a major economic threat to the organics industry, particularly to the processed goods sector, which had to combine many organic ingredients, often from multiple suppliers and processors, into a finished product. Future investments in the industry also would be threatened if the number of organic products and their markets were restricted.

Various organics organizations attempted to work together to build consensus for a new rule to be submitted to the NOP and to

Congress, but agreement was elusive. The Organic Trade Association, the industry's main lobbying group, then took action. It avoided congressional debate or compromises by working with key members of Congress to insert new language into the 2005 agricultural appropriations bill after the final conference committee meeting between House and Senate negotiators. This process was unusual—and effective. A conference committee is only supposed to work out the differences between the versions of legislation passed by the House and the Senate; it is not supposed to add provisions that neither body has debated and voted on. If party leaders and lobbyists circumvent the legislative process in the name of speedy action, we lose the value of expert testimony, deliberation, consensus building, and legitimacy. The new law essentially overturned the circuit court ruling, allowing the NOP to permit the use of synthetic processing aids under restricted circumstances, and also allowing synthetic food contact substances to be widely used.

Policy Option One: Leave Things as They Are

Despite the fact that the USDA is the governmental agency that produces the guidelines a grower must follow to achieve USDA certification, actual certification is provided by a group of independent certification agencies. These agencies may require growers to meet more stringent standards than those imposed by the USDA. This is a benefit of the current system. After all, if an organic grower isn't satisfied with the rigors of a particular certification agency, he or she can just pick a different certification agency that is more to the grower's liking, and these certification agencies often have their own label posted right next to the USDA label. The consumer who cares about these stricter rules will know what they're getting.

Fundamentally, the requirements for organic production promote safety and sustainability, which is why organic production allows so few pesticides and fertilizers to be used. Additionally, for organically produced livestock, the drastic reduction or elimination of antibiotics and hormones is reason enough to eat organic meat, eggs, and dairy. The more humane treatment of animals, which organic production incorporates by allowing animals access to the outdoors, is another strong reason. For fruits and vegetables, the reduction (though not elimination) in the use of nonrenewable resources and pesticides could be sufficient reasons in and of themselves for claiming that today's organically produced food is better than conventionally produced food.

By giving organic growers the ability to label food produced in this natural way, the government is actually pointing to a way that consumers can eat more healthily. The reason the government refuses to acknowledge outright the superiority of organic foods is because acknowledging this "fact" will irritate big, important agricultural companies.

Regardless of the regulations and actions of executive agencies, what the president and first lady do sends a very powerful message. In 2009, President Barack Obama and his family obviously saw some benefit to using organic growing systems because they decided that their White House garden would be maintained using organic principles. They went so far as to import compost from the Rodale Institute, a nonprofit organization started by J. I. Rodale. This gesture brought legitimacy to organic gardening and farming (though the USDA says that there's nothing wrong with plants grown conventionally).

Right-Wing Rating ★★★ The current system is unnecessary, but, at the same time, it is voluntary and allows farmers to more or less govern themselves. If health-conscious consumers demand organic food, farmers will produce more of it.

Left-Wing Rating ★★ The government regulates what *organic* means and provides a clear signal to consumers that organic is better, but it doesn't actually have much enforcement power. Organic rules cater to agribusiness and do too little to promote locally grown foods or sustainable, nonindustrial production of food. Government needs to increase its funding of science in this area to demonstrate the benefits of organic foods for consumers and the environment.

Policy Option Two: Organic Growing Should Not Be Promoted

When the United States decided to certify food as organic, it opened a can of worms, and the night crawler of the bunch was the fact that the government officially takes the position that there is no difference between the health benefits of organically produced and conventionally produced foods. At this point, science has not shown a clear nutritional benefit to eating organic foods. The possible presence of synthetic pesticide residues on conventionally grown produce is a nonissue to the government and to consumers, since the levels of pesticide residues on our produce is considered too low to cause any harm. Besides, much of it can be washed off easily with hot water. Because organic food can't be proven to be more nutritious or safer, all it really offers is promotion of one sector of the agriculture industry—organic growers and processors—at taxpayer's expense.

The theory that organic food is more sustainable than conventionally produced food because it relies on products that are renewable and are better for the environment remains debatable. As we saw in the discussion of the science earlier in the chapter, nonrenewable fertilizers and potentially dangerous pesticides abound in the organic world, just as in conventional systems. Even if you are willing to accept the questionable argument that the USDA program necessarily results in the production of healthier and more environmentally sustainable foods, many of the foods labeled as organic are shipped in from elsewhere using nonrenewable fossil fuels.

Furthermore, organic food is elitist. Because of the increased manual labor that goes into it and the know-how that is needed to produce it successfully, organic food costs more than conventionally grown food, so only more affluent people can afford to eat it. By promoting the health benefits of organic food, we are telling people who have less money that they can't have access to the healthy foods that wealthier people can purchase. This is obviously a strong message, although organic producers vehemently deny it. And finally, it is far too easy for organic producers to cheat. Currently, record keeping and an annual visit by the certifying agency is all that is required to get certification. If producers want to slip in conventional chemicals, the chances of getting caught are slim and, even if they are caught, punishment is not assured.

Right-Wing Rating ★★★★ Let producers do what they need to do to grow crops. The government shouldn't promote or protect the market share of one set of farmers over another. If consumers demand organic products, entrepreneurial farmers will produce them and profit by doing so.

Left-Wing Rating ✯ The lack of governmental oversight puts consumers and the environment at risk. Consumers want reassurance from scientists and government that organic food is safe and healthy.

Policy Option Three: Tighten Organic Standards

To live up to its promise, organic food policy should change in two ways. First, environmentally sound practices must be required. The government would then be able to say without a doubt that organic foods are more environmentally friendly than conventionally produced foods. And second, more oversight is required to weed out the cheats.

Though organic food is supposed to be produced in a sustainable way, the reality is that some organic food is produced using unsustainable products such as guano and rock phosphate. Organic producers can also use certain poisons that may have a significant impact on the environment, just like conventional poisons. In fact some poisons, such as copper sulfate, will remain in the soil long after it has been applied, since copper is an element and therefore cannot degrade further.

Fresh, local produce is also a key to organic reform. The closer to home something is grown the better it tastes. Storage is the enemy of flavor (except perhaps in the case of pickles). But the advantages of locally produced food may go well beyond taste, as its proponents (often called locavores) tell us. The biggest environmental advantage of local food is that it does not travel very far and so minimizes the use of fossil fuels. Locavores may even prefer that crop inputs such as fertilizers be produced within a hundred or so miles of where the crop is being grown. Other benefits include the ability to know who is growing your food, so that you can decide whether they are trustworthy or not, and the reassurance that the food that you're eating supports the local economy. Seems like a win-win situation for everyone involved.

Yet here is one caveat to promoting locally produced foods. Larger farms tend to be more efficient in their use of fossil fuels than most of our local farms because of the economies of scale in using machinery to plant, harvest, and treat crops. Just as your car gets better gas mileage on the highway than in the city, so farm machinery is more efficient when it is allowed to run over a longer distance. Hence, locally grown foods are not necessarily produced more efficiently in terms of fossil fuel usage than foods grown and transported from farther away.

The USDA could assure us that organic food was produced in a way that is more environmentally sound than conventional production by requiring that it be produced without extensive use of machinery, and be sold only locally and without the use of products coming from across the country or the globe. It should also eliminate the use of nonrenewable resources and all pesticides.

Some organic growers would complain that this approach inhibits them from growing the foods that they choose to grow. Apple growers in the Northeast, for example, would have a tough time growing apples without spraying any pesticides at all. But there are ways around spraying for these apple producers, though these methods may be restrictive because they are labor intensive. Bags could be placed around the apples when they are young to prevent pests from getting inside, or traps could be set out in the fields to catch many of the pests that infect apples. Or, if those crops are so difficult to grow in some places, then perhaps they shouldn't be grown there. After all, if we don't grow oranges in Maine because of the weather, how is this different from not growing organic apples in Pennsylvania because of the insects?

Right-Wing Rating ★★ Our conventional methods of mass production and distribution of food are more energy efficient than the alternatives. Imposing more-stringent regulations and intrusive oversight on organic foods beyond what is currently required would limit options and increase costs for farmers, while restricting the choices of consumers.

Left-Wing Rating ★★★★★ Everyone is better off if government can assure us that organically produced food is superior to conventionally produced food. Buying locally not only helps the environment, it helps the local economy too.

The Bottom Line

If you believe that the current methods of production that are feeding the world are just fine and aren't concerned about synthetic chemicals, then you're probably irritated at the organic system. After all, the government refuses to say that there's any benefit to eating organic food. If people really want their own chemical-free food why don't they just grow it in their own backyard or go out to the farmer's market and get it from a farmer who doesn't use chemicals? Why do we need to spend the taxpayer's money and the legislature's time worrying about this nonissue?

Furthermore, while synthetic pesticides certainly have some drawbacks, no one has ever shown that the amount of these pesticides typically found on food is detrimental to humans—and besides, you can wash off the fruit. Organic producers use all kinds of chemicals themselves, albeit organic ones. Our current agricultural system feeds an astounding number of people and to imply that it isn't working by acknowledging organic production is not only a mistake, but potentially elitist. And finally, if you believe that the conventional system for producing food is broken because of the amount of fertilizer and pesticides used, then the answer isn't to have two separate methods of producing food—organic and conventional—but rather to change what conventional farming means.

Depending on your values, it's certainly reasonable to believe in either the USDA certification as it now exists, or in doing away with certification altogether. But we also see a third option that might be an even better fit with your beliefs.

For those who believe that organic growing holds great potential, but that this potential has not been achieved by the current system, by far the best system would be for the government to require practices that are known to be sustainable, and to declare that these practices are better for the environment. The government should install a new system for the classification of how a food is grown—superseding the organic program—that supports local and sustainable food production. In fact, there are already programs that do this, such as the Certified Naturally Grown program, which is a nongovernmental program catering to farmers who market their produce locally and who focus on using safe and sustainable practices. While this program shares a few of the same problems that exist in the USDA's program, especially in terms of enforcement, its focus on local production means that consumers are assured that the food that they are eating only traveled a short distance to get to market and so is potentially more sustainable. If consumers are concerned about the use of chemicals or the trustworthiness of the producer, then they can visit the production location themselves and check things out. A government program that required a reduction in the use of mechanized equipment, required producers to use only local fertilizers and feed, and banned *all* pesticides (not just synthetics) would really make a difference. Add stricter oversight and you've got a program that really works. A program like this would certainly reduce the number of organic farms, make organic food more expensive (paying for more oversight wouldn't be cheap and neither would an increase in the use of hand labor), and limit the offerings that could be supplied from these farms (you wouldn't get organic oranges in Maine), but it would also mean coming closer to reaching the ideals upon which organic farming was originally built.

CHAPTER 3

★★★

Pesticides: How Dangerous Is Dangerous?

WHAT WOULD YOU do if you discovered that the sandwich you're eating contains over 700 milligrams of a pesticide that is known to have mutagenic effects? And that according to its manufacturer, there is some evidence that the compound might increase the toxemia of pregnancy and cause adverse reproductive effects and birth defects in animals? This stuff could even kill you outright if you ingested as little as three ounces. Would you stop eating? Well, if you're eating a Big Mac hamburger, then you're ingesting over 700 milligrams of the herbicide sodium chloride, otherwise known as table salt.

Even taking the previous paragraph into account, we doubt any of you will seriously consider cutting salt out of your diet (unless you already do so for other medical reasons). We are all familiar with salt. Our parents used it, our grandparents used it, and we like what it does to the taste of our food, so most of us are comfortable using it. But all of us also know that a diet high in salt isn't good for us, and besides, it can taste bad. So we regulate our salt intake to some degree. Salt, despite its potential for damage, is still deemed safe. But for chemicals that we're unfamiliar with, and that have weird and scary names such as 2,4-D, atrazine, imadicloprid, and permethrin, we don't have the same history to fall back on.

The town of Hudson, Quebec, took a completely different approach to pesticides in 1991 when it decided that dandelions were preferable to toxic chemicals and became the first place in North America to ban the use of pesticides for so-called cosmetic purposes. Chemlawn and Spraytech, two lawn care companies, were apparently not impressed by this and applied chemicals to lawns in Hudson despite the new laws. They were fined $300 for their efforts. In retaliation, the companies sued for their right to spray chemicals, but they lost in every court they entered, including the Supreme Court of Canada in 2001. This cleared the way for any province or municipality in Canada to ban the use of pesticides if they so wished, and many did. In 2006, the province of Quebec entered its final phase of pesticide restrictions, banning the most commonly used household pesticides, including the insecticide carbaryl (also known as Sevin). Ontario banned most pesticides that were used for cosmetic purposes in 2009.

Meanwhile, as many Canadians enjoy less exposure to pesticides (and more exposure to dandelions and crabgrass), the United States sits by and watches. True, the EPA bans particularly nasty chemicals, but by and large, people in the United States are allowed the freedom to use whatever chemicals they deem appropriate to kill the weeds and insects that they think are taking over their backyards.

There are many people in the United States who consider synthetic pesticides a danger that poses unreasonable risks to the environment and to humans, and who would support pesticide bans similar to those in Canada. Sometimes it's difficult to see an argument for the other side—until you look at your lawn and the food on your table. Simply put, pesticides are the easiest and least time-consuming way to rid a lawn, garden, or field of those unsightly weeds, obnoxious insects, and plant diseases that all of us hate.

Yards and gardens are only the most obvious places where pesticides are used, and since we own them, we control them. But pesticides of one sort or another are also used in orchards, on farms, in federal and state buildings, around schools, in lakes and streams, and in parks. These killers are ubiquitous! They can even be detected on organic fruits and vegetables, as we pointed out in the previous chapter. It wasn't always this way. Once upon a time, these chemicals were considered valuable and used very sparingly simply because it was tough for people to acquire them. Pesticide use on lawns and gardens was almost unheard of. Back then, if you wanted to keep weeds out of your lawn, you'd actually have to use your hands to do something more than squeeze the trigger of a bottle.

A Brief History of Pesticides

Pesticides first emerged during Roman times when sulfur was used to control various problems in fields and homes, and salt was used in warfare to kill crops. Since then, and before the advent of what we now call synthetic pesticides, many other chemicals were added to our palette of tools for killing pests, including pyrethrum, a natural chemical that comes from a type of chrysanthemum, and arsenic, another natural compound very poisonous to insects (as well as people). In the 1800s and early 1900s, lead arsenate, calcium arsenate, and hellebore (made from the roots of *Veratrum viride* and *V. album*) were dangerous chemicals that are rarely, if ever, used today because of their toxicity and their relative inefficacy when compared to modern pesticides. Herbicides included salt and vinegar, and compounds such as sulfur and Bordeaux mixture—which is a combination of lime and copper sulfate—were used to control plant disease. But after World War II, things changed. War has always forced humans to innovate, and that war was no different. It provided many new chemicals for pest control, some of which are still being used today.

At the beginning of the war, a number of new chemicals were introduced that were highly effective and relatively safe, especially when compared with something like lead arsenate. These included the insecticide DDT, introduced in 1939, which had a profound effect on lice and the transmission of diseases among troops, and the herbicide 2,4-D, a wartime secret that targeted broadleaved plants, such as dandelions and clover, but left grasses relatively unscathed. Though it was never used during World War II, it did find a place in the Vietnam War as an ingredient in the defoliant Agent Orange. The organophosphate insecticides—chemicals based on the chemistry of nerve gases that were used against humans—were also first identified around the time of World War II. As a group, these chemicals were far superior to their predecessors in terms of efficacy and, in most cases, safety, which led to their widespread use. But this use was often uncontrolled and overly enthusiastic, and it was just a matter of time before our irresponsible application of these poisons caught up with us.

Dangers Emerge

The potential dangers of pesticides were first brought to the attention of the United States, and to a lesser extent the world, by Rachel Carson's 1962 book, *Silent Spring*. The book was required reading in nearly every high school, and it's a shame that it isn't more popular today. The author dramatically described the negative effects of DDT on majestic birds of prey and on humans, and warned of a bleak future if aggressive action wasn't taken to ban the most dangerous pesticides and to reduce the use of pesticides in general. Rachel Carson was not completely opposed to pesticide use, just their gross misuse. As she wrote, "It is not my contention that chemical pesticides must never be used. I do contend that we have put poisonous . . . chemicals into the hands of persons largely or wholly ignorant of their potentials for harm."

Human exposure to pesticides and the associated health risks occur in a number of ways, including in their application or misapplication, or simply by eating a fruit or vegetable from a farm where these poisons were used. Agricultural workers, who are exposed to the chemicals regularly, and infants and children, who have lower tolerances to poisons than adults, are particularly at risk. Consequently, since the 1940s, the government has been actively involved in trying to determine which chemicals are safe, which are safe if used under specific and limited conditions, and which are so risky that they should be banned entirely.

Rachel Carson was not completely opposed to pesticide use, just their gross misuse.

Though many people would like to see pesticides disappear, a somewhat less vocal but extremely powerful group considers them necessary. The government's attempts to ban or limit their use are viewed warily by chemical manufacturers and farmers, who see these chemicals as critical to producing mass quantities of food at low cost. They are concerned that their livelihoods are threatened by scares whipped up by the media or environmental groups rather than by scientific evidence of the effects of a chemical on humans or the environment.

The Science

Pesticides offer one simple thing to their users: they get rid of pests by poisoning them. The poisons present in pesticides vary widely and have many different effects on the intended target. With herbicides, which kill plants, the poison may shut down photosynthesis, stop the plant from producing an amino acid, supply an overdose of a plant-specific hormone, or destroy any cells that the herbicide touches (as is the case with salt). Insecticides may kill insects by interfering with their nervous systems (these tend to be very dangerous chemicals), by preventing the insect from eating, by interfering with the ability to grow, or through a variety of other devious means. Fungicides can change the pH of the surface of a leaf, prevent a cell from dividing or a spore from germinating, or do a host of other things to knock out a disease.

While there are certainly other ways to get rid of pests, nothing else is quite as quick and efficient as a shot of poison. Over the years, pesticides have served us in a variety of ways, from insecticides that have helped us control malaria and yellow-fever-carrying mosquitoes, to herbicides that have helped us control the weeds on our property, some of which—water hemlock and nightshade, for example—are deadly poisons. Conservative estimates of how many lives have been saved by controlling disease-carrying insects with insecticides are in the millions. Pesticides also allow us to produce the copious amounts of food needed to feed our country. Many of the crops that we enjoy, such as apples and peaches, have so many potentially devastating pests that it would be almost impossible to produce them in any quantity without using pesticides. Even crops like corn and wheat depend on applications of herbicides to control weeds, insecticides to control insects, and fungicides to stop dangerous diseases. Without these pesticide applications, we would be left with only a fraction of the food that we currently grow.

The United States spends about 13 billion dollars on pesticides every year, which saves about 52 billion dollars worth of crops and keeps us rolling in unblemished foods. Still, there are many potential dangers involved with using pesticides. These dangers are usually classified and measured in three ways. First, acute toxicity, which is a measure of how much of the poison is needed in a single dose to kill you. Second, chronic toxicity, which is a measure of how repeated exposure to sublethal doses of the poison will affect you. And finally, environmental effects, which is an overview of how the poison will affect nontarget organisms such as bees or fish. We will look at each of these in turn.

Acute Toxicity

Of the dangers posed by pesticides, the most obvious and easiest to measure is acute toxicity. How toxic is a single dose of a poison? It is usually calculated by exposing rats, mice, or rabbits to various concentrations of the poison and then expressing the results as the milligrams of the poison needed per kilogram of the animal's weight to have a 50 percent chance of killing it. This is called an LD_{50} (LD stands for lethal dose and 50 stands for 50 percent). LD_{50} ratings can be further categorized by how the dose is administered. In other words, what is the difference if the poison is administered by mouth, to the skin, or, in some cases, through the air? Regardless of how the dose is administered, the lower the LD_{50} is the more dangerous the chemical is. It is unfortunate that one of the fundamental ways to determine the toxicity of pesticides is by using them on animals. Currently there are no other testing options that are as universally accepted.

While there is quite a range of LD_{50}s among pesticides, most of the pesticides that you are likely to encounter on garden center shelves will have LD_{50}s that are quite high. In fact, the caffeine in your morning coffee probably has a lower LD_{50} (in other words, it is more acutely toxic) than any chemical that you or your fastidious neighbors have ever sprayed on a lawn. Caffeine has an oral LD_{50} of 192 mg/kg in rats, while four of the most common lawn herbicides—2,4-D, dicamba, mecoprop, and triclopyr—have rat-based oral LD_{50}s of 375, 757, 431, and 630 mg/kg. Of course you still need to examine the concentration at which these chemicals are applied. After all, it would take somewhere in the neighborhood of 100 cups of coffee to kill someone. The caffeine in your coffee is more diluted than the herbicidal chemicals we named above, right? Wrong. Actually, right out of the spray tank, these herbicides are at roughly the same concentration as the amount of caffeine in your coffee. Of course, these are just some examples. There are pesticides that are much more and much less toxic (and more and less concentrated coffee), but it is worth noting that one of the most toxic pesticides ever known, the now-banned Black Leaf 40, an insecticide that worked by affecting an insect's nervous system, was based on the insecticide nicotine (the "40" stood for 40 percent nicotine sulfate), which is still legal for you to inhale or put between your cheek and gum.

Chronic Toxicity

If our only concern about pesticides had to do with their acute toxicity, then the stigma currently associated with their use probably wouldn't exist. But what happens to a person when they are repeatedly exposed to a poison again and again over months or years? The fear is that pesticides will have chronic effects, the most disturbing of which is cancer. There are two ways to establish the likelihood of a pesticide causing cancer. The first is through animal testing. This testing involves feeding test animals the highest dose that they can handle without showing an obvious effect (called the NOEL, for No Observed Effect Level) repeatedly over days, weeks, or months. Frequently, this involves force-feeding, as the NOEL dose is often quite high and may be distasteful to the animals. Notes are taken on how the animals fare (sometimes including their ability to reproduce) and then, at the end of the experiment, the animals are dissected. Evidence of cancer is the most significant of the problems that researchers are looking for, but malfunctioning or oversized or undersized organs, such as the kidneys or liver, are assessed as well. Generally, if a pesticide causes cancer in animals during these tests, that pesticide never reaches the garden center shelves. (Pesticides already on the shelves will be removed if tests demonstrate they cause cancer.)

Epidemiological studies are the second way that a pesticide is examined to see whether it causes cancer or other terminal illnesses. These studies examine people who have been exposed to a pesticide, and then track their health over several years. Some of them are pretty scary. In one 2000 study examining pesticide use around homes, it was established that exposing children to pesticides may increase the likelihood of that child developing non-Hodgkin's lymphoma. More recent research found a relationship between the herbicides pendimethalin and EPTC and pancreatic cancer. While these links may not show the remarkable correlation that tobacco, for example, has with cancer, they are still statistically significant and need to be acknowledged. Other problems with pesticides may include a slight increase in risk for Parkinson's disease, as indicated by one large study that included well over 100,000 participants. Another study saw a correlation between low-birth-weight babies and women who were pregnant when they were exposed to pesticides, particularly chlorpyrifos, an insecticide (now illegal) for use around the home.

The problem with just accepting these studies and others like them as proof positive that pesticides are killing us is that epidemiological studies don't always agree. The Agricultural Health Study, which followed (and is continuing to follow) more than 80,000 pesticide applicators and their spouses, is run by the EPA and compares these subjects to the general population. In fact, this is the study that demonstrated the link between pancreatic cancer and some herbicides. Despite that correlation, on the whole the pesticide applicators fared well when compared to the general population. They have a tendency to survive longer than the population at large, a result that perhaps can be attributed to the daily exercise of many pesticide applicators (who are often farmers).

Epidemiological studies are valuable tools, but they just don't provide the unambiguous science that proves that pesticides, as a group, are bad. For example, while one study showed that chlorpyrifos has a weak relationship to the onset of rectal cancer, the same study showed that dichlorophenoxyacetic acid (2,4-D)—one of the most commonly used herbicides around the home for weeds like dandelion and clover— was associated with a slight decrease in colon cancer.

In general, studies into the carcinogenicity of pesticides show only slight, insignificant increases in the risks of certain cancers as they are associated with the use of pesticides, if they show anything. Even when these risks are found to be significant, they are usually linked to one particular pesticide, rather than pesticides in general, and they usually show that people who are exposed to more of a particular pesticide are more likely to be affected.

Environmental Effects

Acute and chronic toxicity of pesticides represent just the beginning of the problems posed by pesticide use. Certain pesticides have demonstrated themselves to be quite harmful to the environment around us. Many pesticides that we use are known as broad-spectrum poisons, meaning they kill the pest that has been targeted as well as many other innocent bystanders. Over the years, numerous pesticides have been banned because of their effects on creatures they were never meant to kill. DDT, for example, was banned in large part because of its effects on the ability of birds to reproduce (exposed birds produced very thin-shelled eggs), while the insecticide diazinon, once a very effective ant killer, was banned in large part because of its deadly effects on birds, fish, and mammals. One of the most widely used pesticides in the world, atrazine, is an herbicide that kills weeds before they emerge from the ground. This poison is also well known for its propensity to get into groundwater, where it appears to have hormonal effects on frogs and potentially other amphibians, causing them to become hermaphrodites.

Misapplication or accidents add another layer of potential problems. We know that if the popular pesticide glyphosate (Roundup), for example, is applied to a small pond or even a puddle where tadpoles are playing, there is a good possibility that those creatures will be killed. With many insecticides—even if they are properly applied—beneficial insects such as honeybees and predator insects are likely to be killed. Many of the pesticides we use are also highly toxic to aquatic organisms if the pesticides find their way into a pond, lake, or stream. Rotenone, once a popular organic insecticide, has now been relegated to use as a fish poison. Some pesticides, such as the organic fungicide copper sulfate and various synthetic herbicides, may even build up in the environment as they are used over time, potentially causing future problems. But we are now discovering that some of the scariest problems, environmental and otherwise, are those that occur even at very low concentrations.

Low Doses

Most of us are willing to take the responsibility inherent in our use of pesticides when we spray them or apply them to our yards, just as we take responsibility for other risky pursuits, such as driving a motorcycle or taking a drink of alcohol. But pesticides aren't quite the same as motorcycles or alcohol because most of us are exposed to pesticides every day in ways that we aren't aware of and can't control. Everything from the food we eat, to the grass we walk on, to the water we drink may contain pesticides of one sort or another, at one concentration or another. As we discovered in the previous chapter, even organic food may be contaminated with synthetic pesticides. Fruits and vegetables are notorious for having large amounts of insecticides and fungicides, both organic and synthetic, applied to them to ward off insects and disease, and lawns—our neighbor's, if not our own—are sprayed with herbicides to control dandelions. Pesticides used on farmland can leach through the soil to reach our drinking water, or run off into nearby streams and ponds. The more we test the world around us, and the more sensitive our testing equipment gets, the more it becomes obvious that we are constantly in contact with low doses of pesticides.

How are we to know, when a piece of fruit contains 5 parts per million of an insecticide, whether this level of poison is sufficient to cause harm to someone who eats it? Even if it doesn't cause us any obvious harm, what if we continue to eat fruit with this pesticide for days, weeks, and years? In other words, what does chronic exposure to these extremely low doses of poison do to us? There is no data proving that any of our currently used poisons are dangerous at the levels that we would typically find them in fruits and vegetables or on our lawns. But how can we really know? Likewise, while we get extremely concerned when an herbicide such as atrazine is discovered in our water supplies, there isn't actually any hard data available that will tell us exactly what that atrazine will do. Rather, we're worried about it simply because it seems reasonable to worry about it. The government provides information on what it considers to be unsafe levels of various contaminants, but can we be certain that lower levels are really safe? After all, it is impossible to know exactly how a pesticide will affect any given animal in any given circumstance. There is no data on how eating an apple a day with five parts per million of a new pesticide that was just registered for use is going to affect us in thirty years. On one hand, it seems better not to have these poisons at any level in our food and drinking water. But on the other hand, if no evidence can be found that these poisons are dangerous, and there are compelling beneficial reasons to use them, such as a weed-free lawn or the ability to grow valuable crops, then why should we lose the use of these poisons?

There is no data proving that any of our currently used poisons are dangerous at the levels that we would typically find them in fruits and vegetables or on our lawns. But how can we really know?

Although there is little data on the effects on humans of extremely low doses of pesticides, there is some data from amphibians that should make us sit up and take notice. Experimenting with frogs, Tyrone Hayes, a researcher at the University of California at Berkeley, found that atrazine, an herbicide used on many crops, especially corn, will cause frogs to change their sex. This occurs at an extremely low dose, which might be found under typical conditions in a pond, or even in groundwater located close to an agricultural field. Other researchers have also found that very low concentrations of commonly used pesticides may dramatically affect aquatic communities. Rick Relyea, a researcher at the University of Pittsburgh, discovered that a mixture of very low doses of ten commonly used pesticides would kill leopard frogs but not gray tree frogs, though the tree frogs grew twice as large as they normally would. The mixture included the insecticides malathion and carbaryl (nerve toxins used around homes and schools as well as on commercial farms), and the herbicides 2,4-D (the most commonly used herbicide on lawns, best known for its ability to kill dandelions) and glyphosate (Roundup). Similar mixtures of commonly used insecticides and herbicides at concentrations likely to be found in streams and rivers are also known to affect the ability of salmon to sense the world around them, damaging their olfactory sensors (basically their noses), with the potential for drastically affecting their lives. And these are just some of the findings that show the effects of low concentrations of pesticides on living creatures.

But these findings don't necessarily have anything to do with humans. We are mammals after all, not amphibians or fish. Still, our organs are basically the same as those found in frogs or salmon, so it is hard not to speculate about what atrazine and other poisons might do to young, developing boys and girls. While we have no powerful evidence at this time that low concentrations of pesticides are hurting us, neither do we know for sure that repeated exposure to a low dose of any given pesticide or mixture of pesticides is perfectly safe.

Government Policy

National government regulation and inspection of food began in 1906 with the Pure Food and Drug Act and the Meat Inspection Act. President Theodore Roosevelt pushed Congress to pass the Meat Inspection Act in response to public outcry about the working conditions and health hazards in the meatpacking industry as depicted in Upton Sinclair's novel, *The Jungle.* This act empowered the Department of Agriculture to inspect food processors, and was supported by many food manufacturers who wanted to purge unscrupulous operators from the business. While it didn't restrict pesticide use, the act did open the door for the government to have a say about the quality of the food that we buy.

By the late 1930s and 1940s, technology was revolutionizing farming. Synthetic fertilizers and pesticides came into widespread use, theoretically making food production cheaper and more efficient. But farmers were worried that this new technology might be ineffective or dangerous. The chemical companies themselves wanted government to screen out fly-by-night operators and believed that national standards were preferable to a patchwork of state regulations. Congress initially responded with the 1938 Food, Drug, and Cosmetics Act, which required manufacturers to file test results for new products with the Food and Drug Administration (FDA). However, companies could declare test data or chemical formulas to be trade secrets to avoid providing them to the FDA. Even worse, the 1938 act prevented the FDA from testing and clearing a product before it hit the market. To remove chemicals from the market, the FDA had to prove in court that they were dangerous. The product was literally considered innocent until proven guilty. This understandably concerned many people because some highly toxic substances were being used at the time, including many that contained arsenic. Most people who were aware of the situation knew that stronger legislation was needed.

The Federal Insecticide, Fungicide, and Rodenticide Act (FIFRA) of 1947 was tougher than its predecessors on the pesticide companies. It balanced the economic potential of the new methods of pest control with the potential human and environmental costs of those methods. FIFRA stated that pesticides should not cause "unreasonable adverse effects on the environment," but it also required regulators to account for the "economic, social, and environmental costs as well as the potential benefits of the use of any pesticide." All farming chemicals had to be registered for each of their intended uses, and manufacturers were required to provide adequate data from tests of the chemical's effects on human health and the environment.

In 1954 the Food, Drug, and Cosmetics Act (FDCA) was amended to require the FDA to determine "tolerances"—the maximum levels of chemical residues—that would be allowed on all raw and some processed foods. The 1958 Delaney Amendment (to the FDCA) went further, banning cancer-causing chemicals on commodities used in processed foods. Although it seems reasonable and obvious that cancer-causing chemicals should not be allowed in the foods we eat, the practical effects of the Delaney Amendment became increasingly stringent—and controversial. Over time, testing equipment had become more advanced, which made lower levels of potentially cancer-causing chemicals detectable, even though such low levels would not be likely to cause health problems. Additionally, the different standards applied to raw and to processed foods became increasingly problematic as the number and varieties of processed foods increased, and more kinds of raw foods were used to produce them. The final use of many raw foods was hard to determine ahead of time by the farmer, so it was difficult for the farmer or processor to know exactly how to handle the raw food to meet the proper standard. It also was hard for the government (or manufacturer) to trace an ingredient in a processed food back to its origins to ensure that it had been treated properly.

The FDA announced in 1969 the beginning of a two-year phase-out of DDT for all but "essential" purposes. It was the first time the government had forbidden the use of a pesticide because it inherently posed potential dangers, not because it was mislabeled, adulterated, or misused. In some ways, however, DDT was an easy target. In addition to the public concern generated by *Silent Spring*, its effectiveness had been declining as many insect species developed resistance. This made its future look increasingly unprofitable. Besides, chemical manufacturers could be assuaged by the fact that farmers would need to shift to costlier replacements that were coming onto the market.

In the 1970s, the government's concern with its environmental image led to the creation of the Environmental Protection Agency (EPA) and the Federal Environmental Pesticide Control Act (FEPCA) of 1972, which allowed the new EPA to determine what data chemical manufacturers needed to submit with each application to evaluate the safety of their product for the ecosystem. In essence, the same pesticide would have to get approval from multiple agencies: the FDA evaluated the effects that consumption of food residues had on humans, the EPA evaluated environmental impacts, and the Occupational Safety and Health Administration (OSHA) evaluated workplace safety, among other agency reviews. FEPCA had multiple goals and forced the EPA to ensure that chemical pesticides were safe, environmentally benign, *and* effective. Each of these goals is obviously worthwhile, but they also have the potential to be conflicting. For example, a chemical may be effective at killing pests, but not safe for humans or the environment. Unfortunately, this act gave the EPA little guidance on how to resolve such contradictions. Under FEPCA, the EPA had to register products, including those already on the market, without having a standardized system for evaluating them. Studies for some products were ten to twenty years old. To speed up registrations, the EPA ended up skimming through files for the *presence* of test data and made little effort to verify the validity of the information.

The next twenty years brought a policy stalemate as producers and environmental and consumer groups struggled over how the EPA should evaluate pesticides and their food residues. Then, in 1989, the Alar scare brought things to a head. Alar was a chemical

EACH federal agency charged with addressing the dangers of hazardous chemicals has its own mission, priorities, clientele, and way of viewing the world. Often, there are significant barriers to cooperation among these agencies. The USDA, for example, sees the world from the perspective of the farmer and is most concerned with producing an abundant food supply. The EPA sees the world from an ecological perspective and is most concerned with the health and environmental effects of the chemicals that farmers use on their fields. The FDA sees the world from the public health perspective and is most concerned with the health and safety of food products.

The multiplicity of agencies involved in regulating hazardous chemicals is not unusual, nor are the problems created by trying to coordinate policy across multiple agencies. Congress creates the agencies at different times and for different purposes. When it passes a new law it tends to add a new box on the existing organizational chart rather than fighting battles with existing agencies and their clienteles to create a more streamlined organizational chart.

used by apple producers that made all of their apples ripen at the same time. This saved a great deal of labor at harvest time. Unfortunately for apple producers, studies began showing up that suggested Alar was carcinogenic. Not all studies indicated this, and the number of apples that an individual would need to ingest to cause a problem was quite high, even in a worst-case scenario. Nonetheless, major news outlets including *60 Minutes* aired the story, causing a tremendous backlash against the use of this chemical and an intense concern about the residues of other chemicals. The stalemate broke in the early 1990s as federal appellate courts ruled that both raw and processed foods must meet the strict Delaney standard, substantially limiting the presence of chemicals in food products. The court's 1992 ruling in *Les v. Reilly* would have forced the EPA to follow the Delaney clause and cancel the use of several commonly used chemicals. It was never enforced, however, because the Clinton administration proposed a single standard for raw and processed foods, removing the requirement that economic considerations be taken into account when determining food safety regulations, and replacing the Delaney

Amendment's ban on cancer-causing chemicals with requirements based on the amount of risk posed by the chemical. Congress unanimously passed the Food Quality Protection Act (FQPA) of 1996.

The Food Quality Protection Act directs the EPA to review all pesticide tolerance rules to ensure that they adequately protect children and infants, since children may be at greater risk than adults at previously accepted levels of pesticide residue. The act also requires the EPA to analyze the combined toxic effects of multiple pesticides for an individual's "aggregate exposure"—both dietary and occupational (including use on lawns). In place of the Delaney clause, the FQPA requires a "reasonable certainty" of no harm from residues on food, defining reasonable certainty as a one in a million chance of the residue causing cancer or another major health ailment. Other food additives would still be subject to the Delaney clause's zero risk standard. In essence, Congress told the EPA to figure out which chemicals were "too dangerous" and let the EPA take the political heat from those who thought particular chemicals were being treated too leniently or too stringently. Congress established a timeline for the EPA, giving it until 2006 to review the tolerances it had established prior to the FQPA to ensure that each met the new standards. The challenge for the EPA was that it would have to review the tolerances of 9700 chemicals. Just a small bit of homework for the EPA, in addition to its other responsibilities. But in August 2006, the EPA announced that it had met the FQPA deadline for reassessing pesticide tolerances.

The FQPA also preempted any state standards on food residues, meaning that pesticide manufacturers and users had to meet one national standard rather than many state or local government restrictions. Nonetheless, state and local governments can regulate pesticides for other purposes. California, for example, banned the pesticide lindane in 2002 for pharmaceutical use. The FDA, however, still permits this insecticide to be used by physicians for treating lice and scabies. Different executive agencies can and do reach different conclusions about the risks and benefits of a pesticide.

The Political Dynamics

Members of Congress are not chemists and would prefer not to make judgments regarding which chemicals are unsafe. Most members do not want to antagonize farmers, chemical manufacturers, or retailers who conduct business in their districts or who contribute to their campaigns. Nor do they wish to be seen as less than enthusiastic about protecting the health of their constituents. Many members of Congress would be perfectly happy if scientists came before them and all agreed that "this pesticide is safe, allow it" or "this pesticide is unsafe, ban it." They would then have a clear policy direction and would trust the evidence on which they were making that decision. But scientists rarely develop a quick consensus, leading politicians to trust their own predispositions rather than expert advice. As political scientist Christopher Bosso concluded in his study of pesticide regulation: "That scientists of equally impressive credentials disagreed vehemently about the side effects of pesticides . . . very likely forced members [of Congress] to base their decisions more on initial biases than on the weight of scientific evidence."

Fortunately, members of Congress have a way out. By passing laws that order executive branch agencies to implement the legislation and make the tough choices, they can pass the buck and effectively get themselves out of potentially sticky situations. FIFRA, for example, orders the USDA to take action against environmentally damaging pesticides, *and* to make sure that their actions have minimal economic impact. The USDA has to make the tough calls about how to balance the hazards of pesticide use against harm to the economy, not Congress. After the USDA has acted and local farmers (or environmental activists) complain, then the local member of Congress can swoop in and criticize the agency regardless of the decision it has made. Similarly, Congress stalled for years in its consideration of the Food Quality Protection Act, with members unable to agree which pesticide residues posed a health risk. Once the federal courts forced their hand, Congress passed the buck to the EPA and ordered them to review all chemical residues and determine which ones failed to meet the new standards of the law.

Congress usually requires that all affected parties be able to participate in the executive branch's decision-making processes, which means that the disagreements the various groups had during congressional debate, when the law was first constructed, will not go away as the agency decides how to implement the law. Environmental organizations actually quit the EPA's Pesticide Advisory Board in April 1999, claiming that the EPA was moving too slowly and was caving in to chemical manufacturers and farmers as it tried to develop methods to evaluate pesticide residues and comply with the Food Quality Protection Act. Meanwhile, the agency often does not have the funding or staff to undertake its current mission effectively, let alone do the new activities required by Congress under the deadlines and restrictions it has imposed. Inevitably, someone is likely to be upset—whatever decision the agency makes—and appeal the decision to Congress or the courts.

The courts then step in to interpret the law and determine whether or not the agency is acting in a manner consistent with the law passed by Congress. Court decisions also spur Congress to act, as occurred in the Food Quality Protection Act, following a court's ruling that the Delaney amendment—banning cancer-causing chemicals from food items—must be applied to both raw and processed foods. The court's action dramatically increased the cost to both Congress and the chemical manufacturers of a failure to compromise, and a compromise quickly ensued.

The main problem caused by the morass of agencies and rules

CONGRESS can choose to follow science closely or disregard it completely, depending on whatever its members believe their constituents, parties, or consciences want. But the Supreme Court has set high standards of scientific proof for agencies of the executive branch in issuing regulations. In *Industrial Union Dept., AFL-CIO v. American Petroleum Institute* (1980), the Court ruled that agencies must demonstrate a factual basis, not merely a well-reasoned professional judgment, to justify proposed regulations. To meet these standards, executive branch agencies often develop organizational structures to gather and use scientific expertise in their policymaking. The EPA, for example, has a Science Advisory Board of independent experts drawn from a number of fields and backgrounds who advise EPA administrators on scientific issues, a Science Policy Council of EPA scientists who advise EPA administrators, a peer review policy to make sure that scientists who provide external reviews of EPA policies are qualified and independent, and staff that monitors the scientific quality of the research done by EPA specialist scientists (in air pollution or toxics, for example).

regulating hazardous chemicals is that there is no clear and consistent definition of acceptable risk in federal law. Congress has either allowed agencies to define acceptable risk for themselves, or it has listed so many criteria for risk determination that the decisions get bogged down while an agency tries to decide which criteria have priority. It's not uncommon for different agencies to allow different levels of exposure to the same chemical, depending on the purpose for which the chemical is being used. The result is that there is no single, straightforward answer from the government to the question, is this chemical dangerous? It depends on the purpose the chemical is used for and the risk standards that apply to that purpose. Food residues are subject to low standards of risk, while using chemicals on your yard or field are subject to higher levels of risk.

Several trends in the politics of pesticides are clear. First, more types of groups are getting involved, which is increasing the level of conflict and making compromises harder to forge. Prior to the 1960s, decisions regarding pesticide policies were usually made by the farming and chemical manufacturing communities, with the goal of producing effective pesticides. Since then, environmental and consumer groups have played a prominent role and have put much greater weight on the possible negative effects of pesticides. Second, the burden of proof is shifting toward chemical manufacturers having to prove that their products are safe and environmentally benign before they are labeled for use. Policy is increasingly protecting the public from chemical products rather than protecting manufacturers from government bureaucrats run amok. Third, science itself has developed much more sensitive and sophisticated ways of measuring and analyzing the presence and effects of chemicals, so we are becoming more and more aware of the possible negative effects of pesticides. Today, for example, scientists can analyze not only whether DDT kills birds or causes cancer in humans, but also whether it is an endocrine disruptor, a chemical that interferes with hormones responsible for normal functions such as brain growth and sexual development. As scientific understanding changes, so does the application of government regulations that are based on science. As a consequence, legislation governing the regulation of pesticides is a long way from being complete, as is the interpretation of this legislation by the EPA, FDA, OSHA, and other agencies.

Policy Option One: Leave Things as They Are

Right now, the EPA and state organizations are doing a pretty good job of regulating pesticides. Our agricultural system provides abundant, healthy food. If people want food grown without synthetic pesticides they can buy food labeled USDA Organic. When a pesticide is identified as a danger to society or the environment, it is removed from sale from most, if not all, of its uses. Though many people like to clump pesticides together as a group, there are many different types of pesticides that represent many different levels of risk, and the federal government goes to great pains to establish which pesticides should be allowed and which shouldn't. If the federal government fails to catch a harmful pesticide, state governments have the authority to step in and ban a pesticide for home use.

The EPA does not have ironclad evidence that pesticides are harming those applying them, much less those eating the food. If the agency were to impose stricter tolerances for crops, farmers would be less able to grow crops the way they see fit. It is also possible that by eliminating some pesticides we might actually hurt more people than we help. While some people would no longer be exposed to trace amounts of poisons that have negligible toxicity, they also might not have the same access to fruits and vegetables that often require more intensive pesticide use.

Further restricting or even banning pesticide use for aesthetic reasons would restrict our freedom. We are a country based on the concept that we should be free to do whatever we wish as long as it does not infringe upon the rights of others. The pesticides that we use on and around our homes have not been conclusively proven to cause damage in the amounts at which they are normally applied. Sure, if we use them incorrectly someone could get hurt, but that's true of almost anything. We regulate pesticides like we do cars (crash tests and speed limits for cars; concentration limits and use instructions for pesticides) but we stop short of banning cars even though it's clear they kill thousands of people a year.

If pesticides are applied according to the instructions on the label, and if at-risk people and animals don't go near them, then pesticides have not proven to be dangerous. Why are we so worried, when most of us will never see anything close to the doses that pesticide applicators see, and when those who apply pesticides show only very slight increases in particular cancers if they show anything at all? It seems reasonable to expect that people who have an occupation that puts them in contact with a substance that is considered dangerous will be more likely to be affected by that substance. People whose jobs force them to be outside in the sun are more likely to get skin cancer. Additionally, people who smoke cigarettes are more likely to get lung cancer than people who are exposed to pesticides are likely to get any type of cancer. How can we even entertain the thought of banning products that make our yards more attractive and help us produce food?

Some plants that are controlled by pesticides are quite a bit more toxic than the pesticide itself. One of the pesticides most likely to be banned for home use is 2,4-D, which has been around for quite a while and which is one of the most important tools we currently have in controlling noxious weeds. This chemical can be used on poison ivy, Canadian thistle, kudzu, and many other plants. It can also be used on toxic weeds such as nightshade, water hemlock, and tansy mustard. Losing a pesticide that controls noxious and invasive weeds in public areas has obvious ramifications. While small parks close to urban centers may be able to use volunteers to weed by hand, what will a large public park do if it can't control its poison ivy? The risk of a lawsuit by someone with an allergy to this plant has the potential to lead parks to shut off particular portions of their land where they can't control the undergrowth. If we were to ban the pesticides in wasp sprays, would it lead to more wasp stings, perhaps even to someone with an allergy to these stings? Have lives been saved by pesticides because they have rid a yard of poisonous plants or insects that might otherwise have harmed or even killed a young child? It seems more than likely.

Right-Wing Rating ★★★ People generally have the freedom to use the chemicals that they need to both grow crops and maintain their yards. No one wants chemicals that are a public safety hazard used without proper training and equipment. But we should be able to use some of the more effective pesticides that have been banned with relatively little evidence against them. Banning these chemicals has increased food prices and restricted our ability to maintain our land.

Left-Wing Rating ★★★ Current policy controls the worst chemicals, but it should do more. We don't know for sure what effect low doses of pesticides have on people or the environment, especially over long periods of time. We should err on the side of caution and avoid using pesticides unless we have clear evidence that they are safe. Chemical manufacturers have too much power to delay the government from acting on scientific findings.

Policy Option Two: State and Local Governments Need to Provide Greater Protection from Pesticides

Follow Canada's example and ban, or at least heavily restrict, pesticide use for ornamental purposes at state (or province, in Canada's case) and local levels. Such a ban would have little effect on farmers' use of pesticides, instead concentrating legislation on controlling pesticides that are used for aesthetic purposes. There have already been some efforts in this direction. A bill was proposed in New York in 2009 to ban pesticides for ornamental purposes in yards, parks, school grounds, and elsewhere across the state. This type of legislation makes sense, especially at the local level. Across the United States there are communities that value aesthetics more than they fear the risks associated with properly applied pesticides. There are other communities that value not having to worry about being exposed to potentially dangerous pesticides. Why not let each community establish their own tolerance for pesticides? (The big problem with this, of course, is that people can drive over to the next county and buy a pesticide where it has not been banned. There are no pesticide police checking to make sure that no one in a particular locality is using a particular pesticide, and unless you're testing for it, it is entirely possible that the presence of these pesticides would never be known—though we do wonder how it would look if all of the yards in a neighborhood except for one were choked with dandelions.)

A community that believes in the precautionary principle—if a practice might cause serious harm, then we should avoid it regardless of the scientific certainty—should be allowed to ban pesticides. No one can know all of the possible problems with all of the different chemicals that we use and the problems that may occur if they are mixed together.

While not every pesticide we use is likely to cause cancer or some other chronic illness, some might, and it may be years before the connection between a particular pesticide and the disease is made. It is prudent for us to decrease our use of these chemicals so that we can avoid finding out the hard way. Killing a few dandelions just doesn't seem worth the risk.

Right-Wing Rating ★★ Encouraging communities to ban pesticides would be encouraging greater government interference in our lives. We need more evidence of harm from pesticide use before individual freedoms and property rights are curtailed. Local governments have no scientific capacity to evaluate the true risks of chemicals and would be too influenced by hysteria driven by the media or environmental groups. Varying local restrictions would be a nightmare for manufacturers and farmers. On the other hand, communities would have the freedom to allow pesticides.

Left-Wing Rating ★★ Community regulation is fine if you live in a community that offers protection, but everyone has a right to a healthy community. Historically, local governments have been too easily intimidated by deep-pocketed business interests. Local regulation should be encouraged only where it exceeds the federal standards.

Policy Option Three: More Regulation at the Federal Level

Federal regulation is necessary to protect all people and the environment as a whole. The way our food system is currently structured, it is practically impossible, short of growing your own food in filtered greenhouses, to eat food that is completely and thoroughly devoid of any synthetic chemicals. This is a danger we didn't ask for—a danger not of our own choosing. Even some organic foods have synthetic pesticide residues in or on them, which probably came from plants that were grown near conventional production or were processed in facilities that also processed conventionally grown produce.

There are sufficient alternative methods available today to take care of many of the pests that have irritated farmers for centuries—without using pesticides. These methods may be more labor intensive or expensive than pesticides in some cases, but that is a small price to pay for removing unwanted contamination.

Over the coming years and decades it is necessary that the federal government become stricter in its regulation of pesticides allowed in food. Year after year the EPA restricts the use of more and more pesticides, and while new ones also find their way onto the market, these pesticides tend to be safer, and usually more effective at lower doses, than their predecessors. As with the pesticides used by farmers, the EPA has the right to limit the pesticides available to people for their home use. The EPA should use these powers aggressively.

Some of the most intense pesticide applications occur not on farmland but rather on the land that surrounds our homes. These pesticides are applied to control dandelions in the grass or insects that are eating our flowers, for example. Whether or not we kill these weeds and pests, their presence or absence isn't likely to make us any healthier. So, what if our federal government decided to limit our use of these pesticides in much the same way that it limits our use of, say, prescription medication? No access without a prescription, and while this prescription might be easy to get, the process of getting the prescription would itself limit the amount of pesticides used on lawns. And it just might create a higher bar for pesticide use.

While most farmers have an excellent idea about which pesticides to apply for which pests—and when not to apply them—the same cannot be said about homeowners. People misidentify problems in their lawns and gardens with stunning frequency, and regularly apply chemicals without identifying problems in the first place. Many people would not bother to get the prescription, regardless of whether they can identify the problem or not, because they see it as too much of a hassle. They would rather live with the nuisance. This factor in itself might drastically reduce pesticide use.

In a prescription scenario, the federal government would mandate that local or state governments be responsible for diagnosing and prescribing pesticides. Or, it could delegate this task to private institutions (somewhat similar to how it delegates organic food certification, as discussed in the previous chapter) and have them prescribe the pesticides. This would greatly diminish the misuse of these chemicals. Pesticide companies certainly wouldn't like the concept of reduced pesticide use and would probably need to raise their prices, at least for those pesticides used around the home. Higher prices might be a further disincentive to homeowners considering pesticide use.

Right-Wing Rating★★ Forcing people to have a prescription before they can buy pesticides takes away individual choice and establishes a new bureaucracy. The prescription approach relies on hassling and discouraging people, rather than sound and scientific limits. And the delays and costs of the prescription approach might delay the purchase of a pesticide and the control of a pest, unfairly affecting small businesses and individuals.

Left-Wing Rating ★★★★★ The federal government would control the use of potentially toxic chemicals and we'd see a reduction in the overuse of pesticides. Only the government has the ability to make public health and environmental protection uniform and effective.

The Bottom Line

Judging the dangers inherent in pesticide use is extremely difficult. Pesticides are a diverse group of chemicals with widely varying effects on humans and the environment. Making government regulation issues even more tricky, these dangers can be surprisingly similar to those posed by what many of us consider everyday items, like salt and coffee. While the science certainly raises concerns about pesticides, it is difficult to draw a line in the sand as to which pesticides should and shouldn't be allowed. Yet that is exactly what the government has been asked to do.

The question for policymakers is how much potential damage they are willing to tolerate. In the future it seems most likely that local and/or state governments will be more involved in regulating use. But right now, the federal government is in charge, and our current pesticide laws do seem to be controlling pesticide use reasonably well. They are certainly not perfect, but the laws are banning pesticides as it becomes obvious that they are dangerous, while allowing pesticides that seem to be *reasonably* safe when used as directed. Still, it would be even better if people were more aware—how many people really read the entire label on a pesticide package before they start spraying the stuff willy-nilly across their yards?—and reduced their pesticide usage for pests that they may or may not even have.

Certainly, there is less of a chance that pesticides will cause cancer than will smoking tobacco or spending time outside without using sunblock.

If you believe in the precautionary principle and are concerned that pesticides might be a problem, you are unhappy with the current system. But, right now, there isn't a lot of evidence that the typical person who uses a pesticide, as most of us do occasionally, will hurt themselves in any way by using these products. Large studies of licensed pesticide users show very little, if any, increase in the incidence of cancer and other health problems. Certainly, there is less of a chance that pesticides will cause cancer than will smoking tobacco or spending time outside without using sunblock. And how, exactly, will we keep our yards free of weeds (especially noxious weeds, which we'll examine in a later chapter) and wasps without these tools? Pesticides are poisons that have the potential to hurt us and our ecology, so we need to treat them carefully, use the safest ones we can, and use them as infrequently as possible. But the stress caused by an overzealous media that loves to instigate pesticide paranoia at the drop of a dime is probably worse for our health than the pesticides most of us encounter in our everyday lives.

CHAPTER 4

Fertilizers: Good for the Crops, Bad for the Water?

IN 2002, MINNESOTA, the so-called land of 10,000 lakes (there are actually more than 11,000) decided that it was time to protect its lakes from its inhabitants. A statewide ban went into place preventing the use of phosphorus—one of the most overused fertilizers—on lawns unless there was a demonstrated need. This nutrient was suspected of contributing to a buildup of algae in lakes, which can cause severe damage to their ecosystems. This ban was instituted quietly and prompted very little outrage. Most people had no idea whether they needed phosphorus on their lawns anyway, so when they were told they didn't need it, they didn't make a scene. In garden centers throughout Minnesota, most lawn fertilizers are now phosphorus free, though it is still legal to use a phosphorus fertilizer on your lawn if it is newly planted or if you have a soil test showing the need for it. There are no fertilizer police in Minnesota, nor do the regular police take any time away from their ordinary duties to enforce the phosphorus law. Nonetheless, there was a 48 percent reduction in the amount of phosphorus used on lawns between 2002 and 2007, and over 80 percent of the fertilizer used is now phosphorus free. Meanwhile, the lawns in Minnesota look as good today as they did before phosphorus was removed from their fertilizer palette. By 2010, Wisconsin and New York had joined Minnesota with similar bans.

A Brief History of Fertilizers

Prior to the use of fertilizers, the only way that a plant would receive nutrients was through natural cycles. Fallen leaves and other waste from plants, along with the waste from animals that fed on those plants, would return nutrients to the soil where they would be taken up again by the plants, which then used these nutrients to produce more leaves, and the cycle would continue. Fertilizers allow us to short-circuit that system. Today, we can take nutrients from one place—a strip mine in Florida (a source of phosphorus), a bat cave in Jamaica (where guano, which contains nitrogen, phosphorus, and potassium as well as other nutrients, is mined), or even the air (from which we derive nitrogen)—and put them in another place, where they can provide what the plant needs to speed its growth.

Like pesticides, fertilizers have been used since Roman times to promote the growth of crops. Over the centuries, many different ingredients have been used to enrich the earth, from pigeon dung, which was considered one of the best Roman fertilizers, to synthetic nitrogen, which is made from a reaction between natural gas and the nitrogen in the air. We have always looked for ways to make our plants grow bigger, faster. Farmers have increased their use of fertilizers as the production costs of these products have decreased, transportation over great distances has become easier, and the fertilizers themselves have become more necessary to efficient crop production. The use of synthetic nitrogen is a major part of what has allowed the world's population to skyrocket from a little under 1.7 billion in 1900 to almost 7 billion today (though some believe that naturally occurring nitrogen could have provided for all of our needs, a highly debatable theory). But this use of nitrogen, along with the increased use of other fertilizers, especially phosphorus, hasn't been all good news.

Fertilizers pit two groups against each other: one group that wants to protect the water, and another group that wants to grow crops or have nice lawns. These interests certainly aren't mutually exclusive. Farmers and people who use fertilizers in their yards can take steps to minimize their impact on our water. But these activities usually cost money and land, and so, depending on how you feel about the importance of producing food and the importance of aquatic life, you may well find yourself favoring one side or the other.

Fertilizers pit two groups against each other: one group that wants to protect the water, and another group that wants to grow crops or have nice lawns.

The Science

The impact of soil fertility on crop production, for everything from grass and beans to corn and oranges, has been well documented. Depending on the crop and the type of soil that is being fertilized, an acre of land (43,560 square feet) may be fertilized with anywhere from 50 to 500 pounds of nitrogen, along with other nutrients such as phosphorus and potassium, usually at slightly lower levels. Particularly with heavily used land, additions of fertilizer may increase crop production by two to three times—or even much more, depending on the crop and the quality of the soil. Land that has been newly cleared of trees or other plant material is typically very rich in nutrients because of the natural cycling of plant and animal materials back into the soil; thus, it needs little fertilization for maximum production. Farmland that has been producing crops for decades—or centuries—will usually need large amounts of fertilizer to produce a decent crop. Here in the United States, we have much more of the latter than the former.

As we've placed more and more nutrients into the soil, we have fertilized not only our farms and lawns, but also our lakes, streams, and oceans. Many of the nutrients that we apply never make it to the crops they're intended for, but rather disappear in a variety of ways, including flowing with the rain into bodies of water. Much of the rest is lost to leaching, or a host of other natural processes, some of which create nitrogen gases that may increase global warming. Cereal crops, such as wheat, corn, rice, and barley, use about 33 percent of the nitrogen that is applied worldwide. Tree crops, such as apples and oranges, are typically even less efficient. Once nutrients leave a farm and reach a watershed, they turn into bad players. They feed algae the same way that they might have fed plants on land, but these algae create big problems. Plants, fish, aquatic insects, and other creatures that live in the water need oxygen to survive. Unfortunately, when water is full of nutrients (which are usually in shorter supply under natural conditions), algae grow and reproduce extremely rapidly and, eventually, they die. Their decomposing bodies use up the oxygen in the water to the point that other creatures can't get enough oxygen to live.

In addition to the damage in lakes, sea creatures have also been disappearing from the Gulf of Mexico—even before the oil spill of 2010. A dead zone a little bit larger than the state of Connecticut is caused by water coming from the Mississippi River and exiting into the Gulf after having picked up nutrients from some of the largest farming regions in America. Fertilizer runoff from farms and lawns all the way from Minnesota to Mississippi find their way into this river and eventually get expelled into the Gulf. There are dead zones all across the United States, wherever water is overfertilized with the nutrients that feed algae. In 2009 there were about 150 dead zones in the oceans—mostly off the European and North American coasts—which is double the number in 1990.

Nutrients that destroy creatures living in water don't just come from farms, however. Backyards, schoolyards, parks, and other places contribute nutrients that eventually make their way into a body of water where they can do damage. A common misconception is that applying fertilizers to our lawns creates more runoff of nutrients than leaving lawns unfertilized. Actually, a thick, dense, healthy lawn is better at holding the soil and taking up nutrients from fertilizer than both weaker stands of grass and agricultural land. Hence, while it's obvious that huge applications of fertilizer might lead to nutrient runoff, the regular, judicious use of fertilizers around homes might actually be needed to encourage the growth of grass and other plants that hold the soil, which might otherwise erode into a body of water or from which nutrients might escape as runoff. As Christoph Gross and his colleagues concluded in a study on runoff from grass-covered soil, or turf, "properly managed and judiciously fertilized turf is not a significant source of nutrients or sediment in surface or groundwater." This study also showed that more nutrients escape from agricultural land than from the same size piece of land that is covered with turf.

Mitigating the Damage

A number of factors determine how much fertilizer will contribute to the runoff from a farm or landscape. One of the most important is the weather. Fertilizers tend to wash away more quickly with excessive rainfall, so farmers can help prevent nutrient runoff by not fertilizing right before a heavy rain (but a light rain helps the fertilizer work its way into the soil). Likewise, there are a number of ways to manage land to minimize the amount of fertilizer runoff. A row of plant material, called a buffer strip, placed between the area where fertilizer is to be applied and a body of water, such as a lake or pond, slows the movement of fertilizers from the field to the water. Additionally, farms with better soils will typically hold nutrients better than farms with poor soils, and farmers who till their soil are more likely to suffer soil running off of their land and finding its way into the water system than farmers who don't.

Buffer strips were first suggested in the 1940s by C. B. Brown, who recommended their use to remove sediment from water runoff by filtering it through a screen of vegetation before it entered a reservoir. For the next thirty years or so, these strips were considered handy ways to filter runoff from roads or streets, but not much thought was given to their other uses. Then, in the 1970s, a number of researchers started looking at how well these strips of greenery could remove nutrients that would otherwise enter an aquifer, and lo and behold, they discovered that that these strips could, in some cases, remove 90 percent or more of the phosphorus in runoff water. Today, the use of buffer strips is a well-established—though underused—method of filtering nutrients out of runoff before it enters a body of water.

Most buffer strips include grasses, shrubs, and trees and provide at least ten feet of vegetation between the body of water and the farm field. Generally, the larger the buffer strip the better, because a larger surface area allows for more plants and plant roots to be collecting nutrients from the water. Buffer strips thirty to one hundred feet wide or wider are best, if and when that is possible. The biggest problem with buffer strips is that they often take up land that could otherwise be used for producing crops and this can cut into a farmer's bottom line.

Today's farmland is not as capable of holding the nutrients delivered by fertilizers as it once was because, over the years, our soils have lost organic matter to erosion, without having the opportunity to build levels back up. Organic matter is nothing more than carbon-containing compounds that, in soils, usually come from dead animals and plants that build up over many years. This material is very good at holding nutrients in the soil for plants to use. When we harvest our crops year after year without returning vegetable material to the soil, it loses the ability to hold the nutrients supplied by fertilizers. Additionally, the tried-and-true practice of tilling can itself lead to nutrient runoff. Tilling the soil loosens it, allowing it to erode more easily and to eventually find its way into a stream or lake. New techniques that do not involve tilling the soil and that decrease the chance of nutrient runoff are becoming more popular. Called reduced tilling or no-till practices, these techniques push a seed into the ground and then use herbicides or other weed control techniques, rather than tilling, to make sure that the crop that was planted sprouts from the ground, rather than weeds. The use of genetically-engineered, herbicide-resistant crops makes no-till practices easier to implement.

Government Policy

In the garden or on the farm, pesticides and fertilizers are often used in tandem. Fertilizers help the garden grow; pesticides keep unwanted weeds and critters away from the garden. They are the yin and the yang of modern, industrialized farming. But if farmers and gardeners see them as complementary, the federal government treats them as near-opposites. Pesticides are subject to numerous laws and regulations, as we saw in the previous chapter. They undergo safety tests by the manufacturer and are cleared for public use by the government. Fertilizers, on the other hand, face no government clearance and almost no direct regulation by the federal government. (The only direct regulation restricts the amount of ammonium nitrate you can buy. Congress instituted the limit in 2007 to make it more difficult for terrorists to buy enough fertilizer to build bombs.) The different legal treatment of the two products is a consequence of their basic functions. Pesticides purposely kill things (hence, they are potentially dangerous to humans, wildlife, and ecosystems), while fertilizers help things grow. Pesticides are sprayed directly on foods, where their residue could be dangerous to consumers; fertilizers are applied to soils and are rarely present on the foods we eat. It is rare for state or local governments to regulate how much fertilizer a person or farmer can apply to their home or field.

Because of their effects on clean water and aquatic ecosystems, fertilizers are governed as "nonpoint source pollution" under the Water Quality Act of 1987. Nonpoint source pollution comes from many different places as opposed to a single point. The pollutants are picked up by rainwater and transported to a common collection point where they do their environmental damage. Focusing on nonpoint sources was the result of an evolution of water policy. The Clean Water Act of 1972 (CWA) had focused on point sources of pollution—discharge pipes from factories or municipal sewer or water treatment systems. The law required point sources to obtain permits for discharges into waterways, and regulated the development and dredging of wetlands. The 1985 Farm Bill created the "Swampbuster" program, which barred farmers from federal subsidy programs if they converted wetlands into croplands. Both laws created exceptions for projects that included actions to compensate for the loss of wetlands. These laws addressed the most visible sources of pollution and helped to clean up U.S. waterways, but 40 percent of the waterways did not meet the CWA's goal of being "fishable and swimmable" thirty years after the law had passed.

The Water Quality Act addressed nonpoint source pollution by requiring states to identify "impaired waters" that fail to meet the state's own water quality standards and to develop priority rankings of the impaired waters. States are required to update their lists every two years. The states are also required to calculate a total maximum daily load (TMDL) for each of the impaired waters. The TMDL is the water's "pollution budget," or the maximum amount of pollutant the body of water could receive in a day and still meet water quality standards. States then develop management plans to improve water quality and the EPA must approve the plans.

The EPA has calculated TMDLs for certain states that did not have the appropriate expertise or resources. The law did not contain a deadline for the states to calculate TMDLs, so when a number of states failed to do so, environmental groups sued the EPA, asking the courts to order the EPA to calculate TMDLs rather than waiting for the states. Suits filed on behalf of thirty-nine waterways succeeded, as of 2009, with the EPA reaching an agreement to do the calculation or receiving an order from the court to do it.

Who Cleans Up?

The EPA has no authority to issue regulations or to undertake any enforcement activity to address nonpoint source pollution directly (we'll explain why in the next section). The regulations' teeth are therefore based on the state's willingness to execute its management plan. If the "fertilizer police" are in your yard, it's state or local police, not the feds. The management plans imposed by the states may do a wide variety of things, from regulating farmers' use of fertilizers to encouraging farmers to use new techniques to reduce their runoff. Two of the states that have been most active in regulating fertilizer—Florida and Minnesota—are states with extensive wetlands and waterways, and with tourist industries that thrive on water recreation. Minnesota, in addition to banning the use of phosphorus fertilizers on home lawns unless they are newly planted or a soil test shows the need for one, has also mandated the use of buffer strips between cropland and waterways to reduce the amount of fertilizers and other pollutants that enter the water. Florida hasn't been terribly aggressive on the state level, but municipalities have produced their own regulations that restrict such things as when fertilizer can be applied, what concentration of nutrients can be in the fertilizer, and how much of the fertilizer can be used during a given time. As an example, Pinellas County passed an ordinance in 2010 that banned homeowners from applying nitrogen or phosphorus fertilizers to their lawns from June 1 through September 30, and prevented stores from selling these fertilizers during that time. This ordinance goes on to restrict the amount of fertilizer that can be applied, and prevents the use of fertilizers within ten feet of a waterway. Professional applicators need to take training courses and become certified in fertilizer application. Golf courses and vegetable gardens are exempt.

Some states, including Nebraska and Illinois, use monetary incentives to reward those who plant grass buffer strips to separate farmland from adjacent bodies of water. This is a great way for farmers to have their cake and eat it too. They get to use normal levels of fertilizer, and by sacrificing some growing land for use as a buffer strip (for which they're compensated), they capture both nutrients and pesticides before they reach the water.

Other states have taken different routes to protecting critical waterways. Maryland, Virginia, and Pennsylvania, as well as the District of Columbia, signed the Chesapeake 2000 regional compact to protect the Chesapeake Bay. The states and the District agreed to buy and protect wetlands that serve as a filtering system for the bay, and to reduce the amount of farmlands and woodlands lost to development. Other states that have extensive wetlands, but whose economies are dominated by resource extraction, such as Louisiana, have taken much less assertive approaches to dealing with nonpoint source pollution.

In 1999, the EPA issued a proposal to revise the TMDL regulations. The revisions would have required states to submit schedules for TMDL calculations and implementation plans for their TMDLs, among other things. States objected to the burdens this would place on them. Point source groups fought with farm groups—each attempting to ensure that they wouldn't be the ones who had to clean up their act. And environmentalists (who supported making the regulations tougher and more specific) thought states were given too much time before having to make water quality improvements. Without strong support and with many strong opponents, the EPA revised the proposal in 2000, but then withdrew it entirely in 2003 (after the Clinton EPA had become the Bush EPA). The regulations have not been acted on since.

The Supreme Court has recently complicated the EPA's regulation of point and nonpoint sources of water pollution even further. In two separate cases, *Solid Waste Agency of Northern Cook County v. Army Corps of Engineers* (2001), and *Rapanos v. United States* (2006), the Court took the EPA to task for regulating waters beyond those explicitly required by the Clean Water Act's "navigable waters" language. The EPA had traditionally interpreted this wording broadly, to include large wetlands and any waters that flow into navigable waterways or that cross state lines, because such waterways affect drinking water, fishing, and other public uses that the act was designed to protect. The Court called the breadth of this interpretation into question, specifically arguing that waterways within a state, creeks that sometimes go dry, and lakes unconnected to larger water systems are not navigable waters and thus do not qualify for EPA regulation. The rulings injected tremendous amounts of uncertainty about which waterways the EPA could regulate—and thus who it could punish for polluting them. States were not immediately in a position to regulate or enforce laws on these waters, since they had relied on EPA regulation and enforcement for the prior forty years.

The Political Dynamics

A high priority of the federal government is ensuring an adequate food supply, and crop subsidies are a major policy used to achieve this goal. If protecting our water from fertilizers and pesticides were one of the government's highest priorities, in contrast, we wouldn't have crop subsidy programs. Understanding these subsidy programs is vitally important to understanding why we use as many chemicals as we do.

Crop subsidy programs have been in place since the Great Depression in the 1930s to ensure that the nation has an adequate supply of food, and that farmers have some protection against natural booms and busts of the farm economy caused by things outside of their control, like the weather and the national economy. The government uses a number of techniques to do this, from providing direct payments to

LARGE corporate farms receive most of the farm subsidies and have most of the political clout in Washington, but they use the family farmers to make the argument to retain subsidies, since family farms are a potent symbol of America's pastoral past. It would be extremely hard for public opinion to support a policy that causes regular folks to lose a farm that had been in their family's hands for generations, in the name of cold-blooded economic efficiency. Small family farms would be affected by the loss of subsidies because they have a smaller margin for error. Moreover, farmers' spending supports the farm supply and equipment sales people, the banks, the insurance agents, and others throughout the rural economy. For politicians, subsidies are a small price to pay to keep the rural population quiet. Both Democrats and Republicans compete for the votes of rural residents, and neither party wants to alienate them.

farmers if the price of a crop drops too low, to buying surplus food for antipoverty programs, to allowing farmers to set up regional monopolies to prevent lower-priced goods from entering their markets. The government does this because farmers face a basic problem: the better the yield, the less the farmer earns. If all farmers who grow the same crop have a good year, there is a lot of supply on the market. The greater the supply, the more the price of the food drops. Consumers don't eat more (or not that much more) just because more food is available or because it is cheaper. If some farmers go bankrupt and lose their farms—which would help to decrease the supply of food, increase the price, and keep the remaining farmers profitable—the risk is that there won't be enough food in the next bad year, when the weather or the pests don't cooperate. That's not a risk the government is willing to take, not to mention the major job losses that would occur in small-town America.

So the government steps in to even out the booms and busts. It attempts to protect farmers when there is too much production and prices drop too low for farmers to earn a living. But no good deed goes unpunished; this system creates perverse incentives. By essentially guaranteeing farmers that all of their produce will be sold and that they will receive a minimum price for certain foods, farmers are encouraged to grow as much as possible. The more they produce, the more money they can get from the government, regardless of whether consumers are actually buying their products. But more production drives the price down even further, making it more difficult for the farmer to make money without government support. Because taxpayers pay the costs of overproduction, however, farmers have an incentive to keep finding ways to produce more. More production means more fertilizer and more pesticides, which then have their unintended side effects on health and the environment.

Attempts to reign in farm subsidies have failed miserably. The Federal Agriculture Improvement and Reform Act of 1996, better known as the Freedom to Farm Act, tried to institute some free-market principles, but the next farm bill (the Farm Security and Rural Investment Act of 2002) basically reinstated traditional subsidies, and the Food, Conservation, and Energy Act of 2008 expanded those subsidies to fruits and vegetables. Farmers are well organized and have an intense interest in protecting their benefits; individual taxpayers would only save a little bit if subsidies were reduced, so they have little incentive to mobilize against them. Environmentalists essentially side with farmers on the subsidy issue. They don't support the subsidies per se or the overproduction that results, but the subsidies give them leverage over farmers to get them to obey environmental regulations. That is, the subsidies give the government the ability to say, for example, "If you want to keep your subsidies, you must not fill in wetlands on your property."

The Politics of Dirty Water

Federal water quality rules are written so that their ineffectiveness is practically guaranteed. On one hand, the Water Quality Protection Act sets the goal of decreasing nonpoint source pollution. On the other hand, the act doesn't give the EPA direct authority to do anything to control or minimize nonpoint sources. It passes the buck to the states. Yet most state environmental agencies do not have the resources or the expertise to develop TMDLs or management plans, let alone enforce them. Even when court orders force the EPA to calculate the TMDL, it still doesn't have the ability to do anything to decrease pollution in waters that fail to meet the standards. And a state agency without the resources or motivation to calculate the TMDLs on its own is unlikely to develop the will to crack down on nonpoint source polluters just because the EPA has identified standards. It's a recipe for frustration on all sides.

Despite the fact that they are largely implementing federal laws, states issue more than 90 percent of environmental permits and conduct more than 75 percent of all environment enforcement actions. If you take your car to be tested for emissions, for example, you are dealing with state officials. When a local factory gets a water discharge permit, the permit comes from the state government.

Essentially, this matrix of policies is based on the logic of the federal structure of the United States. State governments have primary authority within their states, and Congress cannot just order them to do whatever it wants. Constitutionally, Congress is limited to addressing domestic issues that affect "interstate commerce." Land use policy has traditionally been a core responsibility of state and local governments. The Clean Water Act's navigable waters language was Congress's attempt to apply federal law to waters involved in interstate commerce. Besides, from a practical standpoint, states are in a better position than politicians in Washington, D.C., to know or to find out the sources of water or air pollution, and states are in a better position to determine what strategies would be most effective in cajoling their citizens to cooperate in decreasing pollution. When the federal government sets national priorities, it must entice states to implement them by providing incentives (such as providing technical support and money) or threatening them with penalties (such as losing federal money).

Providing carrots to get states to do what Washington wants is fine as long as the states want the same thing. Dealing with point sources of pollution is an example of how the states and the federal government can be on the same page. In point source pollution, a drainpipe from a factory or water treatment plant dumps polluted water into local streams. It's easy to send a camera crew to film the muck and generate outrage from the public. And likewise, it's easy to send a government inspector to the plant to make sure they've installed appropriate cleanup technology and to test the water coming out of a pipe or the air out of a smokestack. Since there are clear benefits to taking action, the states can take Washington's money, clean up their water/air/toxic waste dumps, and win public approval for doing so. As hard as it is for government to take on "big business" that provides lots of jobs and tax revenue, it's easier to take on "big polluters" than to take on the ordinary people who create nonpoint source pollution.

Nonpoint source pollution is a different ball game from point source pollution because it comes from so many different places. Few people understand how the runoff from their yards and driveways or runoff from farms or industrial sites affects bodies of water many miles away. Such diffuse effects are hard to document and publicize, unlike the Exxon Valdez spill or garbage washing up on beaches. Nonpoint sources are also hard to regulate because inspectors can't just check a few sites. Instead, policy must encourage a large number of people to change their behavior, which to each of those people seems inconsequential in causing water or air pollution. Farmers, for example, are having outsiders tell them to change tried-and-true methods used on their own properties in order to have a minute effect on algae growth hundreds of miles away. It's hard to expect enthusiastic cooperation, especially when the changes can be expensive and risky. Of course some farmers in some states do implement techniques to decrease their nutrient runoff by taking government incentives, but this raises another question: will the incentives need to be made permanent to ensure that these practices continue? Would it be better to follow the model that we have for air pollution and use a whipping stick along with some carrots?

In addressing one nonpoint source of air pollution, Congress has found ways to get around the problem of enticing thousands of individuals to cooperate. It has mandated that car manufacturers change the way cars are constructed. States and cities that do not meet air quality standards will lose their federal highway funds. Since states want to keep their federal money, they develop plans to decrease air pollution by increasing mass transit options, by working with employers to develop changes in work schedules, and so on. But as of 2010, Congress has not shaken the stick at states to get action on nonpoint sources of water pollution in the same way. States that have other priorities aren't forced to do anything because there are no deadlines and no penalties for not complying with the law. They can live in their dirty water—until it flows downstream and becomes the next state's dirty water.

Policy Option One: Leave Things as They Are

While it's hard to argue that there aren't currently some problems with the amount of fertilizer that we apply to our lawns and to farm fields, this problem is largely taking care of itself and doesn't need more regulation by federal, state, or local governments. The free market system is at work reducing the amount of fertilizer that we can afford to apply. The synthetic nitrogen that most of us use in our yards is based directly on the price of natural gas and energy (since these are needed to create nitrogen fertilizers). Hence, as natural gas and coal prices increase, so will the cost of nitrogen fertilizer. Other elements in commercial fertilizers, such as phosphorus and potassium, are usually mined (or at least start their journey to becoming a fertilizer in a mine), and so their cost also increases with scarcity. It has been suggested that by around 2030 the world will reach its peak in phosphorus production and that supplies of phosphorus will start to dwindle. (In fact, it has been suggested that we may have mined all of our mineable rock phosphate within the next fifty to one hundred years.) And so prices will rise. Because of these cost considerations, farmers continually need to find new ways to use fertilizers more efficiently. Farmers already have a number of techniques at their disposal. No-till and reduced-till farming practices avoid loosening the top layer of soil so that it is less likely to erode. Incorporating more organic matter from manure into soils allows the soil to better absorb more nutrients. And using buffer strips between the fields where fertilizers are applied and any nearby waterways prevents runoff from reaching those waterways. Incentives being offered by some states and the federal government are also encouraging these techniques.

The rising cost of fertilizers isn't as likely to affect their use around homes as it is on farms because homeowners aren't balancing their fertilizer spending against proceeds, but rather against their sense of aesthetics. The lack of government control over fertilizers applied around homes isn't an issue because there is no evidence that a healthy, properly fertilized lawn produces more runoff than a poorly fertilized one.

Finally, dead zones caused by runoff are certainly significant, and fertilizers contribute to the problem, but the oceans are large and when these dead zones are measured against the total size of the oceans, they just aren't that significant. Besides, nature has its own dead zones, like the Dead Sea.

Right-Wing Rating ★★★★★ We are all making the choices we need to make to keep ourselves in business and to keep our lawns green.

There are lots of things that can affect aquatic ecosystems; picking on fertilizers is not the solution. More regulation would impose a huge cost on farmers and do very little to help the environment.

Left-Wing Rating ★★ Science clearly shows the damage that overuse of fertilizers has on aquatic ecosystems. The problem may be difficult to solve, but government inaction is inexcusable. Action by a few states and municipalities is insufficient to combat problems that affect entire watersheds.

Policy Option Two: The EPA Should Firmly Regulate Fertilizers

Because nonpoint runoff is important, we need to do something about it. The laws passed by states and municipalities are going to be few and far between, and history has already shown that they're not going to be appropriately enforced. The federal government needs to get involved, not just in an advisory role, but rather as the rule maker and the enforcer. Some of the regulations that the EPA could enforce include restricting when and how often crops and yards could be fertilized. Most fertilizer runoff occurs during storms soon after the fertilizer is applied. By restricting fertilization to times when heavy storms are less likely, nutrient runoff could be reduced. Restrictions should apply to lawn care companies and to individuals, and should also restrict the amount of fertilizer that people buy per year. Fertilizers containing phosphorus should be prohibited unless people have a soil test. Parks and forests could be required to implement strategies to use less fertilizer.

The EPA should also require farmers to implement buffer zones wherever their land butts up against a swamp, stream, river, or lake. More extensive restrictions could be placed on lagoons in which factory farms dispose of vast quantities of animal manure, to ensure that runoff does not cause the lagoons to overflow into neighboring waterways. Farmers should be required to apply a certain percentage of their fertilizer as natural manures, composts, or other materials. This would, over time, increase the soil's ability to hold nutrients and reduce the amount of nutrient-rich wastes that might reach a delicate water system. Farmers should also be required to use reduced tilling techniques.

Right-Wing Rating ★ The federal government is going to restrict me from fertilizing before it rains? Can we even predict when it will rain? Such rules are unenforceable. And we're going to pay bureaucrats to read records of how often and when I fertilized? What a waste of time and money! Just get off my lawn!

Left-Wing Rating ★★★★★ Water (and air) does not respect the niceties of jurisdictional boundaries. Your dirty water becomes dirty water for everyone else downstream. Strict federal rules are the only way to ensure drinkable, swimmable water for everyone. Also, if we're going to be concerned about the economy, we should be concerned about fishing and tourism, not just farming.

Policy Option Three: Give States a Deadline for Developing and Executing a Plan for Reducing Nonpoint Pollution

States can have different methods of controlling their nonpoint source pollution, but if a state does not implement a plan then they should be punished by cutting off all crop subsidies to that state. There are so many simple strategies that could help to reduce fertilizer runoff that the states could figure out which ones were most relevant for their situation and require farmers and homeowners to comply. Federal air pollution laws are already enforced this way; there is no reason that water laws should not be enforced the same way.

Right-Wing Rating ★★ The federal government should not abuse its power by pushing the states around. States need to be trusted to know what is best for their own citizens; the farmers and homeowners need to be trusted to know what's best for their land.

Left-Wing Rating ★★★★ Having the means to get states to follow their own plans is important, but we also need to ensure that all states are as strict as possible, since the water from one state flows to its neighbors. One weak link can break the chain.

Policy Option Four: Do Away with Crop Subsidies

Getting rid of crop subsidies doesn't directly affect the use of fertilizers, but if the free market were allowed to control the price of our food, an indirect result would likely be a reduction in the use of fertilizers. Without subsidies farmers wouldn't have the incentive to plant every last inch of their land in subsidized crops (such as corn), which deliver some of the lowest dollar figures per acre and require heavy inputs of fertilizer.

Right-Wing Rating ★★★★ Farmers do not want to be dependent on the government. Subsidies are a tremendous waste of taxpayer money.

Left-Wing Rating ★★★★ Cut subsidies to corporate farms, but give assistance to small family farms and to poor people who need assistance buying food.

Each to the Other: *"You first!"*

The Bottom Line

Our current system is broken. In practice, states just don't have enough incentives to clean up our water system and the intent of our laws is being skirted. With the laws that currently exist there is very little enforcement to control runoff from farms and yards into larger areas of water. Some local and state legislation restricts the use of a few fertilizers and offers incentives to install buffer strips to catch fertilizer runoff, but these actions have not changed the big picture.

With the laws that currently exist there is very little enforcement to control runoff from farms and yards into larger areas of water.

We currently do not have a firm grasp on exactly how much pollution is caused by any specific nonpoint source and so we're doing a lot of guessing when we look at options. Not that our efforts will make things worse, but it's possible that they won't help as much, or as quickly, as we think they will. That said, we should start with simple-to-implement techniques that would mitigate the problem, including no-till and reduced-till farming and buffer strips. We can take these steps while we continue to debate what farmers and homeowners should do of their own accord and what the federal and state governments should regulate and enforce. Meanwhile, the rising cost of fertilizers will begin to cause a reduction in their use.

CHAPTER 5

★★★

Alternative Energy: Is Ethanol Overrated?

DURING THE 2008 presidential election, T. Boone Pickins, a billionaire from Texas who made his money running Mesa Petroleum, a large, independent oil and gas company, bought ads promoting his energy plan. Unlike most ads during campaign season, the energy plan was not a Trojan horse to promote or disparage particular candidates or political parties. Pickens's plan would rely heavily on natural gas (intended for automobiles), nuclear power, and alternative energy sources—primarily wind power—and would, theoretically, greatly reduce our country's need for oil. Because of its reliance on wind power, this plan would increase the number of power-generating wind turbines across the midwestern United States. These commercials touched a chord with many voters worried about gas prices approaching $4 a gallon. Candidates of both parties promoted their own plans to increase energy production—including the use of alternative energies—to address the public's anxieties.

In 2008, more than 83 percent of the energy in the United States was supplied by fossil fuels, around 8 percent by nuclear energy, and just over 7 percent by alternative sources of energy such as wind, solar, and biomass power. We all know that we cannot continue to depend on fossil fuels indefinitely. How rapidly the supply of fossil fuels will disappear is an open question, but as long as we continue to use these resources at our current rate, the ultimate ending is a foregone conclusion.

Various groups are convinced that wind, biofuel, tidal current, solar, hydroelectric, or nuclear power will offer the solution to our country's energy needs. Most scientists think that it's some combination of all of the above, as well as some as-yet-undiscovered fuel sources. Still others think that the ultimate answer will necessarily include a considerable amount of conservation. All of these ideas have their benefits and drawbacks. The government itself has focused much of its efforts on funding biofuel research, which is a very interesting decision considering that biofuels have drawbacks that put them at odds with other policies our government has implemented (see the chapters on global warming and fertilizers).

The Science

Alternative energy possibilities are diverse but are generally categorized into one of two groups. The first group is transportation fuels, those that might be used to run an automobile. Not that these fuels couldn't be used to run a power plant, they certainly could, and sometimes are—the first ethanol-based power plant was opened in Brazil in 2010, for example—but that is not currently seen as the primary use of these fuels. The second group of alternative energies includes those intended to produce electricity. While electricity certainly could be used to run a car, its primary purpose is to run such things as lights, television, and video games.

Transportation Fuels: Ethanol and Biodiesel

There was a time when using biofuels would have meant burning wood, which was a good way to warm a house, heat a boiler on a train, or cook a meal, but not a great way to fuel a car or bus. Today, the term *biofuel* generally refers to something just a little more sophisticated than a hunk of wood—but not quite as sophisticated as you might think. Energy from biofuels generally comes from either processing a crop to produce an oil (usually soybean or palm oil), which is called biodiesel, or, more commonly, fermenting the crop (usually corn in the United States) to produce easy-to-burn alcohol (usually ethanol, exactly the same type of alcohol that is in your evening glass of wine, beer, or scotch). The basics of fermenting harvested plants into alcohol are anything but new. We've had beer, wine, and whisky for a long, long time. There are a number of problems with using this source of energy though; the most important is the frequently ignored question, just how much fuel can we actually get from plants?

A reasonable estimate is that even if the entire United States corn crop were dedicated to nothing but producing energy, it would only provide about 12 percent of our current demand for gasoline. While 12 percent is certainly quite significant, we need a lot of that corn for other purposes, such as feeding ourselves. Fortunately, biofuels can be derived from other crops, too. One popular option is using soybeans for biodiesel. Diesel fuel has been around for years, but biodiesel hasn't really been used much, at least not in comparison to regular diesel. Biodiesel has its limitations, though. If all of the soybeans in the United States were converted to biodiesel, only 6 percent of the diesel fuel needed by this country would be generated. Still, every gallon counts, and, if we're going to replace corn as the primary source of biofuel, then we will need to utilize many different sources.

Almost any vegetable product that you can think of can be fermented to make alcohol, which can in turn be used as a fuel. Here in the United States, corn is king, though sugar beets, potatoes, wheat, or even blueberries could be used to produce ethanol. Across the world, there have been some remarkable success stories using biofuels. One of the best is the story of fermented sugarcane in Brazil. Brazil produces an abundance of this crop and uses it to produce ethanol, which supplements gasoline in cars driven in Brazil. In 2010, the world's first power plant driven by ethanol was put into service in Brazil as well. The great thing about sugarcane ethanol is that it takes much less energy to produce it than it takes to produce alcohol from other sources, most notably corn. In fact, for every bit of energy used to produce alcohol from sugarcane, the resulting alcohol produces 3 bits of energy, while for every bit of energy used to produce corn ethanol, less than one bit of energy is returned, according to some analyses, and that's a problem. David Pimentel, an emeritus professor of ecology and agriculture at Cornell University, and other scientists claim that the corn we use for ethanol production should not be considered a renewable resource because of the fossil fuels used to create it, and because producing corn requires more pesticide use and causes more soil erosion than any other crop. Pimentel's calculations actually show that corn requires 29 percent more energy to grow and make into ethanol than the energy that the ethanol itself can produce. Not everybody agrees with this number, though. Other estimates claim that corn ethanol can yield 25 percent or more energy than the energy used to produce it—still a long shot from the efficiency of sugarcane. Biodiesel has a much better rating,

Almost any vegetable product that you can think of can be fermented to make alcohol, which can in turn be used as a fuel.

with estimates of a yield of almost 95 percent more energy than what is used to make it. Though this lags behind sugarcane and its three-to-one return, it is substantially better than corn ethanol.

Biofuels have an advantage over fossil fuels in that they burn cleaner than oil or gasoline. Burning biofuels, and ethanol in particular, releases water, carbon dioxide, and little else. Carbon dioxide is considered a pollutant, as we will find in the upcoming chapter on global warming, but the net result of burning biofuels should affect global carbon dioxide concentrations less than burning fossil fuels. It takes many millions of years to create crude oil, while ethanol and biodiesel can be produced much more quickly. While crude oil, or any other fossil fuel for that matter, is forming, it stores carbon. When these fuels are burned, the result is a net increase of carbon dioxide in our atmosphere, derived from carbon that hasn't seen the light of day in many millennia.

Growing, harvesting, and converting corn to ethanol leaves an immense ecological footprint.

Technically, biofuels are supposed to be carbon neutral, with the plants that they are made from taking up the same amount of carbon dioxide during photosynthesis as the amount given off when the biofuel is used. However, this balance doesn't take into account such things as the fossil fuels needed for the production of fertilizers or the fuel used by farm tractors. More importantly, though, if we were to expand our use of biofuels, we would increase cropland at the expense of forestland. Since trees store carbon much more efficiently than annual crops, which are only in the ground for a year or less, we would have a large net increase in carbon dioxide emissions. Growing, harvesting, and converting corn to ethanol leaves an immense ecological footprint, and it becomes bigger as we turn more land over to corn in order to make ethanol a more significant fuel source. Exactly how much land would be needed to meet our fuel needs is not easy to nail down because no one knows exactly how much corn would be used for ethanol and how much ethanol we would end up using for fuel. No one suggests that greenhouse emissions would be worse if we used biofuels instead of fossil fuels, but don't think for a minute that switching to biofuels would be a perfect solution to controlling greenhouse gasses.

A final concern about ethanol production is that it comes at the expense of farmland used for producing food. While there are many contrasting opinions about how much food is actually sacrificed in the use of corn for ethanol, researchers at the University of California, Berkeley, have calculated that, in 2007, if we were not using ethanol in our gasoline, gas prices would have been 1.4 to 2.4 percent higher. The use of crops for biofuels, however, resulted in the price of soy increasing somewhere between 10 and 20 percent, and the price of corn increasing between 15 and 28 percent. Using crops for fuel instead of food has a significant impact on the cost of food.

One promising solution for biofuel production is cellulosic ethanol. Cellulosic ethanol comes from parts of the plant that normally aren't converted into alcohol. In corn, sugarcane, grapes, or any other fruit or vegetable, the sugars contained in the plant are converted into alcohol during the fermenting process. Unfortunately, the structural part of the plant—the cellulose—is not digested into alcohol. Cellulose is made of complex sugars that aren't easily broken down by the microbes normally used to make ethanol; as a result, many of the sugars present in plants are wasted. There is a method to process this structural material, but it is more complex, and researchers are still working to make it more efficient. Currently, the preferred crops for this process are switchgrass and other grasses that produce a lot of structural biomass quickly (in other words they grow fast). This method promises to make ethanol production much more efficient. The U.S. Department of Energy says that cellulosic ethanol produces 80 percent more energy than is needed to manufacture it, compared to their estimate of a 20 percent return for corn.

Another type of biofuel that is starting to receive some attention is biodiesel derived from algae. Algae can be converted into diesel fuel just like other oil-producing plants, including soybeans and palms. Diesel fuel from algae is attractive because it is produced in areas where crops aren't grown. Ideally, vertically oriented clear sheets of light-transmitting materials such as plastic or glass are built to hold and grow algae. The algae are then harvested and the oil is extracted. This form of production is much closer to carbon neutral than the production of ethanol, and it can produce much more fuel per unit of land than any other system. Soybeans produce less than 100 gallons of biodiesel per acre per year, while an acre of algae could produce as much as 10,000 gallons of biodiesel in that amount of time. This much oil production is possible because of the vertical orientation of the algal colonies, and because many generations of algae can be grown each year. Right now, the biggest hurdles for this technology have to do with finding the best ways to harvest the algae, and figuring out ways to get carbon dioxide to the algae more efficiently. Pumping gas through this system takes a lot of power, so without technological advances, this system will not be economically efficient for some time.

Alternative Energies for Producing Electricity

Considering the problems associated with ethanol and biodiesel, we should consider spending our research dollars on a number of other technologies as well. Technologies exist that provide energy for more than just transportation. The sun, tides, wind, and geothermal energy are all sources of power that should last about as long as the earth as we know it. Tidal and geothermal power can be efficient, but they have high startup costs, and they are only useful near where these resources naturally occur, limiting their usefulness. Energy needs usually peak at night, making solar energy a bit of a pain. The wind doesn't always blow, which is a problem with wind power. Because solar or wind power is only realized when the sun is shining or when the wind is blowing, a method needs to be in place to store the energy from these sources. Unfortunately, methods for saving this power are far less than 100 percent efficient. Think of your car battery, which is charged by the car's alternator every time you run your car. Sure, it lasts five or six years, but eventually this battery will lose its ability to hold a charge and you'll be stranded somewhere. Obviously this is an even bigger problem with larger energy sources: that's a lot of batteries to change when they go bad.

The cost of energy from alternative sources is decreasing and the cost from fossil fuels is increasing. In 2005, it cost between 3.1 and 4.3 cents per kilowatt-hour (kWh) for geothermal energy, 11 to 15 cents for solar, between 18.8 and 31 cents for photovoltaic cells (another form of solar), and between 4.3 and 5.5 cents for wind power. Energy from fossil fuels cost 1.2 cents for coal and 3.5 cents for natural gas. But these numbers aren't the end of the story. As you might expect, some of these alternative energy sources are likely to become more cost efficient, especially as the technology advances, though others may have already reached a plateau. When solar energy was first introduced, it might take as long as ten or fifteen years to recoup the power that went into making the solar cell. In other words, making solar cells was very expensive and didn't yield much in return. Today, it might only take a year or two for a solar cell to return the energy that was expended to make it—and the cost of solar cells is decreasing. Research by Melissa Schilling and Melissa Esmundo at New York University concluded that there are two technologies poised to outperform fossil fuels in terms of cost: geothermal and wind. Furthermore, their work examining research dollars invested as compared to how cheap the energy will become reveals that these two technologies are underfunded, especially relative to funding for solar power, and that greater funding may well lead to prices that will make these technologies even cheaper than fossil fuels.

Government Policy

Ethanol is not a new fuel. It was first used in 1823, along with turpentine, to run New Hampshire mill owner Samuel Morey's internal combustion engine, and it was popular with pre-Civil War farmers who could turn crop waste into fuel using their own stills. Its popularity, however, has risen and fallen based on government policy. During the Civil War, the Union slapped a tax of $2 per gallon on ethanol to fund the war. Our ancestors didn't like taxes any more than we do, so they switched to kerosene fuel. In 1906, Congress lifted the tax on ethanol just in time for it to compete with other explosive liquids as the fuel of choice for the newly mass-produced automobile. Henry Ford's Model T could run on ethanol, gasoline, or a combination of the two, so removing the tax allowed the two fuels to compete on their own merits. The use of ethanol peaked during World War I at 50 to 60 million gallons per year, as demand for all fuels was high. Then in 1919 the ratification of the Eighteenth Amendment—better known as Prohibition—made the distillation and transportation of grain alcohol for fuel difficult. By the repeal of Prohibition in 1933, gasoline dominated the market, and, since gas prices stayed low until the 1970s, ethanol fuel was commercially unavailable. Biodiesel was invented in 1893, but never became popular because of its high cost.

The oil crisis of the 1970s led Congress and the Carter administration to promote energy conservation and research into alternative fuels. Amoco, followed by other oil companies, started to sell alcohol-blended fuels to reduce the cost and extend how far a gallon of petroleum would go. Congress provided tax breaks for ethanol producers starting in 1980 and protected domestic producers by placing tariffs on imported ethanol. Consumers never really took to ethanol, though. As oil and gasoline prices fell in the late 1980s and 1990s, there was little in the way of financial pressure driving consumers to demand the change, or the government to require the use of ethanol. There was, however, some pressure from environmental groups that appreciated ethanol as a cleaner-burning fuel. Congress did enact ethanol-friendly policies in several energy and farm bills and in amendments to the Clean Air Act during the 1990s. These pieces of legislation continued to provide tax credits for the production of ethanol, required alternative-fuel vehicles in government car fleets, mandated wintertime use of oxygenated fuels to minimize carbon monoxide, exempted alternative fuels from certain excise taxes, and imposed tariffs on imported ethanol to keep ethanol production within the United States. In addition, as state governments began to ban the use of the rival fuel additive MTBE because it contaminated groundwater, ethanol emerged as the dominant alternative fuel additive.

The 1992 Energy Policy Act encouraged state governments to restructure their electricity markets and to promote alternatives to fossil fuels. Many states responded by deregulating electricity to allow consumers a greater choice of providers, including green options. States also developed and implemented Renewable Portfolio Standards (RPS) to require utilities to offer a specific percentage of power from renewable sources.

After the terrorist attacks of September 11, 2001, energy issues reemerged as a high priority. This wasn't an energy issue as much as a national security issue: we needed options to make us less dependent on oil from the Middle East. Meanwhile, consumers were reacting negatively to gasoline prices of more than $3 per gallon and to the subsequent volatility of oil prices over the next several years. Ethanol's status as the only renewable fuel produced in any quantity, due in part to government assistance and the abundance of corn in the United States, as well as ethanol's claim to be carbon neutral, made it a natural alternative to oil.

Unfortunately, ethanol's preeminent status as the top renewable vehicle fuel is something like winning the largest shrimp award in an ocean full of whales. As of 2003, it accounted for just 1 percent of U.S. fuel consumption; by 2007, it had only risen to 2.6 percent.

In addition to the low prices of oil and coal, there are other barriers that have limited ethanol's market penetration. In the United States, ethanol is not available to any great degree outside the Midwest (except in whisky bottles and beer cans) because it corrodes pipelines and therefore must be shipped in small quantities by train, truck, or barge. One of the ethanol industry's major priorities is lobbying Congress to help pay for special pipelines to transport ethanol. Its usage is also limited by the fact that, while it can be used as a gasoline additive, ordinary vehicles cannot run on it alone. Without the wide availability of ethanol-powered cars, there's little incentive for gas station owners to invest in pumps and storage tanks to distribute it. The most likely scenario for an increased availability of ethanol at gas stations nationwide is for automakers to produce more flexible-fuel vehicles as an alternative to hybrid vehicles. Flex-fuel vehicles are cheaper to produce than hybrids because all they need is a slightly modified engine rather than a complete redesign of the vehicle to accommodate both electric and gasoline engines.

As scientific research raised questions about whether the amount of energy consumed in producing ethanol was worth the energy obtained from burning it, whether it raised food prices, and whether it could be transported out of the Midwest in sufficient quantities, Congress invested more federal funds into research, development, production, and distribution of other alternative fuels including solar, hydrogen, geothermal, wind, biofuels, and cellulosic ethanol, in a series of energy and farm bills in 2005, 2007, 2008, and 2009. Congress also set and expanded a federal Renewable Fuel Standard to mandate that utilities increase their use of renewable fuels.

The Political Dynamics

Corn-based ethanol's status as the top dog in the renewable energy world is due in part to its merits relative to its competitors. It is a very flexible fuel that can power vehicles or run electric turbines. Corn is so abundant in the United States that many would argue that it is overproduced, which is why the government helps to create a market for it by turning it into ethanol. In contrast, the other crops commonly talked about in relation to biofuels—switchgrass or fast-growing trees for cellulosic ethanol, and vegetable oils and animal fats for biodiesel—wouldn't be able to supply more than a fraction of the energy needs that corn can in the near future.

Corn-based ethanol's advantage is also political. The Corn Belt runs across the upper Midwest, stretching roughly from Kansas to Ohio. It includes twelve states, several of which are frequently among the most competitive in presidential and congressional elections (Ohio, Iowa, Missouri, Michigan, Wisconsin, Minnesota). More critically, the top corn- and ethanol-producing state is Iowa. The Iowa caucuses are the first event in the process of nominating presidential candidates for the Democratic and Republican parties. Candidates spend months in Iowa trying to win the favor of Iowa voters, hoping that the media coverage of their victory will provide them a critical boost of momentum to win primaries and caucuses in states that follow, paving the road for them to win their party's nomination and then the presidency. The influence of Iowa takes on mythical proportions in the minds of presidential contenders. First, Iowa; next, Mount Rushmore. And since approximately 99 percent of U.S. senators think they are running for president on any given day (only a slight exaggeration), protecting the interests of Iowa corn farmers has a larger effect on the dynamics of U.S. energy, agricultural, and environmental policy than we might reasonably expect. Given the political dynamics of the Midwest in presidential and congressional campaigns, neither party is willing to risk offending corn farmers. Whatever its policy merits, ethanol has built-in political support that other alternative energy sources do not.

As Congress became more interested in finding additional sources of renewable fuels in the 2000s, it might have noted that the ethanol industry was growing rapidly, and therefore concluded that ethanol no longer needed government support. Yet Congress did not level the playing field between ethanol and its competitors by removing ethanol's subsidies and tariff protections. The political rationale for protecting ethanol's benefits was too strong. Instead, Congress solved the unfairness problem by providing subsidies to other renewable energies too. In the future, we will undoubtedly find that these subsidies are nearly impossible to get rid of, regardless of the success or failure of the energy source itself. If the fuels do not compete successfully in the market, their proponents will argue that the failure is because they have received insufficient government support or faced barriers that their competitors did not face, and thus they require even more support from government. Those fuels that succeed will develop significant bases of employment (producers, distributors, retailers) and consumers who rely on them and who can lobby members of Congress to maintain their benefits. To avoid alienating constituents who care intensely about their benefits, it's easier to keep providing the goodies regardless of whether there is an economic rationale, especially since the savings from eliminating the subsidies from the federal budget would not be noticed by taxpayers. Whether or not new programs or subsidies are hard to create, they are nearly impossible to kill once they've started.

We all know that the more effective way of decreasing pollution or reducing our dependence on foreign oil is to use less fuel of any kind. Raising fuel efficiency standards or promoting conservation would achieve these goals efficiently. The problem is that Americans have traditionally favored dispersed residential patterns (dare we say "sprawl"?) and large vehicles to transport themselves (and their kids) to work and play. Until 2007, automobile fuel efficiency standards had not been raised since 1980, as the automakers were consistently able to persuade members of Congress that there would be a backlash if drivers thought they were being forced into smaller, less safe cars. And even in 2008, when consumers increased their purchases of smaller

MOST economists argue that it is more effective to tax things we don't like (such as pollution) than to subsidize things we like (such as particular kinds of alternative energies). In 1993, the Clinton administration proposed a BTU tax (British thermal units are a measure of energy) on energy sources as a means of decreasing the budget deficit and encouraging energy conservation. This proposal was blocked by a few Democrats in Congress who represented oil-producing states and sought to protect jobs back home in alliance with Republicans who didn't want tax increases. Members of Congress from competitive districts who voted for climate change legislation in the House of Representatives in 2009 were immediately attacked in radio commercials for voting to increase their constituents' energy bills. Raising taxes is unpopular; giving someone a subsidy is popular among its recipients—and nonrecipients usually aren't aware of what's going on. Thus, as a nation, we tend to choose the economically less efficient route.

cars as gasoline rose above $3 a gallon, most of the political pressure focused on getting the price of gas down ("Drill, Baby, Drill" was the chant at the Republican National Convention in 2008).

Besides taxing energy, it would be more efficient economically to remove tariffs on foreign ethanol. This would lower the price of foreign ethanol and provide greater incentive for U.S. companies to use it as a gas additive. Foreign-produced ethanol is often based on sugarcane and sugar beets, which produce energy with greater efficiency than corn-based ethanol. But foreign ethanol producers and the farmers who supply them do not vote in the United States, whereas U.S. farmers and producers who benefit from the protectionist tariffs do.

There are many other sources of energy besides ethanol, of course, and various levels of government have been proactive in promoting them. For example, California implemented the Million Solar Roofs initiative to assist homeowners who installed solar cells to help power their houses. Without this subsidy it is unlikely that most homeowners who installed solar panels would have done so. After all, while solar energy can drastically reduce a power bill, the cost of solar panels for a 2,000-square-foot home would probably be over twenty thousand dollars if there were no rebates. (State and federal governments, in many cases, offer tax incentives and subsidies for using solar power.) Without subsidies it would take a decade or longer for the cells to pay for themselves, depending on the specific sunlight exposure and energy usage of the home.

The question isn't whether we need alternative energy sources, but how soon we need to implement their usage; which energy sources we should pursue; and what, if anything, the government should do to facilitate the transition. Of course the free market could govern which alternative energy sources come out on top. Currently, the only alternative fuel that is close to fossil fuels in terms of cost to the consumer is ethanol from corn, and that's largely because of government subsidies for corn growers. (Although if the free market truly reigned, we'd have to get rid of the tax breaks that oil companies get, too). Aside from ethanol, alternative sources of energy just can't compete. We would certainly transition to alternative fuels over time, but it is likely that this would take significantly longer than if we offered subsidies for using these fuels.

Policy Option One: Leave Things as They Are

One of our country's greatest weaknesses is our reliance on foreign oil. The power plants that supply electricity to our homes are driven, for the most part, by fossil fuels like coal and natural gas that come from United States soil, or, in some cases, from alternative power sources, such as nuclear power. Our transportation system, on the other hand, is absolutely dependent upon foreign oil, with domestic oil only providing about a third of our needs. Our first priority should continue to be finding a way to reduce our dependence on fossil fuels. Right now, in terms of alternative energy sources for vehicles, ethanol from corn is the answer. Corn ethanol only costs between $1 and $2 per gallon to produce, which is competitive with the cost of gasoline when prices spike—a gallon of gas can cost anywhere from less than $1 to about $2 to produce. Gas prices have regularly been above $3 a gallon at the pump, and emissions from our cars are full of pollutants, so something needs to be done right now. There is no better cure for what ails us than ethanol from corn, which is why the government continues to provide subsidies and money for research. When the cost of gasoline gets too high, adding ethanol can bring the cost down, or even partially replace it.

The United States is already overproducing corn. In fact, roughly 20 percent of the corn that we grow is shipped to other countries. We can use a portion of this corn for making alcohol and decrease our dependence on foreign oil. And every little bit of ethanol that we use as a substitute for gasoline means that much less carbon dioxide in our air. Ethanol burns cleaner than gas and oil, which also means less air pollution.

Right-Wing Rating We're split on this issue.

Economic conservatives ★★ Private companies are best able to determine which investments in alternative energies are worthwhile. Oil is king because it's cheap. As it becomes more expensive and new technologies are developed by private industry, ethanol or other alternatives will take over. This is a perfect free market situation (except for the corn subsidies and, if it were politically feasible, we'd get rid of those too).

National security conservatives ★★★ The United States sends lots of money to oil-rich dictators, some of whom fund terrorists. We don't like government subsidies, but it's a better alternative than the risk of dependence on foreign oil. At least the money stays in America.

Left-Wing Rating ★★★ Corn-based ethanol is better than oil and coal, but isn't as carbon neutral as its proponents would have us believe. Promoting other alternative fuels will provide incentives to develop technologies and distribution systems. This will be a boon to a new green economy.

Policy Option Two: Encourage Biofuels, but Reduce Dependence on Corn

We should concentrate our alternative energy efforts on replacing fuels used for transportation before we start to worry about powering our homes. Unfortunately, right now the only substitute that competes with oil is ethanol, and that's because of subsidies paid to corn farmers. If the powers that be in the Middle East shut down oil exports to the United States tomorrow and we responded by using our entire corn crop to make ethanol, we still wouldn't be able to meet the fuel needs of our society. Furthermore, if we were to convert all of our corn, or even a significantly greater portion of it, to producing ethanol, there would be serious consequences for the cost of food in the United States, as well as on exports of corn to other countries. Corn ethanol just doesn't have the ability to meet our need for transportation fuel. Fortunately, corn is not the only crop from which we can acquire biofuels.

While the ultimate system for producing biofuels in terms of the quantity of energy produced per amount of energy expended is sugarcane, there aren't many places in the United States where we can grow sugarcane efficiently, so it is really isn't a reasonable replacement for corn. However, there are options for producing biofuels that, while not currently economically or technologically perfected, have the potential for replacing corn ethanol. Cellulosic ethanol, which uses otherwise unusable plant materials, and biodiesel from algae both cut into food production much less than corn ethanol, and are more efficient. We need to put money into developing these and other technologies.

Right-Wing Rating ★★ Any energy product that can be cheaply produced and provide us with energy is a good thing. But only corn is available in the quantities we need, so let's not waste a lot of money on options that won't give us much bang for our buck.

Left-Wing Rating ★★★★ This is much better than the corn option, but our government should put more money into energy sources that require less land. Calling forests renewable biofuel, for example, is not a step forward.

Policy Option Three: Concentrate on Truly Renewable Nontransportation Fuels and Conservation

We are misdirecting our efforts when we focus on biofuels to replace gasoline. Every resource that is being used for biofuels, including land and fertilizer, is at the expense of food production. This is true for everything from corn to algae. We need to aggressively develop truly renewable resources like solar and wind power, which will require generous funding. Once a solar cell or windmill is made it will produce power for decades; compare this with ethanol, which is burned up the moment it enters a car's cylinder. Every time the spark plug fires, that's a little bit more fertilizer, a little bit more pesticide, and a little bit more topsoil used up. The electrical energy that is produced from solar and wind sources can power a car as surely as gasoline can, we just haven't yet had enough incentive to make electric cars a popular option.

From wind and solar to geothermal and tidal power, there are dozens of different options for renewable energy. Despite the fact that most of these options currently cost more per unit of power than coal, this won't always be the case. Expanding research will drop the cost of these energy sources quickly. Different power sources make sense in different parts of the country: solar power in California, tidal power along the East Coast, wind power in the Midwest.

Simultaneously, we need to use less power in our daily lives. Reducing our demand for energy is the best way to conserve resources and spare the environment.

Right-Wing Rating ★★ Conservation is virtuous, but we need to develop energy sources to grow the economy. These alternate technologies for energy are becoming more competitive on their own, and consumers will shift to them when the price is right, without government assistance. When alternative technologies are viable, government may have to use its authority to site energy facilities in order to promote economic growth despite the not-in-my-backyard objections of local residents.

Left-Wing Rating ★★★★★ Because of global food shortages, going in a direction other than biofuels is really the only reasonable choice. Conservation must be a big part of the solution because it doesn't require any expense or cause environmental damage.

The Bottom Line

Despite the fact that our government is enamored with biofuels, we're better off treating them as a short-term remedy, rather than a long-term solution. The world's need for food will only increase over the coming decades. Meanwhile, as long as we believe that increasing carbon dioxide in our atmosphere isn't good for us, we need to do what we can to decrease our emissions of this gas. Unfortunately, our alternative energy sources are not currently cost-effective enough to take over for fossil fuels, and so, if our government wants to inspire us to use alternatives, it must provide us with an incentive, or simply wait for the price of fossil fuels to rise naturally as we deplete that resource. Incentives could include lowering costs by subsidizing corn even more than we already do, by subsidizing other crops for biofuels, or by pouring money into other energy sources entirely. We could even increase the use of alternative energy by giving incentives directly to the consumer for purchasing these energies. The biggest incentives would determine which alternative energy sources dominate.

CHAPTER 6

★★★

Genetic Engineering: A Time Bomb Waiting to Explode?

EARLY IN 2001, Dr. Elaine Ingham, then an Oregon State University researcher, was recruited by New Zealand's Green Party to testify before New Zealand's Royal Commission on Genetic Modification about a genetically altered bacterium she had worked with that seemed poised to end the world as we know it. Specifically, she claimed that "the likely effect of allowing the field trial . . . would have been to destroy terrestrial plants." The press immediately latched onto this powerful statement. Headlines read: "GM Bacteria Could Kill All Life," and Dr. Ingham's statements resulted in further digging by reporters and politicians into the specific bacteria that Dr. Ingham had researched. This bacteria, it turns out, was created to convert waste plant material into alcohol. In Dr. Ingham's laboratory tests, conducted in artificial conditions, these bacteria had indeed killed plants. Other researchers, however, strongly disagreed with Dr. Ingham's conclusions—some of them believing that the bacteria probably wouldn't survive for long in a natural setting—and they made their thoughts known. In March of 2001, Dr. Ingham and the Green Party apologized to the commission for submitting what was reported in *Nature Biotechnology* as "false claims about the ecological impact of genetically modified organisms." The discredited claims that Dr. Ingham had made and her subsequent apology raises a larger question: how much of what we hear about the dangers of transgenic plants is hype, and how much is the truth? And implicit within this question is an even larger one: how much do people really know about what a transgenic plant is?

The Science

In practically every university across the world researchers are working with the stuff that makes us what we are. Deep in our cells lies

DNA, a long polymer (which basically just means a very big chemical with many constituent pieces) that provides the coding for almost everything that a person or animal or plant physically is. DNA and how it is constructed, which in turn reveals how it stores information, was discovered in 1953 by James Watson and Francis Crick, at the University of Cambridge in England. At first their discovery was interesting but not particularly useful. After all, knowing that there are little marks on a music CD that can be read by a CD player doesn't mean that we can read the discs ourselves. But knowing they exist does raise the possibility of figuring out what they mean, with enough time and study. After examining the codes for decades, scientists began to discover how to read DNA and how the codes contained in its twists and turns worked to create the various proteins that make a living thing what it is. At first this information was used merely to read the DNA of various organisms. By just comparing the DNA of two different organisms scientists could identify how closely related they are. They could also use DNA to detect genetic problems by identifying genes that weren't properly organized. Later on, scientists discovered ways to manipulate an organism's DNA by introducing new pieces of DNA from one plant or animal into another plant or animal. This is possible because essentially, every living thing uses the same coded DNA.

A short segment of DNA that codes for a particular protein—and hence a trait, like resistance to a disease—can be introduced from one living thing into another by one of a few different processes. None is necessarily better than another, it's just a matter of which works best with the particular animal or plant that you're handling. Perhaps the easiest system for introducing DNA into a plant is the gene gun, which is loaded with very small metal particles instead of bullets. These particles adhere to DNA, so when they are mixed in a test tube with the DNA that you want to add to a plant, what you end up with is a bunch of little bullets with DNA glued to them. These DNA-spiked particles are then shot into a plant using compressed air (it's like a BB gun, but with many very small BBs shot at once) and—voila!—you're done. You've introduced a trait into the plant. The part of the plant that was shot with DNA will then be reproduced using small cuttings, and the resulting plants will be tested to make sure they have the desired DNA.

Another popular method of introducing new DNA into a plant is by putting the DNA into a specific type of bacterium that has the ability to transfer it to another plant. Humans weren't the first organisms to come up with the idea of moving genes from one living thing to another—these bacteria, called *Agrobacterium,* have been doing it for millions of years, naturally inserting DNA into plants where it wasn't found before. In fact, they can even insert their DNA into human cells in certain situations.

Causing plants to produce compounds that they would not normally produce has been a goal of agricultural scientists for as long as there has been agriculture. Genetic engineering is just the newest way to meet an ancient goal. For centuries we have been grafting one plant onto another so that the grafted plant would contain compounds that it would not ordinarily contain. Usually this provides a benefit to the grafted plant (and hence the people who use it), such as insect resistance, but it could also make a perfectly palatable plant extremely dangerous. For example, if you graft a tomato plant onto the roots of jimson weed, the tomatoes will become toxic from poisons manufactured in these roots. Such a graft might actually prove fatal to people who eat the tomatoes. Today, most of our fruit trees are grafted onto roots that imbue the grafted plants with certain traits, such as dwarfing (to increase production and make them easier to harvest) or resistance to certain insects. If you have ever eaten an apple, a peach, or a pear, then it is more than likely you have eaten a fruit from a grafted plant.

By using gene guns, *Agrobacterium,* and other methods, humans have been able to change animals and plants so that they can do things they had never done before. Many different traits have been transferred to transgenic plants, but the most common are herbicide resistance and resistance to insects, particularly caterpillars. Caterpillar resistance comes from a gene that causes the plant to produce a particular protein called Bt (for *Bacillus thuringiensis,* the bacteria from which the gene was originally taken). This protein works in the caterpillar's stomach, basically causing the stomach to split open and the caterpillar to digest itself. This protein is also available as an over-the-counter pesticide commonly called Bt. In the case of herbicide resistance, inserting a particular strand of DNA into plants causes them to be resistant to a particular type of herbicide, most commonly glyphosate, which is the chemical used in Roundup.

It is obvious from the percentage of genetically modified crops grown in this country just how successful genetic engineering has been in the marketplace. Currently, 85 percent of the corn planted in the United States is genetically modified, along with 91 percent of the soybeans, and 88 percent of the cotton.

Americans consume more genetically engineered goods than they probably realize: at least 60 percent of all foods in the United States likely contain some GE material. And in most cases foods containing genetically modified products do not have to be labeled as such. While no GE animals were approved for human consumption (as of 2010, though genetically modified salmon was on its way), dairy products may contain milk produced with GE-BST, the growth hormone for cattle, which comes from genetically engineered bacteria.

There is a great deal of controversy over whether it is moral, ethical, and even safe to transfer genes from one organism to another, and there is no doubt that a lot of money is at stake. Transferring a gene to cotton to make it resistant to a particularly damaging insect transforms that cotton into something very valuable. Likewise, making a crop resistant to a particularly effective herbicide is also extremely valuable. But there are a whole string of concerns that people have about these technologies. First, and perhaps most importantly, is the ethical question of whether it is right to mess with what nature (or God) has created. Second, there is the question of whether altered plants will breed with their unaltered relatives, and whether these new plants become weeds, unresponsive to some of our most effective herbicides because of their new DNA. Third, there is the issue of whether these plants are safe to eat. And finally, there is the concern about whether these plants could negatively affect our environment. Our government needs to take all of these issues into account as it decides what to do, if anything, about the new transgenic organisms we are creating.

Despite extravagant claims, genetically engineered plants tend to have yields similar to their non-GE counterparts.

What's Good About Genetic Engineering

Despite extravagant claims, genetically engineered plants tend to have yields similar to their non-GE counterparts. Often, a company selling GE plants will claim that farmers can increase yield by using transgenic plants. Usually, what they really mean is that using GE plants will reduce their losses to the insect pest that the crop has been engineered to resist, or to the weeds that can be controlled by using a more effective herbicide that the crop is now resistant to. It's a subtle but very real difference that is often more pronounced in developing countries. In these poorer countries, farmers make fewer pesticide applications, while here in the United States farmers generally have the freedom to apply whatever is needed whenever it is needed. Hence, in poorer countries GE crops will often show greater yields because of a reduction in losses, but in the United States, yield numbers are usually similar to non-GE crops because of our ability, through pesticides as well as other, more natural, means, to control pests in non-GE crops very effectively.

A more established benefit of transgenic plants is a reduction in pesticide use.

A more established benefit of transgenic plants is a reduction in pesticide use. The use of transgenic cotton has resulted in a substantial decrease in the use of pesticides for this crop in the United States as well as in China, Australia, and other countries. Chinese farmers reduced their pesticide inputs by almost 80 percent when they used rice varieties genetically modified to resist insects. On the other hand, some people argue that there is actually a net increase in pesticide use, at least in crops modified to be herbicide resistant, because the herbicide that these crops are resistant to, Roundup, is used more frequently. But there is a consequent reduction in the use of other herbicides (like atrazine) that are usually considered more environmentally damaging than Roundup. Indeed, this reduction in pesticide use can have a profound impact on preserving our natural ecosystems in certain sensitive locations near farmland. If a crop suffers an outbreak of pests, in many cases the only choice for a farmer is to spray pesticides. Pesticides often drift, or can be used incorrectly, causing damage to lake or stream ecosystems, or even to forests or rainforests. A genetically altered plant seems like a good choice because it will often preclude, or at least drastically reduce, the need for environment-damaging pesticides.

***

Today's biotechnology allows us to do things that were impossible just a few years ago. On the surface this may seem entirely positive, but what if there are complications that we never thought of? Opponents of biotechnology claim that new chemicals could be introduced into food that would cause it to become poisonous, but that just hasn't happened, and it seems unlikely (unless it is done purposely by some malicious person or government, which is not out of the question). True, soybeans have been transformed using Brazil nut plants, which caused the GE soybeans to contain an allergen, but the problem was discovered before the plants were released and no human was ever affected. As of the writing of this book, we don't know of a single case where a transgenic food was proven to have made someone physically sick because it was transgenic. In contrast, traditional breeding and selection processes have been know to cause injury. For example, people who were handling a new variety of insect-resistant celery developed a reaction when they were exposed to sunlight because of the increased levels of chemicals called psoralens that the plants contained. And lima beans are a crop in which new varieties need to be screened very carefully because of their tendency to have high levels of cyanide.

We don't know of a single case where a transgenic food was proven to have made someone physically sick because it was transgenic.

Despite the lack of evidence that humans are harmed by genetically modified plants, a few studies have shown that other animals may be affected by certain transgenic foods. For example, in one isolated experiment, certain genetically modified potatoes were been shown to be potentially damaging to the digestive system of rats. Other studies have shown that the addition of a bean protein into peas caused mice to exhibit an immune response that could, potentially, be dangerous in humans. More studies on mice have shown that, when fed diets of transgenic foods (corn and soybeans) over many generations, or when older mice were fed transgenic foods, they developed abnormalities in some of their organs. These studies do not provide conclusive evidence that transgenic plants can affect our health, however, and the preponderance of studies show that transgenic plants are safe. But these experiments do support the fear that someday a food that is not safe will sneak by or—just as bad—that some of the transgenic foods that we currently eat will have a negative effect on us that will not be evident for years to come.

There are additional reasons to be concerned about the use of transgenics. One of the greatest fears of farmers and the companies that produce transgenic plants is that their genetically engineered crops will escape cultivation and create races of superweeds. After all, most transgenic plants were created to have resistance to one problem or another, so the idea that these crops could breed with wild crops and make superweeds isn't really that far-fetched. In fact, there is a case of a transgenic crop breeding with a wild relative: transgenic corn grown in Mexico has passed its DNA on to native corn, including the Roundup Ready gene. This is potentially the worst gene that could escape because it allows the plant to resist the most powerful herbicide in our pesticide arsenal, glyphosate, which kills almost anything green.

Though this introgression of the gene for Roundup resistance into wild corn is a bit scary, what is even scarier is that it is not the only case of this type of introgression. Glyphosate-resistant creeping bentgrass, a grass used for lawns, was identified in Oregon in 2006, and the gene for glyphosate resistance was found in field mustard in 2007, apparently transferred from transgenic canola. These are just a few cases of the many where genes have escaped into wild populations, and there are likely more to come.

The genes that we release do not always stay where we place them. None of these crosses, however, have yet produced weeds that impede crop production. Furthermore, though these hybrid plants are resistant to Roundup, they are not resistant to the many other available herbicides, so they are still easily controlled. Besides, it's not as though plants can't be naturally resistant to glyphosate. The Asiatic dayflower, once an ornamental, is now a glyphosate-resistant weed that threatens Roundup Ready corn and soybeans because it can survive exposure to this herbicide. This resistance didn't develop in a vacuum, however, and it can easily be argued that the presence of the Roundup Ready gene in crops accelerated the process.

In addition to the ability of genes to escape boundaries by breeding with related plants, there is also the issue of the genes that we move from one organism to another becoming ineffective. A weed can develop resistance to an herbicide because it acquired this resistance from a genetically engineered relative, but there is also another way: natural selection. If a particular pesticide is used too frequently, then pests will develop resistance to it. For example, cotton bollworm, a pest of cotton, has developed resistance to the Bt gene because of that gene's pervasive use in transgenic cotton. Similarly, the increased use of Roundup to support Roundup resistant crops means that weeds have been under a lot of pressure to adapt. In a nutshell, that's what natural selection does: select for the organisms that can survive certain hardships. In this instance the hardship is Roundup, and natural selection favors the weeds that can cope with the herbicide. Hence, with increased Roundup applications weeds develop resistance to this product faster than they might have otherwise. Fortunately, we already have crops that have been genetically engineered to be resistant to another herbicide, glufosinate ammonium, which can be used very similarly. And when weeds start to develop resistance to that . . .

What happens if nonpest insects are damaged by these transgenic plants? Will our natural ecology be turned on its head? It's already known that pollen from transgenic plants can poison the monarch and many of our most beautiful butterflies. If pollen from transgenic corn plants falls on the milkweed that these butterflies eat while they are larvae, it can kill them. Despite this example, we have yet to see any widespread calamity from transgenic pollen.

Many people understandably feel as though we're just waiting for the biotechnology industry to make a wrong decision in creating a transgenic plant or animal. If this occurs, we could suddenly see problems that we cannot now imagine. Could it occur with an animal rather than a plant? It's possible. Currently there are experimental catfish that have a gene inserted into their DNA that causes them to grow rapidly. If these catfish escaped into the wild, would they have a radical effect on the environment? Some research shows that they wouldn't survive, but the truth is, until it happens, we won't really know.

And then there is the fact that pests tend to be able to get around some of our best laid plans. In many ways, all we're doing when we control pests with pesticides, biotechnology, or any other method is trying to hold our own. Aristotle wrote that nature abhors a vacuum, and that is very true in the case of insects and the resources available to them. When we stop one pest, another rushes in to fill the void. When we inserted the Bt gene into cotton to control caterpillar pests like the cotton bollworm, we opened the door for other insects. Stink bugs are immune to the effects of Bt, so they found the cotton bolls, now relatively free of their competitor, the cotton bollworm, a good place to feed. In other crops the same thing is happening: the damage formerly caused by the larvae of butterflies and moths is being traded for damage caused by stink bugs and flea beetles. Furthermore, the reductions in pesticide applications realized by the use of transgenic plants are very crop specific. This means that with some crops, major reductions in pesticide use are possible, but with other crops the reductions are minor, or there may even be an increase in pesticide use. Transgenic plants may have changed the battle lines, but they have not won the war.

Government Policy

Currently, federal policy treats products created with biotechnology the same as products created with conventional processes. Put another way, products are regulated based on the features of the product (such as disease resistance or color), not the method by which they were produced. Genetically engineered products must meet the same safety and health standards as their traditional counterparts. No more, and no less. This policy was articulated by the White House Office of Science and Technology Policy in 1986, and Congress has never modified it.

★★★

Following this policy, the Food and Drug Administration determined in 1992 that no special label would be required for GE foods, since the foods were substantially equivalent to their traditional counterparts. In 2001, the FDA invited public comments on whether to issue new rules on GE labeling but has not, as of 2010, changed its original stance. The FDA has, however, required intensive review of GE foods if the genetic modification causes the food to have a different composition, nutrients, or toxicity than conventional products. Review is also required if the plant that is the source of one of more of the genes produces allergic reactions; if the modified plants are used to make substances like pharmaceuticals or polymers in addition to food; or if the gene transfer has produced unexpected genetic effects. Simply put, this means that the FDA requires a lot of testing of genetically engineered plants before they can be planted on farms.

In cases where a product (such as an oil) obtained from the genetically engineered organism is sufficiently different from its conventional counterpart, the FDA requires that the modified product be given a different name, but it does not require an identification of its GE production method. For example, the FDA required the renaming of a soybean oil whose fatty acid composition had been altered by genetic engineering. The new name is "high oleic acid," which, while it may be descriptive of the oil's chemistry, does little to tell consumers about the source of this oil.

The Animal and Plant Health Inspection Service (APHIS) of the USDA also has responsibility for biotechnology-based products that are known or suspected to be—or pose a risk of becoming—plant pests. It regulates the handling and disposal of these products to ensure that they do not become a problem. If someone wants to import GE plants, transfer them across state lines, or release them into the environment, they must submit biological information on the genetically modified organism (GMO) and the organisms that supplied its genetic material, as well as experimental and field test data, to APHIS. APHIS then examines this information, paying particular attention to disease and pest susceptibilities and the many physiological factors that may be changed by the introduction of the new genes, including new enzymes and changes to plant metabolism. Information on the GMO is also examined to see whether it acts as a weed or can cross-pollinate or otherwise transfer its genes to other plants or animals. Critics of GMOs are particularly concerned about the potential to create superweeds that essentially act as invasive species and take over native organisms in their habitat. APHIS attempts to ensure that such a scenario will not happen.

Perhaps the most significant complaint about the system as it exists today is that the USDA and FDA review only the conclusions of the manufacturer, rather than conducting their own tests of GMOs. This is true of these agencies' procedures for other products, as well. The EPA is in charge of pesticides, so crops engineered to produce a pesticide (such as Bt) must be approved by the EPA.

***

The U.S. government has not been terribly concerned about GE issues. However, it has had to react to the international politics of biotech foods. The European Union, and to a lesser extent, Japan, have used their domestic environmental laws to block imports of GE or pesticide-treated products from the United States (such as beef in Europe or apples in Japan). The U.S. government has been quite active in trying to get those trade barriers reduced to open up those markets to U.S. agricultural products.

In the 1980s, several European countries imposed bans on beef hormones made using genetically engineered bacteria, due to media reports in Italy that children were growing oversized genitals and breasts because of hormones in veal. Scientific advisory boards found no evidence of health risks from these hormones, but numerous European governments instituted the bans anyway, in response to public pressure. Later, Europeans bore the brunt of the spread of mad cow disease in 1995 and 1996. Though mad cow disease was unrelated to GMO technology, European public opinion and government regulators were cautious about any potential risks to food safety. Environmental and consumer groups had allied with small farmers—who would be at a competitive disadvantage if farmers with larger herds could produce even more beef and milk and drive down prices further—to impose these hormone bans. Facing overproduction of milk and beef, there wasn't any reason for governments to encourage, or even allow, hormone use. The question then became how these governments would respond to imports of U.S. meat from animals that might have been given these hormones.

A major international trade law, the 1947 General Agreement on Tariffs and Trade (GATT), allows countries to restrict imports if "necessary to protect human, animal, or plant life and health." But it doesn't define or set standards for what would be considered "necessary." The United States argued that the hormone ban was not necessary to protect health and safety because there was no scientific basis for it—as the Europeans themselves admitted. The United States also argued that the issue was whether the meat contained harmful residues, not whether the animal was ever fed hormones. And because most U.S. cattle are weaned from hormones well before slaughter, there was little risk of residue contamination. The European Union countered that there was no scientific evidence to prove that hormone-treated meat was *not* dangerous, setting a standard that is nearly impossible to meet, since it's impossible to prove a negative (that a substance is *never* dangerous, or is 100 percent safe). In the end, the United States had little leverage under international law. As long as domestic and imported products are treated the same, countries have substantial latitude to impose restrictions. And since the Europeans imposed the beef hormone bans on themselves, they could impose them on imports too.

The United States settled the matter in 1989 by agreeing to assist in certifying that U.S. beef exports were hormone free (though it would not participate in actual inspections). Similarly, in 2000, the United States agreed to the Cartagena Protocol on Biosafety, which requires labels on genetically modified agricultural commodities shipped across borders, and gives nations the right to refuse imports of genetically modified food if there is little evidence to show that the food is safe. This applies only to exports and not to foods sold and consumed in the United States.

The European Union passed additional GMO rules in 2004. Any product with 1 percent or more transgenic content must be labeled. Each GMO product also must have a paper trail maintained by each handler in the food chain to document where it came from and to whom it was sold, so that any safety problems could easily be tracked and other potentially contaminated products identified. Because few GMO products are being sold in Europe, the costs of these regulations to European producers and distributors is minimal.

The Political Dynamics

The contrasts between policies in Europe, Japan, and the United States on GE products are crystal clear. All are advanced, industrialized democracies, with active environmental and consumer movements, yet the Europeans and the Japanese have placed all kinds of domestic and import restrictions on GE food, while U.S. restrictions are minimal. The key reason for the difference is probably the political potency of small farmers. In Europe and Japan, they are extremely powerful and, particularly in Japan, allied with the historically dominant political party. Farmers are powerful in the United States, but large, corporate farms, which are technologically advanced and therefore allied with the agricultural technology industry and the USDA, are more politically potent than small, family farmers. As they have in Europe, small farmers in the United States have allied with consumer and environmental groups to try to restrict the use of GE products, but this coalition didn't hold. Small farmers feared they would not remain competitive if they didn't adopt the new technology; they also feared that a milk safety and animal rights campaign would trigger consumer backlash. This division undercut the potency of the proregulation coalition.

The other major push in the United States is to place labels on GE products so that consumers can identify the method by which the

THE USE of genetically engineered hormones for cattle has met with some resistance in the United States as it has in Europe, but not enough to stop its use. Small farmers and their allies in Congress wanted the FDA to add an additional stage—a social needs test—to the traditional drug approval process. They were specifically concerned with growth hormones like GE-BST, but this extra step would have applied to any drug. Basically, this proposed step would force the FDA to determine whether there was an economic demand for the drug and cultural acceptance of it before the FDA approved it for sale, the theory being that technology should not be developed if consumers will reject it. The FDA, however, countered that the federal Food, Drug, and Cosmetic Act prohibits them from considering the social and economic effects of new drugs. The FDA only has the legal authority to determine the safety of human consumption of animals that have received the drug, the drug's safety for animals, and whether the drug works as intended. Congress could, of course, change the law to add a social needs test to the FDA's drug approval procedures, but it has not done so.

food as been produced. Consumers may be wary of these "Frankenfoods" (as critics cleverly call them) out of fear or uncertainty about the dangers that genetic manipulation may pose, and there is a push to force producers to identify GE products to enable consumers to make informed choices. Unsurprisingly, the food industry generally opposes labeling requirements because consumers might interpret GE labels as warning labels, implying that the foods are less safe or nutritious than conventional foods. Furthermore, the industry objects to GE labeling because it would require developing parallel production, processing, and transportation infrastructures for GE and conventional products. Not only would this be extremely costly, but it would also be very difficult to do in practice because of pollen drift and the residue of seeds left on farm equipment and grain elevators. In other words, GE foods have become so prevalent that completely separating them from non-GE foods is too difficult (except for when non-GE foods are exported to other countries).

Genetically engineered products gained greater attention from policymakers in the late 1990s and early 2000s (though no new laws were passed) due to three incidents. In 1998, Monsanto announced that it was developing GE "terminator" seeds. These seeds would themselves grow and provide farmers with a crop, but seeds from that crop would not germinate, thereby preventing the farmer from producing another crop with them. This announcement came on the heels of a major consolidation of the seed industry in which the three biggest multinational biotechnology companies—Monsanto, DuPont, and Novartis—rapidly bought up smaller seed companies around the world. Monsanto's announcement reinforced concerns that a few companies were gaining too much control over the world's agriculture. In that context, terminator seeds attracted intense opposition, and Monsanto retreated the following year.

The second incident occurred in 2000 when the environmental group Friends of the Earth reported that numerous corn-based processed foods had been contaminated with a genetically modified feed corn known as StarLink, which was never approved for human consumption. More than 300 potentially contaminated corn products, like taco shells, were recalled from around the world, and major food companies pledged to avoid certain GE foods. The Kellogg Company and ConAgra shut down production lines to remove any traces of StarLink.

The third incident happened in 2001 when small amounts of StarLink were detected in conventional seeds about to be planted. Farmers and grain exporters feared massive losses, so the USDA used disaster relief funds to buy back between 300,000 and 400,000 bags of potentially contaminated corn seed.

Policy Option One: Leave Things as They Are

Without scientific evidence that GE foods are any more of a risk to public health and safety than their conventional alternatives, the U.S. government has not made an effort to prevent their use. Environmental, consumer, and small farm organizations have attempted to persuade the government to impose labeling requirements and social need standards for certification, but have not succeeded to date. Without clear evidence of a substantial problem or a crisis to generate intense public pressure, they have not been able to outmaneuver the agriculture technology community (otherwise known as Big Ag) on biotechnology issues. The advanced technology of U.S. agriculture has given it a major competitive advantage on the world market and the government has been unwilling to risk that advantage without clear threats to public health or the environment.

Currently, there isn't much regulation of transgenic plants beyond the initial testing that the companies introducing them are required to do before they bring the plants (or their products) to the market. While many environmentalists may think that this isn't enough, these tests do have a cost associated with them. A conservative estimate (from an employee of a biotechnology company) is that it costs 50 million dollars or so to provide the data that the FDA now requires to deregulate a crop.

The most compelling reason to let our biotechnology companies continue their work is that our farming system is based on technology, and technology has allowed us to grow more and more crops, more and more efficiently, as our population has expanded. Our use of biotechnology to increase food production is nothing more than the next logical step in our ability to improve crops. While genetically modified crops haven't lived up to their original billing as the answer to all of our farming problems, they have decreased crop losses and overall pesticide use in the United States and across the world This is reason enough for us to allow the continued use of these crops.

Right-Wing Rating ★★★★ The current system works. Products are being tested to find problems before they occur. If there is evidence that GM products are more of a risk than conventional products, then we can consider additional testing and restrictions; until then, there is no need to go much further.

Left-Wing Rating ★★ Genetically engineered plants have the potential to do a great deal of damage, and the fact that they haven't yet is just luck. Lack of evidence of danger means a lack of evidence, not a lack of danger. One day our luck will run out.

Policy Option Two: Transgenic Plants and Animals Should Be All But Outlawed

Without a doubt, the most substantial argument against the widespread use of transgenic plants and animals is that almost every type of bad result that was feared has in fact happened. Transgenic plants have bred with their wild relatives, transferring genes into new populations and potentially making superweeds. Pests have become resistant to the pesticides coded for in the transgenic plants. There is the potential for transgenic plants to alter the life of particular ecosystems. In other cases, transgenic plants haven't delivered all that we had hoped they would. Just about the only problem that hasn't happened is that people haven't been poisoned (at least that we know of) by transgenic plants—yet. While there has been no widespread catastrophe, it might only be a matter of time.

It's no longer just food crops that are being altered. We have come to a point where genes may be placed into another organism merely as a statement. In 2000, a rabbit named Alba had its DNA modified with a protein from a jellyfish so that it would glow. Eduardo Kac had a French geneticist, Louis-Marie Houdebine, create this rabbit for the sake of art. Kac later had his own DNA expressed in the genome of a petunia. To an outside observer, it looks as if the scientific community is playing games with genes. Is it responsible of us to use this powerful tool so frivolously? If we don't stop the creation of these abominations now, when will we stop? The question isn't necessarily whether what we have done so far is wrong, but, rather, whether it is leading us to something much worse, morally and physically.

Of the many potential dangers of genetically modified plants, the scariest scenario allows a dangerous transgenic plant to fall through the cracks because of insufficient testing. Humans could ingest this plant before we realize its dangers, and much of our population will be unknowingly poisoned. While there is no evidence to date that humans have been injured, the fact that transgenic plants containing allergens have been made, such as the GE soybeans spiked with Brazil nut proteins, is a cause for concern. Also troubling are the studies suggesting that GE foods have the potential to be detrimental to the health of animals. Food is a serious business, and if there is any chance that a food might not be completely safe, then it should be banned.

In addition to these unrealized dangers, there are some very real problems that transgenics pose to farmers who choose not to use them. A non-GMO farmer who is growing the same crop as a nearby GMO farmer can get into trouble if the GMO plants pollinate the non-GMO plants (as if the farmer could avoid this pollination). This is because the genes that are used to genetically modify plants are patented. If the non-GMO farmer plants seed that has a genetically engineered crop as one of its parents, then the non-GMO farmer has utilized a patent without permission. There have been lawsuits over this precise issue. Companies that produce transgenic plants have sued farmers who didn't originally plant transgenic seeds, but who replanted their own seed, which happened to have been pollinated by nearby transgenic plants from another farmer's field. The companies have invariably come out the winners, thereby preventing farmers from using the seed produced by their own plants! (See the next chapter on plant patents for more on this topic).

Right-Wing Rating ★ You want to ban genetically engineered products that are central to modern farming without any real evidence of harm? You're paranoid! These products reduce pesticide use and soil erosion substantially. Environmentalists should be for them.

Left-Wing Rating ★★★★★ The government is responsible for protecting public health and safety and therefore needs to regulate potentially harmful genetically engineered crops more carefully. Once there is overwhelming evidence that they are a danger, it will be too late.

Policy Option Three: Label Every Food That Includes Genetically Engineered Material

Biotechnology is being inflicted upon us without our approval. This is not okay. True, there's no definitive proof that transgenic organisms have caused problems for human health, but some studies do point to potential problems. Additionally, and perhaps more importantly, transgenics have a proven potential to affect our environment. Historically, one of the ways that we have protested a business's perceived bad practices is to boycott their products. By not providing information on which products include transgenic ingredients, businesses have stripped us of this form of protest. We can buy organic foods that we know have been produced without transgenic materials—because GE products cannot be sold as organics—but these foods are significantly more expensive. Transgenic foods should be an option we can knowingly choose or avoid. If anyone were arguing that we need transgenic crops to feed our nation this lack of an informed choice might be more understandable, but no one, not even the biotech companies, is making that argument (though they do argue that we can produce more with GMOs, that GMOs can reduce food prices, and that GMOs reduce the use of pesticides). Why not label foods with GE ingredients?

Groups opposed to requiring labeling—most large-scale farmers and biotech companies—complain that this labeling would mean they would need to process these foods separately from foods produced without modification, which would raise costs for food production. They also claim that the addition of a new gene from another organism is no different from adding a new gene through a more conventional breeding process, and there is some truth to that.

An alternative system would be for the government to standardize the use of labeling for foods that *don't* have any genetically modified material in them, similar to what is happening with organics right now. Designate what's not there rather than what is. The private sector is beginning to do this already. In 2009, the organic and natural foods chain Whole Foods announced that it would be partnering with the Non-GMO Project, a nonprofit group opposed to genetically modified foods, to use their Product Verification Program (PVP) to label foods that don't include GMOs. This label will give consumers the freedom to choose foods that aren't made with genetically modified organisms but may still be cheaper than organically produced food. If there is a demand for these nonmodified foods over a period of a decade or so, the government may step in. That is, after all, how the government originally got involved in labeling organic foods.

Right-Wing Rating ★★ While there's nothing wrong with letting the market decide which products succeed, there could be a lot of unjustified damage if the public reacts in ignorance and fear to foods labeled as genetically engineered. This unintended consequence would badly affect farmers who are using this technology to keep their crops going and avoid the use of expensive pesticides. If certification and labeling are warranted, let private industry set the standards; they're the experts and won't impose unnecessary and cumbersome rules.

Left-Wing Rating ★★★★ Letting people know what they're buying is a great idea.

The Bottom Line

So where should the government come down? It's not an easy question to answer. Changing the DNA in a plant or animal makes it into something new that—though not radically different from what it was before—has different qualities. In other words, this could be considered "playing God." Most scientists consider this to be a religious argument against biotechnology, and some consider it to be an irrational one. We beg to differ. If you value your religious beliefs (and here we're including those who might be atheists but who believe that nature is a deity unto itself), then biotechnology may be in direct opposition to your values. You should realize, however, that nature itself changes the genetic code of creatures through mutations, and that some organisms, such as *Agrobacterium*, can insert DNA into other organisms—we're not the only species that uses biotechnology.

Rejecting biotechnology because you fear its potential to end life on this earth isn't realistic, but rejecting it because you think that the drawbacks are potentially worse than the benefits is very valid. The dangers of biotechnology have been widely publicized, and, unfortunately, many of the bad things that have been predicted have come true. But it's also true that the predictions were much more dire than the reality seems to be. If you think that herbicide-resistant weeds have the potential to make our most reliable herbicides useless, then you have a legitimate concern. If you fear that our overuse of Bt as a gene in transgenic crops has the potential to make one of our valuable organic pesticides (Bt) less useful because it will result in Bt-resistant caterpillars, then you also have a legitimate concern. If you fear that transgenic plants will be detrimental to human health, well, that just hasn't happened yet, despite quite a concentration of these products in the grocery stores, and it doesn't seem likely to happen either—though it's impossible to completely discount it as a possibility.

Right now the most convincing arguments about possible negative effects on human health from GMOs come from a few studies on mice. The meaning of these studies is perhaps best summarized by a quotation from the "Report on Safety and Nutritional Assessment of GM Plants" published by the European Food Safety Authority: "The majority of these experiments did not indicate clinical effects or histopathological abnormalities in organs or tissues of exposed animals. In some cases adverse effects were noted, which were difficult to interpret due to shortcomings in the studies." In other words, while we can't ignore the few studies that have shown that feeding GMO crops to rodents can be detrimental to their health, these studies don't clearly show that these crops are bad. People who are very concerned about risky food will nonetheless find that these studies provide enough data for them to make the effort to avoid genetically altered foods.

If the government requires the labeling of food that has a high percentage of GMO material in it, people will assume that the government is making a statement about the health risks of GMO food (which they have not done) simply because there is a label, just as many people incorrectly assume that the USDA Organic label means the government has found health benefits to eating organic food. Private industry labeling of non-GMO foods seems like a good idea, and it's surprising that it has taken so long for it to take hold.

If the government requires the labeling of food that has a high percentage of GMO material in it, people will assume that the government is making a statement about the health risks of GMO food (which they have not done) simply because there is a label, just as many people incorrectly assume that the USDA Organic label means the government has found health benefits to eating organic food.

Unless you're in the camp that believes that using biotechnology is bad in and of itself because it is contrary to nature, then biotechnology is probably acceptable to you for some applications. The next question is, what applications do you find acceptable? Not every genetically modified organism has the same potential for altering the environment, and each needs to be assessed for its own benefits and drawbacks. You can easily argue that some of the things we've already done with this process have been bad. But biotechnology is, like pesticides or fertilizers, a tool for us to keep our crops healthy. The one difference between this tool and the others is that changes to an organism's DNA may be carried on in its progeny. This is reason enough for the government—and all of us—to pay special attention to each new genetically modified organism that we decide to introduce.

CHAPTER 7

Plant Patents: Protecting Plants or Profiteering?

HOW NEAT WOULD it be to have a special plant that you could call your own and that you could plant at your discretion—and no one else could plant it, unless, that is, they paid you? It seems counterintuitive that plants can be owned in this way but patents, specifically plant patents, ensure that they can. Apples such as 'Honeycrisp' and 'Connell Red' were once patented, as was the 'Mars' geranium and many others. The U.S. patent office has been granting plant patents since August of 1931, when a man by the name of Henry Bosenberg received a patent for a climbing rose that kept blooming for substantially longer than other, similar roses. This rose wasn't even bred by Bosenberg, it was just a 'Van Fleet' rose (named for the breeder, Dr. Walter Van Fleet) that he had purchased from someone else and it had the unusual, redeeming quality of reblooming. But Bosenberg propagated it using a stem cutting, and once you propagate a plant and file the paperwork, it's yours. Bosenberg named this rose 'New Dawn', and if you're willing to look around a little, you can still find it in garden stores today.

Is it right for one person to be able to "own" a living organism and to control who grows and sells it? That's a tough question. And it's not just plants that can be owned: all of the *genes* we just read about in the previous chapter can be owned too. This means that if your crop was planted with seeds that came from plants that contained those patented genes, or was even fertilized by plants with those genes in them, then your plant probably has those patented genes and you owe some company some cash. You say it was an accident? Too bad, if the company who owns the patent to the genes that you accidentally acquired decides to sue.

Before 1930, when you discovered or bred a new sort of plant, you had absolutely no control over it other than selling as much of it as you could before someone else propagated it and began to sell it more cheaply than you. This would usually take a year, or two at the most, so there was little incentive outside of universities to breed anything new. But the ability to patent plants meant that the new plant you developed (or discovered) would be yours, at least for a little while. Governmental protection for patented plants does expire, but usually not until the plant has made its creator some money.

A plant patent is just one way, albeit the most common way, to protect a plant. Plant patents can only be used for plants that are propagated asexually—in other words without using seeds—such as Henry Bosenberg's rose. There is a second means of protecting a plant, called the Plant Variety Protection Act of 1970, which is like a plant patent except that it's used for plants propagated by seed, such as corn and oats.

A third means of protecting plants, and the one used with the least frequency, is the utility patent, which is the same type of patent used for inventions like the paper clip and the cotton gin. The utility patent is the most powerful protection. Like the other two methods, it prevents those who purchase a patented plant from selling its progeny, but it can also prevent that plant from being bred to create new plants or from being used for seed within a farmer's own fields. Furthermore, a utility patent can protect more than just one variety of plant. In other words, it might have allowed Henry Bosenberg to patent a whole species, not just the cultivar he discovered.

The plants most commonly protected by utility patents are transgenic plants, because the genes that have been inserted are themselves patented. These patents are obtained by the company that created and is selling the transgenic seed, so that farmers have to buy the transformed corn, soybeans, or whatever, year after year rather than collecting the seed from their own plants, which would already contain the gene. But these transgenic plants aren't the only plants protected by a utility patent, there's another example, too.

In 1999, Donald White, a professor at the University of Minnesota, patented varieties of *Poa annua* (U.S. patent 5,912,412), more commonly known as annual bluegrass. This grass was usually thought of as a weed that had the ability to crowd out more desirable grasses, particularly on golf greens. White decided to develop a variety of annual bluegrass with redeeming characteristics. In essence, he decided that since he couldn't breed something to outcompete *Poa,* he'd breed the *Poa* itself to do the job. Annual bluegrass found in the wild isn't particularly desirable for golf greens because it has the propensity to create too many seeds and it has a lighter green color than most people prefer on a golf course. Over years of breeding, White developed a variety, called 'True Putt', that produced fewer seeds, was darker green, and had other characteristics essential for high-quality turfgrass. Naturally, White wanted to protect the years of research that he had put into 'True Putt', so he patented it using a utility patent. Specifically, the patent covered "novel varieties of *Poa annua* that are perennial and have characteristics desired for a turfgrass, including dark green color, vigor, disease resistance, and restricted flowering." By using a utility patent, which protects the way something is used or the way in which it works rather than a single variety, White had much broader control over this species of grass than if he had used a plant patent or the Plant Variety Protection Act. And since the characteristics that White listed are highly desirable for just about any grass that you can name, he essentially stopped anyone else from producing a commercially useful variety of annual bluegrass. As stated by Eric Watkins, another turf breeder at the University of Minnesota: "There aren't many reasons to develop a variety of this species besides those characteristics which are listed in the patent."

White's patent caused controversy in the world of plant breeding because it so completely cornered the market on a nontransgenic plant. Now, nobody could breed or produce a variety of annual bluegrass that exhibited any of the characteristics that a nice turfgrass would have, without paying a royalty to the patent holder. This raised animosity toward White, who, by the way, is one of the kindest gentlemen you'd ever want to meet. It inhibited his interactions with other researchers, particularly those at Penn State, who were also breeding annual bluegrass and who almost certainly would have soon released at least one variety if they hadn't been hobbled by this patent. On August 2, 1999, David Huff, a Penn State researcher, went so far as to draft a six-page letter to the U.S. Patent and Trademark Office outlining the problems with White's patent. Ultimately, however, the patent was not overturned, and on August 7, 2007, it had run its course and was not renewed. But this conflict brings to a head a larger issue. Is the ability to patent plants a good idea, and should the powerful utility patent be applicable to plants?

The Science

Plants could not be patented if they could not be produced in a way that ensured that the offspring plants would be the same as the parent plant. This is the main reason that plant patents only cover plants that are vegetatively propagated. Vegetative propagation, that is, asexual propagation using only one parent, ensures that all of the genetic material from the parent is present in the offspring. Since sexual propagation results in a mixture of genetic material from two parents, it doesn't make sense to be able to patent a sexually reproduced plant. However, if enough breeding is done, most differences between offspring can be bred out of a population. Just as a Doberman Pinscher can be bred with another Doberman to produce a Doberman, so can a particular variety of wheat be bred with the same variety of wheat to produce that same variety of wheat. The offspring is sufficiently genetically similar to the parent to be protected by the Plant Variety Protection Act.

One of the issues inherent with plant patents is that of deciding how novel a particular plant is.

Utility patents are a bit of a different beast. They were not created with plants in mind, but plants have been found to be patentable by the higher courts. The DNA that codes for all of a plant's unique characteristics seems custom made for protection by a utility patent. Specific chemicals have been patented for a long time, so it's no surprise that specific sequences of DNA—which are really nothing more than very specific chemicals that can be transferred from one plant or animal to another—can be patented.

One of the issues inherent with plant patents is that of deciding how novel a particular plant is. Someone at the patent office who is relatively unfamiliar with plants may have a difficult time making that determination. This unfamiliarity can lead to a problem called biopiracy, which can occur if a person patents something that is already used by a particular culture—for example, if someone decides to patent a nut that a tribe indigenous to South America has used as a food or dye for centuries. Such a case occurred in 1986 when a plant patent was awarded to Loren Miller for a purple-flowered Amazonian plant used by native tribes in their ceremonies. Miller claimed that the purple flowers and the medicinal qualities of the plant made it unique, patented the plant (using a plant patent), and began efforts to produce it. Further research by two groups, the Center for International Environmental Law and the Coalition for Amazonian Peoples and their Environment, concerned that a disservice was being done to these tribes, demonstrated that versions of this plant collected from the wild were very similar to what Miller had collected. This meant that Miller's plant wasn't really unique and so didn't warrant a patent. The patent was overturned in 1999, but was then reinstated in 2001.

Another example of supposed biopiracy is the case of Larry Proctor, who patented a bean native to Mexico. He bought some beans in Mexico, grew them, harvested their seed, and claimed to have invented them. He then patented these beans (using a utility patent, U.S. Patent 5,894,079) and proceeded to sue others who attempted to sell or distribute these beans. It took more than a decade before his patent was finally struck down.

Government Policy

From our country's beginnings we have understood the importance of giving entrepreneurs a way to protect their inventions. Congress established the first U.S. patent system in its very first session in 1790, just one year after the Constitution was ratified. The basic standards for a patent, which still apply today, were established in the Patent Act of 1836 (which is, coincidentally, the year of the great patent office fire, when the patent office burned down and many of the previously filed patents were lost). Novelty and utility were the key requirements of the act at the time. The Supreme Court added a third requirement in 1851 in a ruling that stated that inventions must present evidence of a degree of skill and ingenuity (*Hotchkiss v. Greenwood*). Congress set forth the contemporary standards for meeting each of these requirements in the 1952 Patent Act, and specifically barred patents from being issued if the product would have been obvious at the time of creation to "a person having ordinary skill" in that particular field of knowledge. While the content of the law has not changed since then, Congress did create a new federal appeals court in 1982 to hear all patent cases, in an effort to create more consistent rulings. Lawsuits are a big part of the patent process, and over time, the courts have had as much to do as Congress has with the way patents are protected.

The Plant Patent Act of 1930 provides patent-like protections for plants reproduced through asexual means, but it does not deal with plant varieties reproduced through seeds or tubers, such as potatoes. Plants that are reproduced through seed had to wait until 1970 and the Plant Variety Protection Act; those from tubers had to wait a bit longer, until the 1994 amendment to the Plant Variety Protection Act. This amendment created Certificates of Protection to protect plants that are reproduced sexually (from seeds) and plants from tubers. To receive certificates, plants must meet criteria similar to those for traditional patents: they must be new, distinct from other publicly known varieties, uniform (any variations are predictable and marketable), and stable in their characteristics. Certificate protections last for eighteen years.

Unlike traditional patents, there are three limitations to certificate protections. First, the USDA may limit the breeder's exclusive rights to two years if it deems the product is necessary to ensure an adequate food supply and the owner is unwilling or unable to make the product available at a reasonable price. If the USDA allows others to produce and market the product, they must pay the certificate holder a reasonable compensation, as set by the USDA. The second limitation of a protection certificate is that the plant must be made available for research purposes. And finally, farmers may use some seeds from plants protected through the Plant Variety Protection Act for use on their own farms, though they may not sell seeds to their neighbors. The fact that farmers can save seeds makes this type of protection unappealing to many seed companies that want to monopolize a market if they have inserted genes into a plant.

The process by which a patent is awarded starts when an inventor files his or her application for a patent with the Patent and Trademark Office (PTO) of the U.S. Department of Commerce. The invention must meet several standards to be awarded a utility patent, which can be for anything from toasters to plows and bicycle rims. First, the invention must not be considered obvious, based on the terms of the 1952 Patent Act. The invention must also be deemed novel, or different in some critical respect from a previously patented object or publication, or from information already publically available. Determining whether a product is obvious or novel is not clear-cut in practice and gives inevitable discretion to the patent office. At what point does the patent investigator decide that a particular plant is sufficiently different from other similar plants? Human judgment plays an important role and is a fundamental problem with the patent process that cannot be overemphasized.

Every plant is different from every other plant of a particular species or variety. In fact, even if a plant is propagated from another plant using stem cuttings—an asexual means of reproduction where we usually assume that the plant grown from the cutting is exactly like the parent plant—those two plants will actually be somewhat genetically different. Sometimes this change will be readily apparent, sometimes not. For example, many plants with variegated edges on their leaves (the edges are white or yellow instead of green) originally came from plants with green leaves: a variegated "branch sport" spontaneously appeared on the green-leaved plant, and the sport was then propagated. In this case it is obvious that the parent plant is genetically different from the offspring. Though this genetic difference between the mother plant and the clonal offspring isn't usually so apparent, the differences would nonetheless be very real. Just as two identical twins will have small, but increasingly noticeable differences as they age, so will two plants that are supposedly clones. Knowing that plants that are supposed to be perfectly similar are actually not so similar, where is the patent investigator to draw the line?

The third criterion for obtaining a patent is particularly important for the living organisms that are created through biotechnology. The invention must be "eligible" for a patent—in other words, it must contain the subject matter that patent law was designed to protect. A critical issue of eligibility in patenting biotechnology products is whether the living inventions or genetic material are appropriate to the patent system. A so-called product of nature—a preexisting substance found in the wild—may not be patented. But if the product's natural state has been significantly modified in some way, the altered version is eligible for a patent. In *Diamond v. Chakrabarty* (1980), the Supreme Court ruled that a genetically engineered bacterium capable of breaking down crude oil was eligible for a patent because, in the words of Chief Justice Warren Burger, the bacterium "is not nature's handiwork, but his [the inventor's] own." The courts recognize that patents have long been issued for biotech products, including the 1873 patent issued to Louis Pasteur for pasteurized yeast. The 1980 ruling also allowed plants to be registered for utility patents, as with Don White's patent for annual turfgrass. The ruling of the Court stated that a "living, man-made micro-organism is patentable subject matter as a 'manufacture' or 'composition of matter' within the meaning of the Patent Act of 1952. The fact that the organism sought to be patented is alive is no bar to patentability." This last section is the most important because it says, essentially, that despite the fact that there exists a separate plant patent (something that the dissenters to this case noted in their opinions), the utility patent could still be used for living organisms.

In a second case, in 2001, *J.E.M. Agricultural Supply v. Pioneer Hi-Bred,* the Supreme Court was even more specific, saying that there was nothing in the law that precluded providing utility patents for plants. DNA sequences generated for scientific purposes have traditionally been eligible for patents. A 2010 federal district court ruling invalidated two DNA patents, however, and threw the status of many others into uncertainty by finding that the value of DNA lies in its "information," which is found in nature and is therefore ineligible for a patent. The fact that it was a district court ruling (and thus only applies to a single judicial district) and was so divergent from precedent (and therefore likely to be overturned on appeal) leads many observers to discount the impact of this case.

The fourth and final requirement for a patent, "utility," means that the invention must work as intended and provide a definite benefit. The challenge of meeting this standard in biotechnology is that scientists can create chemicals, compounds, and so forth, without knowing how their creation might be incorporated into a useful product. By requiring that a specific, useful product result from the invention, the law attempts to ensure that whole fields of scientific inquiry are not blocked by monopolies created by legal claims of patent protection. In *Brenner v. Manson* (1966), the Supreme Court declared that "a patent is not a hunting license. It is not a reward for the search, but compensation for its successful conclusion. A patent system must be related to the world of commerce rather than to the realm of philosophy."

If the U.S. Patent Office finds that these four criteria have been met, it publishes a full technical disclosure of the invention in addition to certifying the patent. The patent holder then holds the right to exclude others from "making, using, selling, offering to sell or importing into the United States" the patented invention for twenty years, though the patent will need to be renewed to last the entire time. Plant patents also have twenty-year terms and need renewal. The patent is enforced by the federal courts, which can stop unauthorized individuals from using the product and can assess financial damages to the patent holder. Even the threat of a court injunction—an order to stop doing what you're doing—is powerful, since it may cause a company to shut down a product line. Penalties for violating a patent are no laughing matter. If a patent is violated, the damages may be based on the total value of the product, even if the element that violated the patent protections was a minor part of the whole. Damages can be tripled if the court finds that the violation was committed knowingly and willfully. The status of a patent can be challenged, but the challenger has to present "clear and convincing" evidence that the patent was improperly issued for it to be invalidated. To make a long story short: don't violate patents.

Contrary to popular belief, just because a product is patented does not mean that it can immediately be used or marketed. Often it will need to undergo testing. Plants that incorporate the products of biotechnology, for example, may have to demonstrate their safety to the FDA, EPA, and/or USDA before they become publicly available.

The Political Dynamics

Today, some of the most challenging patent questions revolve around biotechnology. Before a new product becomes available, biotechnology enterprises spend years making large research and development expenditures to run the labs, buy or create rare and expensive lab equipment, and pay their highly trained staffs. According to the Biotechnology Industry Organization, U.S. biotech firms spent $27.1 billion on R&D in 2006. And, given the nature of the scientific process, many initial ideas, and the investments made to research them, will not ultimately pay off scientifically or economically. Unfortunately, it's hard to tell which ideas will work and which ones won't when the big investments are made to get a project started. The firms are heavily dependent on outside investors to pay for their large initial investments—$100 billion between 2003 and 2007. Without patents, which protect their ability to profit on the final product, investors have little incentive to provide start-up funds. The patent itself becomes the valuable good because patent rights can be sold or licensed. Or a larger firm with greater capacity to bring a technology to market may buy the smaller firm that holds the patent, providing a big payoff

PATENTS allow inventors to recoup their investment in and profit from their inventions. Without patent protections, there would be little incentive to pour blood, sweat, and tears—not to mention money—into developing a creative product if some slacker could immediately come along, rip off the essential idea, and sell it for profit. Society would suffer because of the stagnation of efforts put into creating new products and technologies.

Congress has not made significant revisions to the patent process since 1952. Patents are a low priority on Capitol Hill. They're highly technical, and therefore a dimly understood policy area for most members of Congress, who are not likely to take the risk of making changes to the law that might create unintended consequences for the U.S. economy. Unless there is clear evidence that the current limitations of patent law are creating substantial economic problems for their constituents, Congress has every incentive to let the PTO and the courts sort through the current disputes on a case-by-case basis.

for the small firm's investors. In essence, then, the government's patent policy is an economic development policy. It underwrites capital investment in R&D and the development of technology.

These investments are important, some might even say vital, given the increasing role of biotechnology in the U.S. economy. The revenues earned by U.S. biotechnology companies have grown from $11.2 billion in 1994 to $53.3 billion in 2006, by which time they employed 118,000 people in the United States. Their technologies reach into numerous industries: medicine, industrial processes, environmental cleanup, and agriculture. Furthermore, the United States has a considerable advantage in biotechnology in the world market (see the chapter on biotechnology), making the industry critical to the country's economic competitiveness.

Because of the speed with which technology changes, it sometimes overrides the ability of the law, and the courts, to keep up, especially in the Internet, software, telecommunications, and biotechnology industries. These high-tech industries have been advocating changes that would simplify the process of challenging patent applications and limit the penalties in patent infringement lawsuits. They argue that the PTO approves too many questionable patents, so-called low-quality patents (see box), many of which are not for truly novel products. These dubious patents are then used by "patent trolls," essentially to extort large financial settlements from companies using the patented devices. The number of patent lawsuits tripled between 1983 and 2004. Since the courts are generally reluctant to overturn the rights of a patent holder, the companies using a patented device do not want to take the risk of the court issuing an injunction or imposing penalties, even if the company thinks the patent was issued inappropriately. The companies thus have an incentive to pay off a patent troll to avoid a lawsuit. Firms that are frequent targets of patent lawsuits believe the current legal environment creates substantial unpredictably in the development process, and that overly generous damage awards divert resources that could be devoted to innovation.

Pharmaceutical and biotech companies, on the other hand, are generally the patent holders, and to the extent that the current system advantages the patent holder, it works well for them. They believe that strict patent protections are necessary to provide greater assurance that venture capitalists will receive some payoff from the long R&D process in biotech. They are competing for venture capital with high-tech firms that can offer a much faster return on investment.

Perhaps the most significant patent issues today concern patents for biotechnologically advanced plants and the control that the patent holders have over today's agricultural system. Farmers are concerned

PATENT lawyers make a distinction between high-quality and low-quality patents. High-quality patents are issued for inventions that meet all the criteria and the intent of the patent system and thus promote investment and innovation. Low-quality patents are issued to products that are not truly novel, or are "obvious," and thus probably should have had their patent applications rejected. The term also covers patents whose claims are overly broad and thus can be used to claim compensation for elements of the product beyond what was originally deemed novel. Patent law itself and the courts, however, have not made this distinction, contributing to the increase in patent litigation as more low-quality patents are defended in court by so-called patent trolls or other patent holders.

that the patenting of organisms, particularly with the increased development of genetically modified organisms, will lead to large agricultural technology corporations having control over agriculture. This has already happened to some extent. By utilizing utility patents, which are legal for transgenic organisms, companies can sell seeds to farmers and then prevent these farmers from utilizing seeds from their own crops for replanting their fields. This is, naturally, a problem for farmers who like to replant with their own seed, which is substantially cheaper—and besides, they produced the seeds on their own land. Monsanto has sued a number of farmers who have used seeds from crops that Monsanto developed using biotechnology, and the company has come away the winner virtually every time (as we saw in the previous chapter). Because patent holders are able to exclude farmers who don't follow their rules from obtaining their products, farmers' ability to manage their own farms with their own resources is severely limited. For example, manufacturers could require that new seeds be purchased every year, or that only their fertilizers or pesticides be used with their seeds. Farmers would be at the mercy not only of good weather but also of the restrictions of the major agricultural products corporations.

By utilizing utility patents, which are legal for transgenic organisms, companies can sell seeds to farmers and then prevent these farmers from utilizing seeds from their own crops for replanting their fields.

Internationally, our trading partners are increasingly adopting patent systems for biotechnology that are similar to our own. Their systems include our broad definitions of what subject matter is eligible for patenting. Thus, placing greater patent restrictions on our biotechnologies would potentially create trade difficulties, put U.S. biotechnologies at a disadvantage compared to their foreign competitors, or give U.S. companies an incentive to move their product development facilities overseas to take advantage of more favorable patent systems. In other words, things aren't likely to change soon.

Policy Option One: Leave Things as They Are

The ability for people to hold patents that stop others from producing a particular type of plant does one thing very well: it encourages companies and individuals to create these new plants that can then be used for the good of society. The company that sweated and struggled to create the plant or technology is able to reap financial rewards. The two processes by which most plants have been protected, the Plant Patent Act and the Plant Variety Protection Act, have both served their purposes admirably. It is true that certain unscrupulous people have dabbled in biopiracy by patenting plants that might have no right to be patented—such as a plant that has been used by a native culture for centuries. But this is the exception to the rule, and is easily handled by the courts or by the patent office. Reworking a system just to fix a problem that affects a very small population may actually cause more problems than it solves.

Utility patents have also been used for plants since 1980, offering the biotechnology industry a powerful tool that allows them to completely control patented transgenic plants—as well as the offspring from these plants, because they contain the patented genes (the Plant Variety Protection Act, on the other hand, allows farmers to replant seeds). There has been a public uproar over this control, but the reality is that relatively few plants have actually been protected in this way. Those plants that have been protected took a huge amount of resources to create, and the company needs the protection afforded by a utility patent if it ever hopes to make its initial investment back. Patents are temporary, and these companies won't control these genes forever.

Right-Wing Rating ★★★ High-quality patents should be protected to give incentive to innovators and investors; low-quality patents deserve less protection because they waste money on litigation without providing really new or useful products. The rewards for successful high-risk research need to be protected, otherwise technology will stagnate.

Left-Wing Rating ★★ The current system hands over too much control to Big Ag. Let the farmers plant seeds they've paid for.

Policy Option Two: No Patents for Plants

Rewarding the ingenuity of plant breeders for their work with a patent may be a good way to inspire the creation of new plants, but patents on plants are so misused that granting patents is simply inappropriate. Leave the plant breeding to professors at universities who get paid for it. Look at the first plant patented by Henry Bosenberg.

He didn't even breed this rose, he just happened to buy a plant that someone else had put the time and effort into breeding, noticed something unique about it, took a cutting, grew it, and patented it. The idea that one person can control the trade of a natural product, such as a naturally occurring bean, flower, or species of grass, is wrong. Our patent process and judicial system were aptly criticized by Silvia Ribeiro of the Action Group on Erosion, Technology and Concentration, an international group that investigates the socioeconomic and ecological issues surrounding new technologies: "A system that favours patent holders at the expense of the common good and takes more than a decade to right an obvious wrong [referring to the Mexican bean example mentioned earlier] should be considered broken beyond repair."

For those who argue that not allowing plants to be patented will drive creative minds away from these subjects and our plant choices will stagnate, we can only respond that universities will happily be there to pick up the slack. As new varieties of plants are needed, more dollars will filter into the university system to hire more breeders who would once have worked for large biotechnology companies. We wouldn't lose the creative breeders who make all of our transformed crops possible; rather, we'd put them into a different system, where they could do the same work and help society instead of providing their knowledge and labor to large agricultural corporations that then monopolize the market on various crops.

Right-Wing Rating ★ No protection for plants hurts innovation.

Left-Wing Rating ★★★★ There is too much opportunity for patents to be abused, especially as they relate to plants, in our current system. Plants are everyone's property.

Policy Option Three: Utility Patents Should Not Be Used for Living Organisms

Utility patents were conceived, and most of the legislation written, before the advent of modern biotechnology. This technology, which allows for the transfer of genes between two very different creatures, along with the use of the broad utility patent to protect the genetically transformed product, makes certain patent-owning companies just too powerful. Whichever company produces the best gene (or genes) for a particular plant rules the market for that crop. In classic breeding, where the best plants were continually bred together to eventually produce an even better plant, changes tended to be incremental. A new variety was probably better than an older one, but this new variety didn't overshadow the older one to such an extent that the older one wouldn't be planted anymore. Biotechnology offers the opportunity for a particular variety of crop to be far superior to the crops that came before it, and so these new crops suddenly dominate the market.

If transformed crops were protected with the Plant Variety Protection Act instead of regular patent law, farmers would still need to purchase seed from the company that developed the genes, but after that initial purchase they could use seeds from their own plants to plant their crops the following year. This would take quite a bit of the power away from the biotechnology companies, including some of their earning potential. It would also force biotech companies to be more innovative because they could not simply insert a gene into a plant and rely on the royalties from sales of that plant. Instead, they would be forced to continue working on new varieties so that they could release new and better plants more frequently. After the first year, when a premium would be charged for the technologically advanced seed, the biotech companies would be forced to charge a more competitive fee for the seed, because they would be competing with the lower costs of farmers using their own seed.

Also, protecting plants under the Plant Varieties Protection Act would reduce biopiracy. No longer could a plant be patented using a utility patent, thereby preventing the indigenous culture that originally used the plant from profiting from it, and allowing a "pirate" to usurp control over the plant. The Plant Variety Protection Act is very specific in that it controls a variety that has been bred and is propagated through seeds. Because it only controls a variety, it would be impossible for a biopirate to prove that the seeds that an indigenous group had been growing for years were the same as the one the biopirate had patented and to sue them. The utility patent simply offers too much control over a plant, restricting creativity and research. The Plant Variety Protection Act narrows this control considerably, and includes a clause that allows for the use of plants for research.

Right-Wing Rating ★★ Using the utility patent for plants allows companies that take risks to succeed.

Left-Wing Rating ★★★★★ The utility patent is much too powerful and infringes on the rights of others, including other cultures. Using the procedures of the Plant Varieties Protection Act would solve that problem and be much fairer.

The Bottom Line

There are a lot of things to dislike about the current patent systems for protecting plants, especially in terms of utility patents. Though they are used infrequently for plants, they are an extremely powerful tool that can prevent research on patented plants, provide an opportunity for biopiracy, and offer biotech companies an excessive amount of control over what farmers plant in their fields. On the other hand, from a capitalist's viewpoint, these patents allow the biotech companies the greatest return on their research dollars, and it takes a lot of dollars to create these fancy plants, not to mention getting them through all of the government hurdles to get them to market. Realistically, if the big biotechnology companies did not have the protection of utility patents it seems unlikely that biotechnology would have progressed as far as it has in this country (whether you support biotechnology is another question).

Regardless of how plant varieties are protected, our system does need some additional work, especially regarding the issue of how novel and useful a plant needs to be to warrant a patent. The laws also need to do a better job of preventing biopiracy.

CHAPTER 8

★★★

Invasive Plants: Kill the Aliens?

CONTRARY TO WHAT most people assume, the food production system of the United States has very little to do with foods native to this country. Much like its human population, our nation's food system is built almost entirely on plants that came from somewhere else. When European settlers first arrived, Native Americans taught them to use foods such as blueberries, and sugar extracted from sugar maple trees, both of which are native to the United States; and corn, which had been introduced to North America from South America by Native Americans centuries earlier. But Europeans already had a taste for foods from their own homelands, so they introduced wheat, apples, citrus, and many other plants that, if they hadn't originated in Europe, were at least well established there. Other crops with South American origins, but which were introduced by Europeans, were the peanut and potato. Currently, about 99 percent of U.S. cropland is planted in crops that are not native to the United States. Thomas Jefferson was a great advocate of such importation: "The greatest service which can be rendered any country is to add an useful plant to its culture." Unfortunately, not all of the plants (or animals) delivered here from other parts of the world have turned out to be beneficial.

Over the years, humans have introduced numerous plants. Some have behaved themselves, and some have become invasive or noxious weeds. But what is a noxious weed? And how do we know if we have one? Well, the federal government creates a list of these weeds, and various states have their own lists of noxious weeds, as well. The definition of a noxious weed, according to the federal government, is "any plant or plant product that can directly or indirectly injure or cause damage to crops (including nursery stock or plant products), livestock, poultry, or other interests of agriculture, irrigation, navigation, the natural resources of the United States, the public health, or the environment."

Contrast this with the federal government's definition of an invasive species: "Those species whose introduction does, or is likely to, cause economic or environmental harm or harm to human health." As you can see, the big difference is that invasive species are introduced to a region, while noxious species may be native to a region. In general terms, when the government describes a plant using the term *noxious weed,* those plants are considered worse than invasive plants because they tend to be more aggressive, and/or more dangerous to animals, humans, or crops.

Various methods have been tried to restrict the damage caused by introduced plants and their associated fauna, but the most frequent method has been limiting the movement of these plants. During the 1800s, when people across this country first restricted plants from being moved from place to place, the reason was not because anyone was particularly frightened of the plants themselves, but because they were worried about the insects and diseases that might travel with the plants and infest other locales. We have a long history of introducing a new crop, and then inadvertently introducing something that destroys that crop—dating back to 1660, when wheat stem rust found its way to the United States after wheat had been introduced in the 1620s.

The question we need to ask ourselves at this stage in the ecological life of the United States is whether we should use our government to prevent—or to encourage—the introduction of plants and animals onto American soil.

There are many environmentalists who promote the idea of ecologically sound gardening and who prefer using native plants. They usually suggest that natives offer a more stable ecosystem that is worth preserving. Douglas Tallamy, the author of *Bringing Nature Home* (2007), is perhaps foremost among those who propose that we try to plant more natives and avoid exotic plants, because native plants are able to sustain populations of insects that they have coevolved with, while exotic plants cannot. Perhaps that's true, but then those exotic plants would be less prone to insect damage and hence better ornamental plants. And besides, if a native plant can't compete without our help, then isn't this artificial maintenance of its populations just a stalling tactic?

The question we need to ask ourselves at this stage in the ecological life of the United States is whether we should use our government to prevent—or to encourage—the introduction of plants and animals onto American soil. It's not an easy question, and there is a lot of history behind the politics.

The Science

Although much of this chapter is specifically about plants and the pests that attack them, most of the information also relates directly to insects and other animals that are noxious and/or invasive. Zebra mussels, Asian carp, and starlings are all critters that have come here and made space for themselves by displacing native species, and they deserve to be mentioned in any discussion of noxious and invasive pests. In 2000, David Pimentel, then a professor at Cornell University, published an article examining the effects of introduced plants and animals on our economy. He calculated that the cost of invasive species to the United States is about $138 billion per year (and those are 1999 dollars). This includes losses caused by dogs, cats, and rats, all of which are introduced species. The greatest costs, however, come from introduced plants, followed by microbes and arthropods (insects and mites). It's only fair to mention, however, that these costs often relate to their negative effects on crops that were, themselves, introduced. Both dandelions and crabgrass, for example, were introduced into the United States as crop plants: dandelions by colonists in the seventeenth century as an herb for making wine, and crabgrass by the U.S. patent office in 1849 as a forage crop. Today these plants are weeds that infest lawn grasses, most of which were themselves introduced from Europe.

Many plants have found their way to the United States, resulting in a disruption of the country's ecosystems. More than 4200 plants have escaped cultivation, about 8.4 percent of the total number of plants that have been introduced. A list of the most noxious of these plants would certainly include kudzu, a vine introduced in the South to help prevent erosion along stream banks, but which now climbs trees at the edges of forests, shortening their lives and threatening native plants that would ordinarily live in those locations; buckthorn, a shrub that was introduced to the United States because of its attractive structure and functionality in shrub borders, but which now invades forest borders; and Canadian thistle, which, despite its name, is not native to the North American continent, and which parks itself in lawns and fields across the United States.

The fundamental problem with having a noxious or invasive species take over a location is biodiversity. Having many diverse species in a location allows that location to be more productive and healthier than if only a single species is present and native ecosystems tend to be more diverse than ecosystems in which a few species of invasive plants have taken over. In theory, the diversity present in a native ecosystem allows the location to adapt as the environment changes over tens, hundreds, and even thousands of years. One or another of the natives that is more adapted to the change will become dominant, while the other natives take a backseat, not disappearing, but instead waiting for their chance, which will almost certainly come. When a nonnative species is introduced to an area where it can easily outcompete native plants because it is so well suited to that area (and safe from any serious threat from herbivores), the result is not only a reduction in the diversity of plant species, but also a reduction in the diversity of insect and even bird and mammal species.

Not every scientist agrees that diversity is always, or even frequently, threatened by nonnative species. Because nonnative species are different from native species, they can actually increase the diversity in an area. It is commonly accepted that on an island, where native species have nowhere to go when threatened, introduced pests can cause extinctions of native species. On a huge continent such as North America, however, this is very rarely the case. Mark Davis, a professor of biology at Macalester College and author of the book *Invasion Biology*, asks the question, "How many species of plants in the U.S. have gone extinct because of the thousands of nonnative plants that have been introduced?" His answer: "zero." This isn't to say that nonnative species can't negatively affect native species, and nobody is recommending introducing more potentially invasive species to our continent. But those plants, insects, and fungi already introduced here may not be having the deleterious effects on our ecological diversity that we assume they are.

One of the fundamental problems with invasive plants is that we rarely know that a plant is truly invasive until it has established itself, and once it establishes itself it is almost impossible to get rid of. Marcel Rejmanek, a professor at the University of California, Davis, and his colleague Mike Pitcairn at U.C. Berkeley concluded that efforts to eradicate populations of exotic invasive plants established on less than one hectare of land are likely to succeed, while eradicating these plants from one to one hundred hectares will only succeed some of the time, and trying to eradicate a population that covers over one hundred hectares is all but an effort in futility.

A typical example of what an introduced species does to a native species that fulfills a similar role in the environment is the slow overtaking of our native sugar maple by the introduced Norway maple. The Norway maple came from Europe in the eighteenth century as a shade tree, and it grew more quickly and filled in faster than the native sugar maple. It was, and still is, planted in almost any location where quick shade is needed (and wherever it is legal to plant it). The problem is that the Norway maple has escaped its urban and suburban confines and now competes with sugar maples in natural forests, where it fares extremely well because of its more efficient use of light, nutrients, and water. Norway maples can grow twice as fast as sugar maples and cutting down Norways isn't particularly helpful because the seedlings are more likely to repopulate an area than seedlings from native sugar maples. The presence of such an excellent competitor doesn't spell the end for sugar maples, but it does mean that sugar maples are less abundant and less likely to repopulate an area naturally than they were before the Norway maple was introduced.

The Norway maple and sugar maple compete for space in both virgin forests and parking lots. There certainly are a lot more parking lots in the United States today than when settlers first arrived, and, for the most part, plants that we consider invasive seem to like it that way. The United States today is not the country that it once was. Forests have been decimated, soil has been tilled, and even those beautiful meandering streams of the Northeast turn out to have been encouraged by humans who built dams and mills. The plants we now denigrate as invasive and noxious weeds are simply more appropriate for the current man-made conditions and they are being blamed for something that really isn't their fault. It turns out that, as the carbon dioxide in our atmosphere increases (presumably because of humans), weeds that we consider invasive tend to be able to deal with the situation more effectively than other plants. Canadian thistle in particular thrives on high levels of carbon dioxide. It is entirely possible that as our environment changes, plants that were not weeds will become weeds, and existing weeds will become even more of a threat.

It seems that, as Peter Del Tredici points out in his 2006 article "Brave New Ecology," many restorationists (those who favor native plants) have "faith-based" notions of restoration that have little to do with reality. The world is a constantly changing place, and as it changes, different plants may be better adapted for the new conditions than those that were there before. This is certainly true on the small scale. For example, a new building site where the earth has been compacted by the constant movement of heavy machinery won't be appropriate for most plants—except those that the government now considers invasive. It takes something special to be able to infest an area that man has destroyed. But on the large scale, things are shifting too. Changing climates, acid rain, and increasing carbon dioxide in the atmosphere may inhibit the ability of plants that we want to encourage to compete successfully with plants that we consider invasive.

Changing climates, acid rain, and increasing carbon dioxide in the atmosphere may inhibit the ability of plants that we want to encourage to compete successfully with plants that we consider invasive.

Along with the loss of native plants comes the loss of native herbivores and other animals that use particular species of plants for food or shelter. One of the perceived perks that invasive plants enjoy when they arrive in a new location is that they do not have any predators that are adapted to feeding on them. So they thrive, easily outcompeting native plants and animals, which may lead to the loss of the natives. This is true of such introduced plants as purple loosestrife, brought to the United States for ornamental and medicinal purposes during the 1800s, which quickly took hold and began to do its damage. Purple loosestrife is a poster child for invasive species. It produces an incredible number of seeds over a single season, and crowds out native sedges and grasses, reducing habitat for waterfowl, such as ducks and other marsh birds. Besides a few insects that have been brought to this country to control it, there really aren't many things that will feed on or infect it. This resistance to herbivores was one of the reasons that this perennial was such an attractive and popular ornamental for so long, until selling it was banned in many states. Human intervention may be the only help for the many native plants competing with purple loosestrife and the many insects that feed on those plants. The same is true for a whole host of other threatened native plants.

Government Policy

Even before Thomas Jefferson advocated moving useful plants from one place to another, plants were being outlawed because of the damage they could cause. As early as 1726, a law was enacted in Connecticut banning barberries because they were associated with wheat stem rust. Then, in the late 1800s, many states started to restrict the importation of plants to prevent dangerous diseases from hurting their crops. At the national level, the 1912 Plant Quarantine Act gave the USDA's Animal and Plant Health Inspection Service (APHIS) the authority to regulate the import and interstate transportation of nursery stock and other plants that could carry pests and diseases. This act overrode the earlier importation laws drafted by many states. Since then, Congress has expanded APHIS's responsibilities and enforcement tools. The 1931 Animal Damage Control Act gave APHIS control over populations of wild animals; the 1939 Federal Seed Act gave them the power to regulate importation of seeds that could contain noxious weeds; the 1957 Federal Plant Pest Act allowed APHIS to inspect, seize, quarantine, or destroy nonnative organisms that could damage native plants or other natural resources; and the 1974 Federal Noxious Weed Act expanded APHIS's authority to stop the introduction and spread of harmful, nonnative weeds. These laws make APHIS a very powerful agency with the authority to do just about anything conceivable to protect us from foreign plants and animals.

APHIS spends roughly half of its resources attempting to prevent invasive species from entering the United States and the other half on eradicating pests that are already here. It uses three major tools to control the spread of invasive species. First, and perhaps most importantly, it issues permits for the importation or interstate transportation of numerous types of organisms that are potentially threatening to native species. The permits cover nursery stock, seeds, fruits and vegetables, timber, cotton, and cut flowers, as well as protected plants, such as orchids, and threatened and endangered plant species. The use of these permits should, theoretically, keep unwanted species out.

Second, APHIS has developed "pest lists" of organisms that are quarantined. These pests cannot be moved through importation or interstate transportation. APHIS also develops strategies for controlling the pests in the wild and for restoring natural native habitats for the organisms. The pest lists include insects and mites, mollusks, nematodes, plant diseases, and weeds. The federal noxious weed lists cover aquatic and wetland, parasitic, and terrestrial weeds. It can be found online at http://www.aphis.usda.gov/plant_health/plant_pest_info/weeds/downloads/weedlist2006.pdf.

Third, APHIS also participates in border inspections to prevent organisms on its lists from entering the country. Its primary role is not to provide personnel to do the inspections, but rather to train U.S. Customs and Border Patrol agents to identify items on the lists at airports and border crossings. APHIS does have two thousand inspectors of its own, but with fifty thousand ships, one million aircraft, and tens of millions of travelers seeking entry into the United States every year, the task before them is daunting. Put another way, APHIS has the capacity to inspect about 2 percent of the cargo entering the United States. (All border agencies combined inspect about 5 percent of U.S. imports.) Even with its limited resources, APHIS intercepts more than one million potentially harmful plant materials and tens of thousands of insects and other pests each year. Global travel is easier than ever for both humans and the pests that plague us, which makes stopping invasive species increasingly difficult. Organisms can come along for the ride in packing crates, ballast water, and scrap material without APHIS, or anyone else for that matter, knowing they are there—unless an inspector just happens to inspect the right thing on the right day.

For newly introduced pests that can potentially be eliminated, the federal government (usually in the form of APHIS) takes action that can sometimes be very effective. The Asian longhorned beetle is the target of such government work. A serious pest of hardwood trees, it infested regions in and around New York, Illinois, New Jersey, and Massachusetts in the late 1990s and 2000s. Though this pest has not yet been completely eradicated, there is little doubt that its numbers have been drastically reduced by rapid government intervention—removing infested trees, cutting down nearby trees that could harbor the pest, and using chemical treatments. Similarly, the plum pox virus, which affects peaches, plums, and related fruits in Europe, was identified in Pennsylvania in 1999 and was also controlled. Certainly there are other pests that have made it here successfully, but in recent years, our government has generally been able to move fast enough to prevent any major catastrophe.

Environmentalist critics contend that APHIS is overly focused on the contents of containers—the plants and animals that someone is purposely trying to ship into the United States—rather than the shipping materials themselves on which the "free riders" travel. Two major forest pests that found their way to the United States in the 1990s, the Asian longhorned beetle and the emerald ash borer, are both thought to have hitched a ride on packing materials shipped from somewhere in Asia. Though APHIS now requires more care in the treatment of pallets and other shipping materials, enforcement is not particularly strict and not every container can be checked. Concern about the intentional importation of harmful cargo has only increased since the 9/11 terrorist attacks. Security experts have been specifically concerned about the potential for terrorists to transport microbes (for example, foot-and-mouth disease) into the country to damage food supplies.

★★★

Recent changes in the law have been inspired by the zebra mussel infestation in the Great Lakes in the late 1980s. Zebra mussels are originally from Russia and probably hitchhiked their way here on a ship. These mussels grow in dense masses and can clog pipes and orifices. They can crowd out other mussels and other native organisms, and so are very disruptive to natural ecosystems wherever they are introduced. In response to this emerging problem, Congress created the 1990 Nonindigenous Aquatic Nuisance Prevention and Control Act. It retained APHIS's authority as the primary agency enforcing rules on invasive species, but it also gave the Fish and Wildlife Service and the Coast Guard the authority to regulate the ballast water that is carried by ships and in which zebra mussels and other aquatic species have often been transported.

This more protective legislation has been a long time coming. The first species to be introduced to the shores of the United States from Europe many years ago were probably earthworms and other soil-dwelling creatures that were stowaways in ballast tanks on ships. (Many of the earthworms now in the United States are not native, particularly those in the northern portions of the country, where the glaciers from the last ice age removed them from the soil.) Congress went further in the 1996 Invasive Species Act, developing a framework for international negotiations to prevent the spread of nonnative species in ballast water. Though the framework was developed specifically for addressing the zebra mussel, APHIS has used it as a model in working with foreign countries to identify and stop the spread of other invasive species by preventing them from leaving the host country.

In 1999 the arrival of the West Nile virus spurred another initiative on invasive species. This virus is carried by birds and then spread to humans through mosquitoes that have bitten infected birds. It can cause brain swelling in the elderly, which may lead to death, though it is not generally considered fatal to others. President Clinton responded to the outbreak of West Nile virus by issuing an executive order that established the National Invasive Species Council (NISC) to develop recommendations to improve cooperation between federal agencies, state agencies, and foreign governments on invasive species. NISC was also charged with documenting and monitoring the effects of invasive species in the United States. The council includes representatives from the Departments of Agriculture, Commerce, Defense, Interior, State, Transportation, Treasury, and the EPA. NISC issued a "National Management Plan" in January 2001. This plan emphasized that the only effective method of addressing invasive species was to stop them from entering the United States, and recommended that prevention should be the priority of U.S. policy. For species that do reach the states, the plan recommended immediate eradication of the invader and strategies for dealing with long-established invasive species.

The Noxious Weed Control and Eradication Act of 2004 recognized APHIS's personnel limitations and its reliance on state and local government agencies and private organizations as its eyes and ears for identifying and controlling invasive species. The act focused on attempting to improve coordination between these agencies by providing financial grants to state and local governments or to other "weed management entities" (only Congress could come up with that name!) for projects to fight invasive species.

Control of imports and exports to prevent the introduction of potentially harmful species is handled by APHIS at the federal level, while many different state institutions may be involved in controlling noxious and invasive plants, usually the state's agriculture or natural resources department. Control of invasive species that have established themselves is mostly a state issue. States decide which plants are problematic in their own localities, and often draw distinctions between invasive plants and noxious weeds, considering noxious weeds worse than invasive species. Some states require homeowners to control plants that are considered noxious weeds (for example, North Dakota and Minnesota require private and public landowners to control Canadian thistle), while plants that are considered invasive species (like buckthorn) are simply restricted in terms of their transplant or sale. Some localities provide help to homeowners in getting rid of weeds. For example, in Billings, North Dakota, the Landowners Assistance Program will actually provide herbicides at a reduced cost to help control noxious weeds. If you're interested, you can check out the differences between your state's list of invasive and noxious plants and the lists of other states online at http://plants.usda.gov/java/noxiousDriver. New England states tend to be the most aggressive about dealing with invasive and noxious species. In Connecticut, selling sycamore maple, white poplar, yellow iris, Russian olive, and many other species is banned, meaning that they cannot be moved, sold, purchased, transplanted, cultivated, or distributed. (We do think that you're still allowed to look at them, as long as you don't admire their beauty!)

The Political Dynamics

Unlike many of the other policies discussed in this book, the policy debates surrounding invasive species have not been terribly contentious. Few people are going to take the side of invaders or pests who destroy crops, endanger native species, and devalue land. Most of the criticism of the policies is that they are not aggressive enough: the government doesn't spend enough resources combating invasive species, it spends too much time studying potentially harmful organisms and is too slow to list them, and it doesn't do enough to coordinate across multiple federal agencies and among federal, state, local, and international agencies. The complaint that the federal government should do more, do it more quickly, and should ride herd on other authorities can be heard regarding just about any policy one can think of. In the case of invasives, there is a difference between interest group involvement in the politics of the more aggressive attempts to prevent importation of harmful organisms and in the politics of controlling invasive species that are already here.

The highest priority in dealing with invasive species, according to the National Invasive Species Council, should be preventing additional species from entering the country. That recommendation seems obvious, straightforward, and uncontroversial. Yet there are substantial barriers to making it the top priority. One barrier is international trade treaties, which discourage countries from imposing regulations that would inhibit trade (see the chapter on genetic engineering). American companies that engage in international trade are a key domestic constituency that, naturally, supports minimal restrictions on trade. Transportation companies do not want their vehicles, and importers do not want their products, sitting around on docks or tarmacs for extended inspections. Every hour that a product is in transport is an hour that it is not being sold. For plants, food, and other perishable goods, timing is obviously that much more critical. The political stature of national security experts could potentially offset the power of those who advocate against tighter restrictions on imports or more rigorous inspections. But security experts are much more concerned about higher-profile smuggling—such as bombs, or chemical or radioactive materials—than about the import of harmful microbes or diseased materials. Looking for contraband or dangerous materials in the midst of thousands of daily shipments, vehicles, and visitors to the United States is a needle-in-a-haystack problem. There is so much to search, such a low probability of finding something, and such a high cost associated with the searches—both to the government doing the search and the people and businesses being searched—that the result is a lack of a powerful, organized constituency to advocate for more action. On the other hand, there are well-organized constituencies who oppose doing more.

When environmentalists do argue for changes in our national policies for preventing the introduction and spread of invasive species, one of the things they attack most vehemently are the lists of organisms banned from entry into the United States that were developed by APHIS. Environmentalists contend that these lists are too narrow and allow potentially harmful pests into the country. They're particularly concerned about the damage caused by invasive species because almost half of the species on the Endangered Species List are there because of competition or predation by invasive species. Additionally, environmentalists insist that APHIS is focused too narrowly on agricultural pests and gives too little priority to pests that could threaten other industries or the environment in general. They argue that APHIS should develop a list of species that can be imported, and all other species should be banned. That is, rather than assuming that an organism is safe until we have evidence that it isn't, we should consider it guilty until proven innocent. Another less blunt alternative is for APHIS to restrict the half-dozen plant families that are known to contain harmful species, even without specific evidence that a particular species from that family causes problems.

According to NISC, blocking problematic imports should be the higher priority, but there are organized and active constituencies that give a higher priority to dealing with the noxious and invasive species that are already in the country. These constituencies are motivated because of the economic costs that these species have imposed on them, and they have a strong incentive to fight. Hence the success of Great Lakes shipping companies in passing the 1996 Invasive Species Act to deal with zebra mussels. Farmers, ranchers, and private landowners suffer the most from noxious and invasive plants and they support APHIS in devoting its resources to containing and eradicating existing invasive species. Environmentalists argue that APHIS is overly focused on existing agricultural pests because farmers and ranchers are its main clientele and source of political support. Meanwhile, these same environmentalists are also skeptical about farmers' or government's ability to selectively target problem species without going into overkill and doing broader ecological damage that is worse than the damage caused by the invasive species.

Although interest groups provide greater support for controlling

CONGRESS and executive agencies are likely to devote resources to addressing the concerns of well-organized, intensely mobilized constituencies, particularly when there are no similar constituencies in opposition. Without such advocates for devoting resources to battling invasive species, Congress and executive branch agencies will find plenty of other constituencies who are clamoring for money and attention.

invasive species than for blocking their importation, even this support is relatively low-key. Farmers and ranchers have higher-priority issues, particularly protecting crop subsidies and fighting land-use restrictions. Environmentalists also have many higher priorities. There is even some ambivalence in the scientific community over exactly how bad nonnative species are on the whole, and thus a mixed assessment there, too, of whether it is worth devoting substantial resources to fight them.

Policy Option One: Leave Things as They Are

In terms of the goods that are imported into this country, the current system is not perfect, but it works. Federal inspectors control the borders, but when inspectors can only check about 5 percent of the goods being shipped in, something is going to slip by at some point. Inspectors are expensive, and if they do a good job of randomly checking the materials, they will be able to identify those things that are most likely to cause a problem. In other words, right now we have what most people would consider an acceptable trade-off. We also face the law of diminishing returns. Inspectors are currently available to check for the most obvious and dangerous problems. Hiring more inspectors and adding more regulations would not make enough of a difference to offset the additional costs.

The current system for controlling pests that have already invaded our shores is sound, in that it seeks to either limit the spread of these pests or to eradicate them, depending on what the specific situation calls for. The states, rather than the federal government, are in charge, which makes a lot of sense because many plants are problems in one state but not in another. For example, the Norway maple is a fast-growing, invasive tree in the eastern United States but it is relatively well behaved in the Upper Midwest. Massachusetts has the ability to regulate the sale of this tree, while Minnesota has the ability to allow its sale to continue unregulated.

When the federal government does determine that a particular species is a national problem, APHIS can take a role in its regulation. It has done so with such weeds as the catclaw mimosa (a native of the subtropical states) and wild raspberry (a nonnative), for which it requires a permit for importation or interstate movement.

Right-Wing Rating ★★★ The current system of protection against invasive plants strikes the right balance. It allows trade, targets the worst pests, and encourages different governments to work together.

Left-Wing Rating ★★★ The current system does a reasonable job of controlling pests, though more attention should be paid to pests that damage habitats, not just agriculture.

Policy Option Two: Federal and State Governments Should Be More Strict

There are many pests that have made it through our screening process in the last decade and are causing major problems. The emerald ash borer, an insect introduced to the United States from Asia in the late 1990s, is decimating our native ash trees in the Midwest. Japanese dodder, a plant native to Asia, was introduced to California in the early 2000s. It is parasitic on other plants and can even kill them. With examples like these, along with the estimate by some researchers that almost half of our endangered species are threatened because of invasive species, we need better options.

We need more stringent regulations at both the federal and the state levels. These may come in the form of tighter importation regulations or greater attention to invasive species that are already here. Most environmental groups would probably prefer both.

At the federal level, allow plants and animals into this country only if they are on an approved list. This type of limitation would better control potentially problematic species. It would certainly cost a significant amount of money to enforce, but the restrictions might actually be easier to enforce because agents would only need to be familiar with the relatively small number of species on the approved list. Any unfamiliar species would not be allowed across the border. This type of regulation would definitely limit the importation and sale of new plant species.

Controlling invasive plants and noxious weeds once they are here is a much more difficult issue. The biggest question is, are native species worth saving at any cost? The answer is easy: yes. Every species of plant has its own set of genes that, if lost, might well be lost forever. This isn't merely an ethical question. It is possible, and even likely, that native plants in danger of being lost contain chemicals that are useful to us medically or culturally. Indeed, we already know of many native plants that contain useful compounds that could potentially be beneficial to our health. And we would lose not only the plant, but also the animals that depend on it, further threatening the ecosystem.

Plants all have their own niches, or places where they fit into an environment in terms of their preferences for soil type, water, and nutrition. The problem with invasives is that they tend to fit well into the niche of a plant that is already established, or into a niche that is becoming more prevalent. For example, invasives such as buckthorn in the North and kudzu in the South enjoy the conditions that are present at the edges of forests. As we have harvested timber over the last 400 years or so, we have made more and more edges available, creating more environments for these plants to invade. Without human intervention to control these and other invasive and noxious plants, desirable native plants will be unable to compete.

Right-Wing Rating ★★ We can live with some trade restrictions and government eradication efforts that are narrowly drawn to protect our crops and food security. Saving our native wildlife is a worthy goal, but it is too costly to try to eradicate or contain every nonnative species that potentially threatens a native species.

Left-Wing Rating ★★★★★ Greater control of invasives would mean saving our native habitats and creatures. Prevention is the key, because the cost and environmental damage is too great once an invasive takes hold.

Policy Option Three: The Government Needs to Relax

Whether we like it or not, the United States is a part of a global ecosystem. That means that plants, insects, mammals, and every other creature under the sun has been so thoroughly displaced that there just isn't much room for the idea of "native" anymore. While trying to prevent some of the most damaging pests from reaching our shores might be necessary, we should not be attempting to exclude species that we don't even know are harmful. Furthermore, spending money to prevent a native plant from moving between states is a waste of resources.

In many cases, native plants aren't the appropriate plants for our country anymore. We have created a new ecology in the United States.

Our environment simply isn't what it once was, and to use tax dollars to encourage the growth of certain plants just because they're considered native seems a waste of effort. Once regular trips were made to and from the New World, a new reality was created. Our forestland was reduced in size as it was cleared for the production of crops. Plants came in from the Old World and some became naturalized (which means that they reached a state where they could survive in their newly found home without any human help) before anyone even thought about what that meant. As our industries increased in size so did the amount of carbon dioxide in the air as well as other gases that our energy production creates. This country is not what it was 500, 300, or even 100 years ago, and we need to realize that no amount of restoration is going to change that. Not only are the plants different, the physical properties of the soil, the water, and the air have changed as well. We need to move on and stop spending money and time striving to regain what is gone.

Environmentalists refer to native ecosystems as diverse and successful. But European countries have been introducing plants longer than we have, and England in particular makes a nice case study for what happens when alien plants are continually introduced. England has a functional ecosystem, as do all European countries, even though these countries have introduced many creatures that are considered pests. These countries still have plants and animals, even if they're not exclusively the native plants and animals that some might prefer to see. Nature tends to find its own balance. During the millions of years prior to the appearance of people on this earth, the existing trees, shrubs, and flowers would move from one locale to another. People certainly speed this movement, but they're not really doing anything that wouldn't happen anyway.

It is a shame to restrict beautiful ornamental plants from other countries because of their ability to survive in our new ecology. Butterfly bush, buckthorn, and Norway maple are all considered invasive in various states, and their sale is often restricted. When these plants are lost from our nurseries it bites into their bottom line. In fact, growers in Connecticut estimated that restrictions on sales of so-called invasives cost them twenty million dollars during 2003 and 2004.

By restricting which plants and animals can and can't be moved across our borders, we are also hurting the bottom line of companies that we should be encouraging. The time that produce spends on a dock or at an airport is money lost, with a minimal probability that we will have stopped something really dangerous. It's true that if a major pest makes it into the United States that would be a big problem, but for most imported material, we know the major pests we're concerned about and so do the shipping companies. We could have them check their own stock, and even the shipping materials used to transport the stock. And besides, we can only catch what we're ready for. Even if we added a million well-trained inspectors to APHIS, would they be able to catch every problem? The emerald ash borer probably still wouldn't have been caught because it wasn't an insect that inspectors were watching for. What it comes down to is this: when we're aware that something could be a problem if it enters our country, we tend to be ready for it, and we're able to shut it down before it causes too much damage. If it catches us by surprise, then we might or might not be able to control it, depending on how quickly we identify it as a problem. Controlling foreign diseases and insects that aren't caught early is both time and labor intensive, and the fiscal tradeoffs should be seriously considered before we attempt such efforts.

Perhaps the biggest problem with trying to control invasive plants, insects, and other organisms is, indeed, the problem of wasted resources. We cannot satisfactorily control all of the invasive species out there. And we might very well end up creating what amounts to a desert because of the herbicide use it would most likely entail, not to mention the huge amounts of money it would cost to hire all of the people needed to apply the herbicides. About the best we can do is to slow the thing down, and it's worth asking whether slowing things down is worth the effort it would require.

Right-Wing Rating ★★★★ Setting priorities is the key. Invasives that threaten the food supply or the economy must be dealt with aggressively; we don't have the resources to control everything else.

Left-Wing Rating ★ Allowing invasive species to take over upsets the natural balance of the ecosystem. We need to protect our environment.

The Bottom Line

There is hardly a location in the United States that hasn't been touched in some way by a plant or animal from somewhere else. Perhaps the best way to look at those places in this country that are relatively undisturbed by invasive species is as vintage cars. There aren't many of them left, and, for those that have survived, it is worth the extra effort to save them because of the place they hold in our history and our hearts. But, with that in mind, there's no denying that vintage cars, or undisturbed native forests, just aren't the most well-adapted components of our highways or land. Newer cars are faster, safer, and use less gas than vintage cars. Similarly, invasives are able to not only survive, but actually flourish in more disturbed environments than many of our natives. We could maintain and even encourage the use of more vintage cars than we currently do. They would look great, but it would be expensive and they still wouldn't be able to compete with modern cars in most of the parameters that are important to us. Likewise, we can preserve native ecosystems, and even rebuild them to some extent. But without expensive maintenance it will be impossible to keep them completely free of invasives that are equally or even better adapted to the conditions. So you have to ask, is it worth it?

Insects, plants, and other organisms from different parts of the world that can and do alter the native ecosystems of our country are everywhere. Often, we encourage these plants and animals—cows, corn, wheat, dogs, and cats—from other parts of the world, and much of our country has already been irreversibly altered. If you value diverse ecosystems and like to look back at the way things once were, then you should support efforts to stop invasive plants, animals, and insects from coming into our country, and you should also support efforts to suppress plants that are currently spreading and displacing our native plants. On the other hand, if you think we should save money by not trying to control potentially invasive pests, and stick to slowing down the few that could cause real economic harm, you accept that the world has turned into a big blender and all we can really do is sit back and watch it spin.

Ultimately, everyone's answer to what we should do to control noxious and invasive plants and animals falls somewhere on a long continuum between exorbitant spending with excellent control, and no spending with no control. Neither extreme is workable, so the question is, where in the middle do you stand?

CHAPTER 9

★★★

Legal and Illegal Plants: Why Are the Bad Guys Bad?

GOVERNMENT CONTROL OF the plants grown in this country is sometimes most intense in our own backyards. As we saw in the previous chapter, the government controls certain plants—at least to some extent—to prevent them from taking over a particular ecosystem, such as a lake. But there are other plants that are illegal for us to buy or grow, not because of what they do to our environment, but because of what they can do to us. Over the years many battles have been fought over these plants, with proponents claiming that these plants are being unfairly singled out, while detractors point to the fact that they can be damaging to anyone involved with them. We're talking, of course, about intoxicating plants, of which the most (in)famous, and most controversial, is marijuana.

In the early 1990s in the state of Washington, Ralph Seeley was a cancer patient who was suffering. He was undergoing aggressive chemotherapy and radiation treatments to combat the cancer, but they weren't working. To make matters worse, the pain medications prescribed for him did not agree with his system and were addictive. There was only one thing that worked for his pain: marijuana. Smoking this plant relieved the nausea and pain caused by his treatments. Upon hearing this, his doctor prescribed dronabinol, a pill that contains THC, the active ingredient in marijuana. But these pills failed to provide the relief he sought because he would vomit them up before they could take effect. Seeley then acquired marijuana illegally. As a lawyer, he wanted to use it in a legal way, and he wanted others to be able to use it legally, too. So he embarked on a lawsuit against the state of Washington to establish a legal way to acquire marijuana to relieve suffering. Many people had sued to use medical marijuana before, but none had won. Seeley fought hard and wisely and won the right to use this drug in a superior court decision, only to lose in the state supreme court. He died in 1998 without having achieved the right to use marijuana legally, but his efforts helped to pave the way for others to have access to this drug.

To many people, the idea of legalizing marijuana for medicinal purposes just makes sense. And others can't understand why growing this plant is illegal in the first place, since it produces strong fibers that can be used for hemp rope. Many of our founding fathers, including George Washington, grew this crop for just that purpose. Conversely, still others see this plant as a gateway drug that leads its users to try stronger, more dangerous substances. And some view this plant as a terrible evil in and of itself.

As we saw in the previous chapter, both federal and state governments have identified numerous plants that are illegal to carry over the border or across state lines or to sell, for various reasons. Enforcement of laws regulating invasive plants doesn't come close, however, to the exuberant enforcement of laws regulating other illegal plants, particularly those that are controlled in an apparent attempt to protect us from ourselves. A short list of these plants includes marijuana, psilocybin mushrooms (actually a fungus), peyote, iboga, and the poppies from which opiates are extracted.

The Science

Plants that are banned because of what they do to human beings generally have a long laundry list of effects. From hallucination to intoxication, these plants produce chemicals that make us feel and act differently than we normally would, which is exactly why some people seek them out and others try to prevent their use. For most of these plants, there has been relatively little research into all of the things, good or bad, that using the plants can do to a person.

The highs, lows, and side effects produced by the drugs that come from illegal plants vary greatly, depending on what plant is ingested. Some of these plants, such as iboga, contain chemicals that are relatively toxic (ibogaine and noribogaine). On the other hand, it would take a considerable dose of the THC in marijuana to have an effect beyond making the user stoned. But, as with pesticides, it's not just how much of them it would take to kill someone, it's also the other effects that these chemicals could have on users and those around them. Of all of the plants that are illegal because of their intoxicating properties, the most extensively researched is certainly marijuana, which has been shown to cause a number of health problems. Marijuana lowers the birth weights of children born to mothers who smoke it; it may permanently damage the ability of chronic users to perform tasks like reading; and it may impair the ability to drive a car, train, or other vehicle. Chronic users may be permanently damaging their brains. The respiratory stress that smoking marijuana causes is in many ways, similar to, or even worse than, tobacco. And an estimated 40 percent of people arrested tested positive for marijuana in 2004, a statistic that could be interpreted in several ways, including that marijuana impairs judgment, or competence, or both.

Other plants that are banned to protect us from ourselves can make the dangers of marijuana look like a kitten standing next to a tiger. Psilocybin mushrooms can lead to brain damage, kidney failure, and even a heart attack. Ingestion of the plant iboga has the potential to damage the brain, particularly the cerebellum, or it could just kill you.

★★★

But marijuana isn't all bad news. Research has shown that this plant is useful for the treatment of a variety of ailments. It can alleviate nausea (as for Ralph Seeley), stimulate the appetite of AIDS patients, and help in the treatment of glaucoma. Perhaps the most noted benefit of this drug is its ability to help control pain, and at one time, marijuana was the drug of choice for migraine headaches. In a 1997 survey, about 30 percent of oncologists thought that marijuana should be rescheduled (moved to a list of legal drugs), and of those, about one-third thought that they would prescribe marijuana cigarettes once a month or more.

Marijuana is far from the only drug that has the potential to help as much as hurt people. Studies have shown that iboga can help control substance addictions and psilocybin mushrooms can help alleviate depression. Some people who took magic mushrooms even point to their ingestion as one of the most spiritually meaningful things they had done in their lives. And it is well known that the opiates that come from poppies include not only illicit drugs but also the medically useful painkiller morphine, though it is usually created synthetically nowadays.

Government Policy

Harry J. Anslinger is usually given credit for our current system of controlling illegal plants. Anslinger was the director of the Federal Bureau of Narcotics from 1930 to 1962. In the 1930s, he promoted sensationalized tales of drug-induced crimes that became the basis of pop culture crime stories. Heroin was Anslinger's primary target for government restrictions, but he didn't ignore other drugs. Pressure from law enforcement and leading newspapers led Congress, with help from testimony given by Anslinger, to pass the 1937 Marijuana Tax Act. On its face, the act seemed to be just a tax on the buying and selling of marijuana, but it made the documentation of the purchase and sale so complex, and the penalties for not complying so extreme, that it served to make marijuana essentially illegal. Although some of the mythology surrounding Anslinger makes him out to be a lone ranger in the fight against pot, he didn't really do anything that the states hadn't done already. Indeed, by the time Congress acted, all of the states had their own marijuana prohibitions, though promoters of the federal law claimed it was needed because state laws were not vigorously enforced.

But why is one plant deemed illegal and another plant legal in the government's eyes? It's not their ability to kill—if it were, there would be an incredibly long list of prohibited plants and amazingly few choices for our landscape.

Today, the list of restricted plants includes a lot more than just marijuana. But why is one plant deemed illegal and another plant legal in the government's eyes? It's not their ability to kill—if it were, there would be an incredibly long list of prohibited plants and amazingly few choices for our landscape. Rather, the ability of plants to intoxicate is the driving force governing whether a plant can be grown or not. The Comprehensive Drug Abuse Prevention and Control Act of 1970 included both treatment provisions and tougher legal restrictions on marijuana and other plants. It imposed probation for the first-time offense of possession of small amounts of marijuana, and allowed police to conduct "no-knock" searches. Section II of this act is the Controlled Substances Act, which created the drug classification hierarchy and placed marijuana in Schedule I with other substances that had a "high potential for abuse" and "no currently accepted medical use."

The Controlled Substances Act allows the Drug Enforcement Agency (DEA) and the Food and Drug Administration (FDA) to put together a list of chemicals that are considered drugs. This list is divided into five schedules, which indicate how dangerous the government considers these drugs. The most dangerous drugs are listed in Schedule I, while the least dangerous are in Schedule V. To be classified as a Schedule I drug, the plant in question must fulfill three criteria: a high potential for abuse, no currently accepted medical use in treatment in the United States, and a lack of accepted safety for use of the drug under medical supervision. Schedule II drugs must also fulfill three criteria: a high potential for abuse; a currently accepted medical use in treatment in the United States; and abusing the drug may lead to severe psychological or physical dependence. Schedules III, IV, and V include drugs that are less likely to cause dependence and be abused. Anabolic steroids are an example of a Schedule III drug, and Lomotil, a drug used to control diarrhea, is a Schedule V drug.

A person guilty of owning a plant listed on Schedule I isn't guilty of owning a plant, but rather of owning a controlled substance. This seems somewhat hypocritical to groups in favor of the legalization of marijuana, because there is a huge array of weeds and ornamental plants in any yard—castor beans, yews, flowering tobacco, deadly nightshade, and Virginia creeper, among others—that can be used as intoxicants or poisons.

The campaign against illegal drug use kicked into high gear during President Ronald Reagan's administration (1981–1989). First Lady Nancy Reagan made "Just Say No" her personal public relations campaign and it paid off in 1986 and 1988 with the passage of the Anti-Drug Abuse Acts. These laws imposed life sentences for top figures in drug organizations and permitted the option of the death penalty under certain circumstances. The acts also instituted different sentences for crack cocaine and for cocaine powder. Crack cocaine, which was causing violent turf wars among the gangs that were selling it, was given mandatory minimum sentences one hundred times greater than the existing penalties for cocaine powder. These differences became increasingly controversial as the racial disparities in drug sentences became apparent: African Americans were more likely to use crack cocaine and thus receive the harsher penalties, while whites were more likely to use cocaine powder and receive the lighter punishments. These acts also established mandatory minimum sentences for marijuana possession: 100 plants or 100 kilograms (220 pounds) triggered a five-year sentence.

Since the 1980s, policy innovation has occurred at the state and local levels rather than the federal level. Faced with the high expenses of burgeoning jail populations, several states have reduced penalties for first-time offenses for individuals caught possessing small amounts of marijuana. Thirteen states currently impose no jail time and small-time possession does not show up on criminal records. Public and media attention have been drawn to movements for the legalization of marijuana for medical reasons. California gained national attention in 1996 when its voters passed a medical marijuana initiative that allowed anyone to grow or possess marijuana if they could convince a physician to give them permission to use it for medical purposes.

However, these medical marijuana laws set states on a collision course with federal drug laws, which claim that marijuana has no medicinal value and thus cannot be grown or possessed by individuals for any reason. When federal law and state laws conflict, the federal law is the one that counts. The U.S. Supreme Court rejected the Californians' claim that their declaration of medical necessity exempted them from federal drug laws, in *U.S. v. Oakland Cannabis Buyers' Cooperative* (2001). The Supreme Court also rejected claims that Congress could not prohibit personal use of marijuana because Congress is only constitutionally authorized to regulate interstate commerce. In *Gonzalez v. Raich* (2005) the Court found that Congress could trump state and local laws because those who grow marijuana for medicinal purposes could also use it for other illicit purposes. Likewise, the DEA refused a request to remove marijuana from the Schedule I classification in 2001, and the FDA issued a report in 2006 finding that there was no scientific basis for using marijuana as medicine. The federal government gave no ground on the use of marijuana for any purpose until the Justice Department announced in 2009 that it would not prosecute individuals for drug use that was legal under state law.

The control the government exercises over the use of hallucinogenic plants (such as peyote) in religious ceremonies provides an interesting contrast to its control of marijuana. The U.S. Supreme Court ruled in *Employment Division v. Smith* (1990) that the use of peyote was not protected as a "free exercise" of religion, even if its use was part of a traditional Native American ceremony. The Court's logic was that you can *believe* whatever you want, but that does not allow you to *practice* illicit activities. Nevertheless, a number of states responded by specifically exempting Native American tribal ceremonies from peyote and ayahuasca bans. And Congress passed the Religious Freedom Restoration Act of 1993, which makes it harder for the government to interfere with the actions of religious organizations.

The Political Dynamics

Why is the government okay with alcohol and tobacco and not marijuana? The simple answer is cultural acceptance. Tobacco had been used by Native Americans since well before Europeans arrived, and the population of Europe took to the pastime in the sixteenth century. In fact, Sir Walter Raleigh (who is credited with bringing tobacco to England, though it actually arrived there before his travels) convinced Queen Elizabeth to try a puff around 1600. Alcohol arrived in the United States right along with colonization. They were both used by, and popular with, almost all classes of society. Marijuana, opium, and cocaine arrived more recently and were used by immigrant groups or other members of society that were considered socially marginal.

The policy struggle over medical marijuana is evidence of a widening regional split in social acceptance. Pacific coast and New England states are more likely to allow marijuana for medicinal purposes and to have less severe penalties for first-time arrests for possession of minor amounts. Plains and southern states, however, tend to have strict laws and seem highly unlikely to make them more lenient. The fact that some states allow laws to be passed outside of the legislative process has proven very useful for proponents of medical marijuana. Most state medical marijuana laws come from initiatives placed on the ballot by voters themselves, not by changes in laws made by the state legislature. This shows that even though public opinion in these states may be relevantly tolerant, politicians were not going to risk getting ahead of the public or setting themselves up to be the brunt of a backlash from voters opposed to weakening drug laws.

Fourteen states currently permit medical marijuana, nine (64 percent) through ballot initiatives approved by voters. Put another way, 43 percent of the states that allow voters to place issues on the ballot have passed medical marijuana laws, but only 17 percent of states without initiative procedures have passed such laws. Supporters of medical marijuana have succeeded largely when they can avoid state legislatures and take their case directly to the people.

Indeed, the conventional wisdom for politicians says that voting to loosen restrictions on anything that teenagers might smoke is just inviting attack ads in your next election. Politicians and others in public office don't want to be seen as soft on drugs, soft on crime, or soft on hippies. Douglas Ginsburg, nominee to the Supreme Court, had to withdraw in 1987 because he had smoked pot back when he

FOR ELECTED politicians, perception is usually more important than facts. They might try to decriminalize or reduce penalties for a drug that is likely no worse than other substances that are entirely legal (alcohol) or available by prescription (Percocet, oxycodone). But making those arguments is a nonstarter politically.

The political issue really isn't about drug schedule classifications and regulations. The issue—as the politician thinks the voters back home are to going to see it—is about values. Are you for "anything goes" licentiousness, or for self-control and responsibility? It's also about symbolic group associations: are you in the respectable middle class or are you a hippie? And it's not about whether you ever did a few drugs when you were young (since most people can compartmentalize and thus rarely see themselves as being hypocritical), it's about whether you are for protecting children from bad influences or allowing them to take their chances in a dangerous world.

In politics, symbols matter, and when the symbols are powerful, easily accessible, and can be framed in a thirty-second attack ad, the symbols usually have little difficulty subduing solid evidence or reasoned argument. Politicians protect themselves by not giving their opponents an opening to declare that they are soft on drugs.

was a law professor. President Bill Clinton never lived down his declaration about pot that he had "smoked, but didn't inhale." George W. Bush could not escape speculation about cocaine use despite a lack of evidence. Almost all candidates for high-ranking office are now asked about drug use. By admitting their past up front and showing remorse, most are able to overcome the potential risk, but few want to take on additional risk by taking stances that can be portrayed as pro-marijuana.

The most direct route to national legalization of marijuana (or any other restricted plant) would be for the FDA to reschedule the drug. But, like other elected officials, presidents do not want to be seen as being pro-drug and would thus pressure the FDA to avoid the rescheduling. Congress would most likely respond to rescheduling by cutting the FDA's budget or passing a law to directly block the FDA's reclassification. The FDA itself would want to avoid a battle with the White House and Congress over an issue that is so marginal to its overall mission. One way the FDA seems to have accomplished this is by preventing the gathering of data that might (inconveniently) show the safety of marijuana. The FDA can't declassify marijuana from Schedule I without studies that demonstrate its effectiveness and safety as a medical drug. Yet it has not allowed researchers to use its supply of research on marijuana to conduct medical studies (since growing marijuana is illegal, universities can't just grow it for their own research studies). In line with this, the White House Office of National Drug Control Policy has asserted that the reason that approval for marijuana research has not been granted is that it has not received research proposals that meet the general standards for approval of drug research (such as providing for control groups or involving participants who take multiple drugs), rather than an attempt by the government to suppress scientific analysis of medical marijuana.

The good news for those who support the legalization of marijuana and other intoxicating plants is the passage of state initiatives. There is more room for public discussion when the plant in question can serve socially useful purposes other than recreation, though public officials have been loath to join that discussion. The discussion over legalization of medical marijuana in most states revolves around whether marijuana has therapeutic uses for patients with particular ailments and whether it is equal to or superior to other legal drugs in terms of its pain killing ability or lack of side effects. Supporters of medical marijuana have been successful in attracting media coverage to testimonials of patients who believe it has relieved their pain and suffering. There are many Americans who have experienced a loved one's suffering and are sympathetic to potential alternative sources of relief. Without supporters' assertions of medical benefits, or its protection in religious ceremonies, there would be little serious debate about legalization primarily for the purposes of helping the user get in touch with his or her true self.

Although proponents of medical marijuana have clearly developed an effective strategy of using ballot initiatives to bypass state legislatures, there may not be many more direct opportunities to take advantage of favorable public opinion. Of the twelve states that do not currently permit medical marijuana and do allow ballot initiatives, most are culturally conservative plains or southern states, where the grounds for passage are not fertile.

It is tempting to treat California as the exception (indeed, many Americans already do), given their 2010 ballot initiative to legalize marijuana for recreational use. However, the major rationale for the initiative put forth by its proponents is economic: legalization would allow California to tax marijuana, thereby helping the state out of its $20 billion budget deficit. For voters who don't care one way or another about marijuana, taxing something they don't buy seems like a good choice. It might allow them to avoid a sales or income tax hike, or a cut to public services they use (libraries, roads, police). Nevertheless, previous economic downturns in California did not result in a serious debate over legalization, suggesting that the times, they are a-changin'.

Gallup polls show a slow, steady growth in support for legalization of marijuana from 12 percent in 1969 to 36 percent in 2005. Given that the poll also shows greater support (though not a majority) for legalization among younger respondents, public support is likely to continue to increase as antidrug voters are increasingly replaced in the electorate by a generation with more tolerant attitudes toward drugs.

For our money, the best evidence of an evolution in attitudes toward marijuana is the approval of a medical marijuana initiative in Michigan in 2008, a state more associated with old-time union politics than New Age reforms. Similarly, the state legislature of the rather sober state of Minnesota passed a medical marijuana bill in

2009, though it was vetoed by the governor. If Middle America (though still northern America) is increasingly tolerant of medical marijuana, this suggests that a broad shift in public attitudes is under way and the power of absolutist "Just Say No" politics is ebbing. Reflecting these trends, the Obama administration's Justice Department announced in 2009 that it would not prosecute people under federal law for drug possession when their actions were permissible under the laws of their state.

Policy Option One: Leave Things as They Are

The government controls plants that are regularly used as recreational drugs and that have the potential to be damaging to people. There is absolutely no reason for people to try and acquire most of these plants except for getting high. After all, is marijuana a particularly attractive plant that you'd want in your flower garden? What about magic mushrooms? Peyote? These are some seriously ugly plants. While the poppy may be an attractive flower, it's not as if there aren't good replacements for it in the garden. Why should we even consider having these plants be legal? They have some serious effects on human physiology that cannot be ignored. Life's not all just a fun high.

All that said, however, the overriding reason to keep things as they are is that it allows us to control the drugs that have the most potential to hurt both the user and those around them. Some banned plants may be useful in certain medical circumstances, but we should keep them and other plants on the list of nationally banned substances. Medical marijuana is currently allowed by states in the circumstances where it is most needed—without federal government interference. Though state and federal laws may conflict, in practice they allow people who need to use medical marijuana to use it, while allowing the federal government to crack down on other uses and sales.

There is little incentive or need to remove peyote, magic mushrooms, and other drugs from the Schedule I list, except in specific instances where these drugs have religious or medical uses. Peyote can be used in some states for religious rituals.

Right-Wing Rating ★★★★★ Is anyone else suspicious that medical reasons aren't really the primary motivation here? Scientifically proven painkillers are widely available. We don't need to make it easier for people to make self-destructive and socially destructive choices.

Left-Wing Rating ★★ Marijuana is illegal mainly because it was used at one time by unpopular racial minorities. It is arguably safer than alcohol and many legal prescription drugs, and thus should be available at least for medically useful purposes.

Policy Option Two: Have a Longer List of Illegal Plants

There are many, many plants in the United States that can cause harm to people but are not currently regulated by the government. One of the foremost of these plants is castor bean, a noninvasive plant often used as an ornamental, which can produce the extremely deadly toxin ricin. It's arguably easier to make ricin from castor beans than it is to make opium from poppy seeds. Currently, ricin has no accepted value as a medicine, so it should be on the list as a Schedule I drug. If the standard for inclusion on the list is that a plant must not only be dangerous but also a narcotic, then there are still plenty of plants out there that fit this description, including deadly nightshade and *Salvia divinorum,* which is a hallucinogenic drug of choice for youngsters that leaves them in a temporary, though disturbing, stupor. Why aren't we actively adding these plants to the Schedule I drug list, so we can keep them away from users who could potentially hurt themselves or others?

Right-Wing Rating ★★ Adding more plants to Schedule I would dilute our efforts against already existing, and much more prominent, plant problems.

Left-Wing Rating ★ Adding more plants to the list restricts our personal freedoms further without making us significantly safer.

Policy Option Three: Legalize All Plants

If you ride a motorcycle, there's no denying that it's safer to wear a helmet. Still, some people choose to wear a helmet, and some choose to take their chances. Driving laws are largely governed by the state where you live and, while some states make it illegal not to wear helmets while riding on a motorcycle, most think it should be the rider's choice whether their crash results in a minor concussion or a fatality. The government is not so flexible when it comes to plants, though, and it maintains a "do not grow" list that seems arbitrary. You could grow tobacco (it's only killed 90 million people or so), castor bean, deadly nightshade, or *Salvia divinorum,* but you can't grow coca, or the poppies from which opium is made. This is despite the fact that it would take a tremendous amount of plant material as well as a significant amount of chemical know-how to make cocaine from coca or opium from the poppies.

What is clear, especially to gardeners, is the lack of understanding that the government has regarding plants. Poppies are illegal but castor bean, which is used to make ricin (categorized as a biological agent according to the federal Biological Weapons Anti-Terrorism Act of 1989), is legal to grow. It all seems hypocritical or, at best, confused.

The government also takes an inconsistent stance with regard to the drug THC. As of the writing of this book, the drug dronabinol, which has the same active ingredient (THC) as a marijuana cigarette, is legal with a prescription, while the marijuana cigarette itself is not.

As long as the government can't reasonably and consistently decide what is safe and what is dangerous, then it shouldn't schedule any plants at all. There would still be plenty of laws in place banning dangerous behaviors, including driving under the influence of intoxicating substances. This wouldn't change. Laws might even become more stringent to compensate for the legality of these plants.

Decriminalization also saves taxpayers money in several ways. If marijuana, magic mushrooms, and other drugs were legal they could be taxed like alcohol and bring in considerable revenue to state and federal governments. Law enforcement costs for arrest, prosecution, and particularly incarceration of drug users would be drastically reduced, saving governments more money. And crime would decrease, both organized crime and street crime, because drugs could be obtained legally—which means more safely and inexpensively.

Right-Wing Rating ★ It's not about the money; it's about public safety. The good life comes from working hard, not from intoxication. Decriminalizing any currently criminal behavior would reduce crime, but that's an empty and ineffective solution, since the underlying dangers of drugs would remain.

Left-Wing Rating ★★★★★ Use actual scientific evidence to determine which drugs have hazardous effects and classify them and regulate them appropriately on the FDA Schedules. If a drug isn't clearly more dangerous than legal drugs like alcohol, take it off the Schedule and let adults make their own decisions.

Policy Option Four: Legalize Plants for Medicinal and/or Religious Reasons

Many states already allow the use of marijuana and peyote for religious or medical reasons. Unfortunately, the federal government seems to be working its hardest to keep both of these plants on its Schedule I list. The lack of a federal law governing religious or medical uses means that the federal government could arrest anyone using or possessing these plants. Laws need to change so that people who really need marijuana can get it. Additionally, by descheduling marijuana, research grants from the United States government could be made available to start testing it more thoroughly to see how much promise it really has for treating nausea, glaucoma, pain, and other problems. Despite the report in 2006 by the FDA concluding that there was no legitimate medical use for marijuana, there actually have been studies that demonstrate the contrary, and it would be beneficial if the government explored the possibility that marijuana and other currently illegal drugs could be a useful source of medicines.

This option is actually, functionally, very close to the way things are working right now. The one significant difference would be that states that don't allow certain plants to be used medicinally or for religious purposes would be forced to do so.

Right-Wing Rating ★★ Selective legalization for medical and especially religious purposes may be acceptable, as long as the drugs are tightly controlled and aren't made completely legal.

Left-Wing Rating ★★★★ This seems fair, especially when it comes to helping those who are sick.

The Bottom Line

There is no question that there are plants on the list of Schedule I drugs that can cause harm to people. However, there is also no doubt that the presence of certain plants on the list and the absence of others seems to show that the government places plants on the list because of political pressure rather than their real dangers.

Smoking weed is not necessarily a victimless crime any more than drinking alcohol and driving, or smoking tobacco in a bar where others will inhale that smoke are victimless crimes. Yes, many of the plants currently on the Schedule I list have effects that are arguably worse than alcohol, prescription medications, or certain other plants that are legal. But even people who are extremely concerned about the use of harmful recreational drugs see the benefit of allowing terminally ill patients who cannot swallow the more widely prescribed medications to use marijuana cigarettes.

Based on the research that we have and what we know, it seems a questionable decision to continue to list marijuana as a Schedule I drug, though it probably should not be listed as anything lower than a Schedule II drug, until we have more data. We need more information about many of the plants listed on Schedule I, in addition to marijuana. These plants have not been sufficiently researched by our government for their potential uses beyond their ability to give recreational highs. Without this data, their placement as Schedule I drugs seems terribly hypocritical, when so many other plants that can cause intoxication or even death are allowed to remain unscheduled.

CHAPTER 10

★★★

Local Restrictions: Is Your Backyard Really Yours?

THE BEACON WOODS Civic Association in Bayonet Point, Florida, took Joseph Prudente, a man who was a little down on his luck at the time, to court because he couldn't afford to sod his lawn in what was a deed-restricted community. The association had told Prudente repeatedly to fix up his lawn. When he didn't, they decided to force the issue, noting that he had signed an agreement to keep his yard covered with grass. Prudente didn't show up on his appointed court date, and was found in contempt of court. He was jailed without bail on Friday, October 10, 2008, until he could afford to sod his yard. Fortunately, some good-willed neighbors came to the rescue, donating time and sod to the effort, ultimately springing Prudente from the slammer that Sunday.

If the Joseph Prudente case were an isolated incident, we could all sit back, relax, and have a good laugh—but it isn't. Across the United States there are any number of restrictions and requirements that local governments place on your yard. Sometimes these requirements seem to make sense, such as restricting the number of chickens a person can keep in an urban or suburban dwelling, and sometimes they seem to be a bit off the wall, like requiring a particular grass height.

Over the years, a number of court cases have been tried regarding the enforcement of standards on a person's yard, but none has received as much attention as *City of New Berlin v. Hagar*. Unlike Joseph Prudente, Donald Hagar did have the means to maintain a nice suburban yard. But he didn't want to. In 1976, Hagar was a wildlife biologist in the process of creating a meadow on his 2½ acre property in New Berlin, Wisconsin. The creation of this meadow precluded a lawn, which irritated the powers that be in the city of New Berlin and they proceeded to sue him for violating their weed law. They pointed out that Hagar's property included plants that produced allergens, had the potential to spread fires rapidly, and provided shelter for nasty creatures such as the Norway rat. What the city didn't count on was that Hagar had friends who actually knew something about the meadow he was growing, including professors from the University of Wisconsin and employees of the U.S. Forest Service. In court these expert witnesses testified that meadows such as the one Hagar was cultivating did not create shelter for rats and were not particularly likely to spread fire, and that the plants within this meadow were less likely to produce allergenic pollen than the exotic Kentucky bluegrass planted in other yards (despite its name, Kentucky bluegrass is not native to the United States) or trees such as oaks. Finding nothing to support the claims by the city that Hagar's yard was a hazard, the judge ruled in his favor. The court then proceeded to strike down the weed ordinance because the basis on which the law was built was so weak.

As our country has come to understand and appreciate native plants, many of the local laws that once regulated what people could grow in their lawns have disappeared, or at least ceased to be enforced. However, there are still fines that can be levied against those who go their own way. In 2009, Asa Dodsworth, a resident of Berkeley, California, was threatened with fines of $3000 per day for what amounted to growing a vegetable garden and fruit trees in his front yard: vegetation over six feet tall, unpermitted trees, unpermitted garden beds, and obstruction of the right-of-way. While it's true that some of his plants were covering the sidewalk and may have been considered a hazard, $3000 seems a little steep for having a garden instead of a lawn.

At one time a good lawn would have included a good amount of clover and other plants we now call weeds.

The Science

What constitutes a good yard has changed significantly over the years. At one time a good lawn would have included a good amount of clover and other plants we now call weeds. Yards today are filled with grass, and only grass. This didn't come about by chance. During the Second World War, an herbicide was invented that would kill certain plants, like trees and dandelions, while leaving grasses alone. This chemical, known as 2,4-D, was the most effective herbicide known at that time. After the war (during the war it was deemed a wartime secret), it was considered a great tool for controlling weeds, such as dandelions in lawns. The problem was that it would kill clover in the lawn as well. Clover is a plant that collects nitrogen from the air and, when it is cut, provides that much-needed nitrogen to the grass as it grows. Without clover, grass needs fertilizers. It was once the case that you couldn't have a decent lawn without clover, but today, clover is considered a persistent weed in most suburbs, and annual applications of synthetic fertilizers provide the nutrients that a lawn needs.

Lest you get the idea that letting your yard go to weeds is a good idea, there are problems with poorly maintained yards. Lawns that are not mowed can be particularly attractive to ticks, which can spread Lyme disease and make general pests of themselves. Additionally, weedy lawns often harbor invasive and banned weeds. And then there's the whole issue of how an untidy yard looks.

Landscaping that is attractive, or at least acceptable, to a wide range of people does have some real benefits that are frequently ignored. Most of these benefits favor businesses in the area, but some also favor people who live in the community. People who shop in strip malls with better landscaping may pay as much as 8 percent more than they would at strip malls that aren't well landscaped. People will also pay a premium for a nicely landscaped house, which may very well mean that your house is worth more in a well-maintained neighborhood than in a neighborhood that has perennially brown lawns.

Government Policy

Almost all the laws that affect your yard—zoning, building permits, and most uses of eminent domain—are local laws made by the more than 87,500 local governments (including counties, municipalities, school districts, and so on) in the United States. The federal government only rarely gets involved, for invasive species or intoxicating plants, or to protect wetlands and the habitats of endangered species. The greatest interference with your yard is likely to come, not from governments, however, but from rules made by local homeowners' associations.

Though the ability to protect your own property is a fundamental element of your individual rights, most people recognize that what they do with their property has consequences for their neighbors and can infringe upon the rights of others. Since colonial times, local governments have regulated individuals' uses of their property to prevent public nuisances, such as slaughtering animals in urban yards. Likewise, long-standing zoning laws designate whether a particular property is to be used for residential, commercial, or industrial purposes. Beginning in the 1960s, state and local governments decided to expand the possible restrictions that could be put on land use in order to preserve historical landmarks, protect coastal areas, and maintain green space in cities and towns. These newer types of laws might, for example, require property owners to allow public access or use of their property in exchange for building permits. This type of local government restriction, of course, is seen as incredibly intrusive by property owners.

Recent controversies about restrictions on property use generally have focused on one of two activities. The first involves a government "taking" property or reducing the value of property without "just compensation" for the property owner, as required by the Fifth Amendment to the U.S. Constitution. The second is the imposition of intrusive rules by homeowners' associations on their residents. We'll consider each in turn.

The courts, with a few exceptions, have allowed local governments to make land use decisions without much restriction. (Land use, in this context, refers to whether a piece of property can legally be used as a place for a house, a farm, or a business.) Governments also have the power of eminent domain, meaning they can obtain property for purposes that will benefit the general public—roads, schools, and parks—as long as they pay just compensation to the property owner. This power allows the government to overcome the obstruction of individual property owners who are unwilling to sell or who are attempting to extort exorbitant prices for their property. When the land is being converted to public use, eminent domain is usually not controversial.

Local governments have pushed the boundaries of the concept, however. In the 2005 case of *Kelo v. City of New London,* the U.S. Supreme Court allowed the city of New London, Connecticut, to use its power of eminent domain to take homeowners' properties and sell them to private developers as part of the city's comprehensive redevelopment plan. The Court ruled that the benefits of economic growth qualified as a "public use" that benefited the entire community. The ruling generated quite a controversy because such a broad definition of public use puts everyone's property at greater risk.

Fortunately, having the government take property for reasons that stretch the definition of public use to extreme lengths is a rare occurrence. Still, these kinds of government actions have given rise to the property rights movement. Besides arguing against the unreasonable use of eminent domain, these groups also argue that government regulations that restrict the use of property amount to an uncompensated government "taking" of property. Restricting development in wetlands to protect water quality, or banning huge billboards because they are ugly or distracting to drivers, for example, means that property owners can't make money from developing or selling their land in certain ways. Thus, the government should pay for the loss in property value caused by the restrictions. The courts have agreed, but under relatively limited circumstances.

Oregon has the most stringent requirement that government compensate property owners for any loss in property value caused by government regulations. Traditionally, Oregon has had some of the strictest land use laws in the country (especially in the Portland area). However, voters in Oregon approved a ballot initiative called Measure 37 in 2004, giving property owners the right to claim compensation from the state or local government when the value of their property was reduced by environmental or other land use regulations. If the government failed to compensate them after two years of making the claim, property owners could make use of their property according to the regulations in place when they bought it. Critics of the initiative feared that the costs of complying with it would discourage local governments from passing or implementing land use regulations, since they couldn't afford to compensate all potential claimants for all potential losses in property values. The initiative's passage in Oregon spurred copycat ballot measures in several other western states. To date, all of these measures have been defeated by voters or invalidated by state courts. Even Oregon voters have reconsidered: in 2007, they passed Measure 47, which narrowed the applications of Measure 37 by prohibiting subdivisions on high-value farmlands, forestlands, and groundwater-restricted lands, and by preventing property owners from overturning existing zoning laws.

★★★

The second major source of controversy over property use, and the one that puts the most restrictions on what you can and can't have in your yard, comes from homeowners' associations. Homeowners' associations (HOAs) are usually established by the developer of a neighborhood when houses are first constructed. The association has a legal agreement with the local government that the HOA will provide community facilities (streets, sidewalks, and recreational areas) and certain services (street maintenance, trash collection, snow removal, and water and sewer lines). The HOA's articles of incorporation and bylaws are often approved by local planning officials and must conform to federal housing guidelines. Because HOAs have legal obligations to provide services, they have the authority to collect assessments and enforce rules. Unlike most private organizations, HOA membership is mandatory for those who purchase property in the neighborhood.

As private associations, HOAs can make their own rules, though state laws ultimately set the limits on their authority. HOAs often require that landscaping conform to a neighborhood plan, trees and shrubs be limited to certain heights, flowers come from an approved list, fences and decks follow prescribed designs, houses and/or front doors be painted one of a limited number of colors. It's not unusual for them to place restrictions on pets, the age of residents, window air conditioners, swing sets, satellite dishes, when and whether you can hang laundry outdoors, signs in yards (including political campaign signs and flags), leaving garage doors open, parking campers or commercial vehicles in driveways (or your car in front of your neighbor's house), and placing trash cans in the street during certain hours.

Various attempts by homeowners to create environmentally friendly lawns, such as converting lawns to native plants, replacing grass with synthetic lawns, and allowing grass to go brown during droughts have drawn the ire of HOAs, which usually demand that lawns be composed of bright green grass. In a major coup that reduced the power of HOAs, Florida passed a law in 2009 allowing residents to replace grass with native vegetation despite any HOA rules that might exist. Unfortunately for yard rebels everywhere, forty-nine states have yet to follow suit.

The Political Dynamics

Local governments justify land use policies as efforts to provide amenities desired by residents, to protect the public from the harmful effects of private development, and as a means of protecting the property values of others in the community. Local governments have increasingly used policies to limit development, or to require that land be set aside for open spaces or other public purposes because governments lack the funds to buy the property for these uses. The public wants parks, beach access, and well-maintained roads and residences, but is slow to volunteer the resources needed to provide them. Local governments often encourage the formation of HOAs as a way to shift the costs of facilities, maintenance, and resolving disputes between neighbors from the city's overburdened list of responsibilities and budgets to the HOAs. Unfortunately, a problem arises when local governments have to uphold and enforce the punishments imposed by HOAs, despite the fact that they are based on the rules of a private association.

Regulations imposed by local governments are constrained by the fact that much of their revenue comes from property taxes. Thus, towns that limit development or drive residents to find another property in another town because of silly rules badly inhibit their ability to fund their operations and programs. Likewise, compared to individual neighborhoods represented by HOAs, which tend to be eco-

WE ALL want to protect individual property rights—until our neighbor paints their house neon orange, lets the grass grow two feet high, starts to talk about installing a drag strip, or decorates with plastic pink flamingos. One person's freedom runs afoul of another's common sense.

There's a contradiction between our rural, self-sufficient heritage and the interdependence of modern life. At one time in our history, social expectations of what was appropriate may have been sufficient to keep our neighbors in line; now, informal expectations have been replaced by legal contracts. Conflicts between neighbors raise the fundamental question of governing: "who decides?"

nomically and demographically homogenous, local governments are usually elected by diverse constituencies, which makes it more difficult for one group to impose its tastes on another.

While the governing boards of HOAs are democratically elected and make decisions through democratic procedures, they suffer the same problem as most organizations, including the government: the people who care the most (in this case, about the appearance of their neighbors' properties) are the ones who participate, and few others pay close attention until there is a nasty dispute. The question then becomes whether the HOA board members are being busybodies under the guise of protecting property values. Since just about anything could conceivably affect property values, there doesn't seem to be much that can thwart the plans of petty tyrants on HOA boards, other than the risk of being thrown out of office by peeved neighbors who think they've finally gone too far.

That said, homeowners in HOA neighborhoods have the ability to review its rules when they buy property in that location. Just as they can choose to reside in a town that has a mix of tax levels and public services that fits their preferences, they can choose to live in a neighborhood that does not impose rules that they consider inconvenient. Residents sort themselves into neighborhoods that promote the types of conformity they desire (and can afford!). As political scientist Evan McKenzie found in a study of residential community associations: "[residents] place a high value on the restrictions, feeling that the infringement on one's own freedom is a small price to pay for the protection from the potential misdeeds of one's neighbors." HOAs also serve as effective advocates for the neighborhood in dealing with the local government, helping residents resist the petty rules that the government might attempt to place on them, and helping residents obtain the mix of services and tax burdens that they desire from their city or town.

Policy Option One: Leave Things as They Are

One of the nice things about the way things are now is that some places have tight regulations and some don't, and if you do your homework before you move to an area, then you'll have a pretty good idea of what you can or can't do. If you want to live in a place where you can grow your grass four feet high, you can buy a house in that sort of place. If you want to live under HOA rules that ensure that your neighbors will keep their grass green and their trees pruned, you have that option too.

When a government or an HOA decides that everyone's yard should conform to a certain set of standards, it is promoting a particular aesthetic that is, theoretically, endorsed by the people in the community. We all have different ideas about what lawns should look like, and, if the overwhelming majority of people in a community believe that a lawn should have grass that grows exactly so high, is exactly so green, and has exactly so many weeds, then why should one person be able to destroy the aesthetic of the whole community by deciding to grow fruit trees and vegetables or by allowing a prairie to flourish? Majority rule, after all, is how democracies make decisions.

Regulations mean that your neighbor won't be growing weeds that can infest your yard, and the yards in your neighborhood won't look like a quarry because all of the grass is dead. There are sound reasons for neighbors to demand that everyone play their part within a community.

Right-Wing Rating ★★★★★ Local governments and HOAs do a fine job of reflecting what the people who live in an area expect from their neighbors and their lawns. If you don't want to follow their rules, then don't live there.

Left-Wing Rating ★★★ Generally the rules imposed by HOAs are fine, but sometimes they go overboard. People shouldn't have to go to court to be able to plant native plants in their own yards.

Policy Option Two: Federal Laws Should Limit the Authority of HOAs and Local Governments to Control Yards

In this country we prize freedom and the right to do just about anything we want to with our property. Because of that, we should have federal laws that limit the ability of state and local governments and HOAs to regulate what we plant.

The freedom to decide what to do with your yard shouldn't be granted only to those who live outside the suburbs. Everyone should be able to choose to let their yard "go wild" without any care at all, plant a garden of one sort or another (usually either a vegetable garden, flower garden, or native planting), or maintain the yard in a minimalist way. These options have certain benefits for the person who owns the home, and even for those living in the area.

The main benefit of allowing a lawn to go wild is clear: less work. And the person with the wild lawn can claim to be avoiding the use of potentially dangerous pesticides, avoiding polluting the environment with carbon dioxide from lawn mowers, avoiding wasting good clean water on plants that are genetically programmed to go dormant in the summer anyway (most lawn grasses go dormant over the summer months if they're not watered), and avoiding using fertilizers that may run off and pollute nearby lakes and streams. A lawn maintained this way may not please some people's sense of aesthetics, but so what? The person who consciously follows this method of maintaining their yard is not necessarily doing wrong by the environment.

Growing a diversity of things in a wild yard, whether on purpose or simply because of a desire to do less maintenance, is also more ecologically sustainable than growing a single crop. Having other plants mixed in with grass, notably legumes like clover, results in less need for fertilizing because legumes collect nitrogen from the air, and when they are mowed or when they die back over the winter, they return it to the soil.

One argument used regularly by those who prefer that we all conform to having a well-maintained, grass-covered front lawn is that wild yards are dangerous. They harbor creatures that may infest nearby lawns and they contain a large amount of fuel that could feed a fire. But lawns and gardens just don't have enough fuel (dead, dry plant material) in most circumstances to be particularly efficient at conducting fire from one home to another. Rodents often do prefer landscapes with a lot of cover, though these rodents generally include rabbits and voles, which can certainly be pests of trees and vegetables, but they rarely vector human pathogens.

On the other side of the labor spectrum from a wild yard, gardens have some significant benefits over grass lawns, one of the most significant being that you can eat the things that grow. If you eat grass from your lawn you're likely to do the same thing that dogs and cats do when they eat grass—puke it right back up.

Right-Wing Rating ★ Lawn care is definitely not a responsibility of the federal government.

Left-Wing Rating ★★★★★ I never need to mow the grass again! Senseless conformity will no longer stand in the way of ecologically sensitive lawns.

Policy Option Three: State and Local Governments Should Regulate Lawns

The voles and rabbits in one overgrown yard could well come over to a well-maintained yard, as could the seeds from weedy plants. Though Donald Hagar's yard didn't contain many allergens, that isn't to say that a lawn gone wild can't. And there are certainly plenty of potentially dangerous plants like poison ivy that could invade a poorly maintained lawn. We need a way to protect our yards. Just because we don't have a homeowners' association protecting us shouldn't mean that we have to suffer from our neighbors' actions and watch our property values drop.

It is up to local governments to provide these restrictions. The federal government does not have constitutional responsibility for land use, and as a practical matter, it covers too many geographical regions. State and local governments cover smaller, more homogeneous regions and could pass reasonable laws to ensure that yards are maintained to a certain set of minimum standards, enabling all of us to enjoy a better aesthetic as well as increased property values.

Right-Wing Rating ★★ We like our yards neat, but local and state government regulation is no better than federal government regulation.

Left-Wing Rating ★★★ State and local governments are best positioned to identify ecologically sensitive ways to manage our lawns, but beware of governments that mandate green-grass-only lawns. Laws must be sensitive to ecological issues, too.

The Bottom Line

The federal government is not going to legislate exactly which plants you can and can't have in your yard, with the exception of noxious or intoxicating weeds (which we discussed in depth in earlier chapters). Local governments and HOAs will probably continue to regulate them. How tightly you think these institutions should regulate your yard (and your neighbor's yard!) depends mostly on your sense of aesthetics, your concern about your property value, and how much you worry about pollen, weed seeds, rodents, and other critters.

People will be people, and there's no accounting for taste in music, clothing, or yards. We can certainly understand the comfort of living in the familiar aesthetic of the suburban yard, and, knowing that, can appreciate the fact that some people want to ensure that they will have this aesthetic around them for their entire lives. But doesn't a small fine, maybe $20 or so a week, seem like enough of an incentive to keep people on the straight and narrow? If a garden is really invading a sidewalk to the point that it isn't useable, then why not just have the city's park board or maintenance crew come in, chop it away, and charge the owners of the property for the work?

CHAPTER 11

★★★

Global Warming: Natural or Man-made?

OVER THE PAST few decades, all sorts of environmental problems have arisen that threaten the well-being of our globe, and that we can prove have been caused by our industrial exploits. For example, it was easy to put our finger on what exactly caused acid rain—a prominent environmental problem brought to light in the 1980s—by collecting the rain and testing it. These tests showed minute traces of sulfuric and nitric acids within the rain. By connecting this finding with the knowledge that acid rain occurs mostly around cities that spew nitrogen and sulfur compounds into the atmosphere as waste, it was easy to discern acid rain's cause. In fact, the connection was actually made way back in 1872, when Robert Smith published his book *Air and Rain: The Beginnings of a Chemical Climatology*, in which he noted that the rain around the industrial city of Manchester in England was acidic, especially in the areas where the most soot was found.

Likewise, the thinning of the ozone layer, which was theorized by scientists in the 1970s and later proven through satellite imagery, could be connected with our release of chlorofluorocarbons (CFCs) and the known fact that they react with, and break down, ozone. The connection between CFCs and the thinning ozone layer was confirmed when we sampled air from the upper atmosphere and found it included these synthetic gases.

The newest problem that we are apparently causing is global warming. But unlike acid rain and the hole in the ozone layer, we don't have a gun that is clearly and unambiguously smoking, so it would be somewhat cavalier at this point to name a cause. After all, the earth's climates regularly changed before humans came along. There were ice ages, and periods where most of the world was in what we would now consider the tropics. So how do we know that anything abnormal is happening, much less that humans are causing it? And, even if we are causing it, should our government actually try to reverse it? Isn't there anything good to be said about global warming? For citizens who are frustrated by the writers of letters to the editor who assert that the previous day's weather is definitive proof for or against global warming, an assessment of what science does and doesn't tell us about climate change is in order.

The Science

There are certain places where a warming trend is blatantly obvious: the disappearance of glaciers in the Arctic, South America, the Himalayas, and in Africa over the past hundred years or so. Temperature readings across the globe also tend to support this warming trend, as do a variety of biological indicators, including the movement of trees up hills over the past few decades, presumably to find cooler climates. There is also evidence that the tropics are expanding.

Despite these examples, there are some regions across the world—portions of the Antarctic, for example—that do not seem to be warming. And there may be reasons, besides large-scale climatic ones, why temperature sensors read higher temperatures now than long ago. For example, as an area accumulates humans, those humans do things like build houses and put down asphalt, causing heat to accumulate and form a "heat island," or a small area of land where the temperatures read by thermometers will be higher than in other nearby regions. Over time, it is possible to get an inaccurately inflated picture of how much warmer an area has become because temperature sensors can't tell whether increases in heat come from a new highway or from natural causes.

Scientific investigations of the soil, ice buildup at the poles and on tall mountains, fossils, and living plant material allow us to infer how climates have changed over the years. Through this research, we have established that climates do change naturally. Minnesota, for example, was once tropical. In fact, it seems as though it is more common for the climate of Earth to change than to stay the same. But many scientists find it more than coincidental that the recent warming trends correlate so well with an increase in atmospheric carbon dioxide, which seems to be caused primarily by humans burning fossil fuels.

There isn't much argument about these facts, though different groups argue their relative importance. Disagreements occur regarding how much humans have contributed to this warming trend, and how much work we should do to control the activities that are apparently causing this warming.

The (Simplified) Science of Warming

As the earth heated up during the last part of the twentieth century, the amount of carbon dioxide in the atmosphere increased. One of the most famous charts from this period is Dr. David Keeling's measurements of the amount of carbon dioxide in the air in Mauna Loa, Hawaii, from 1958 to today. These measurements demonstrate that over the past fifty years the amount of carbon dioxide in the air has risen from less than 320 parts per million in 1958 to about 390 parts per million in 2009.

The theory that humans can influence the climate by putting carbon dioxide into it is not new. Svante Arrhenius, a scientist of the late nineteenth and early twentieth centuries, theorized that the carbon dioxide we put into the atmosphere would slowly warm up the globe. Infrared radiation, which comes from the sun, is absorbed by carbon dioxide here on earth, and this absorption causes the earth to warm. The higher the concentration of carbon dioxide in the earth's atmosphere, the more infrared radiation captured, which results in greater heat. While carbon dioxide is the chemical that we're most concerned about when we talk about global warming, there are actually many chemicals, such as methane, that can intercept infrared radiation even more efficiently than carbon dioxide. Chemicals like methane and carbon dioxide are called greenhouse gases. Because there's less methane and other greenhouse gases in the air than carbon dioxide, these other chemicals are usually considered a significant, but secondary, concern. When scientists discuss controlling global warming, lowering the levels of carbon dioxide in our atmosphere is usually the goal. For a full rundown of the supposed interactions between carbon dioxide and global warming, check out David Archer's book *Global Warming: Understanding the Forecast.*

Humans have developed two activities that increase the amount of carbon dioxide in the atmosphere. The first is the consumption of fossil fuels. Fossil fuels are basically energy stored as carbon. Over millions of years, as living things (mostly plants) have died, the energy that was stored in them has been converted through natural processes into various types of carbon, such as coal, natural gas, and oil. These carbon-containing fuels can be burned to create energy. The problem is that the carbon in these fuels doesn't just disappear with burning. Instead, burning releases water and carbon dioxide. Even the "cleanest" engine will still emit carbon dioxide because it has to. The carbon has nowhere else to go. (Though it's not directly related to fossil fuels, an underappreciated source of carbon dioxide is concrete. During the production of concrete chemical reactions occur that contribute an estimated 5 percent of the carbon dioxide that humans release into the atmosphere).

The second major way that humans increase the amount of carbon dioxide in the atmosphere is through the destruction of the places where atmospheric carbon dioxide would normally go. Trees and other plants absorb carbon dioxide while they grow and use it to create sugars from which the plant is built. Sunlight drives this process, which is more commonly known as photosynthesis. Trees are particularly important because they store carbon over long periods of time. Bodies of water are also capable of holding carbon, as are sedimentary rocks. Limestone, for example, is composed largely of calcium carbonate. Rocks currently store more carbon than the air, the ocean, or plants and animals. But the carbon that man has the most control over is that carbon contained in living organisms, especially plants.

Over the years humans have seen fit to destroy forests and replace them with agricultural land, which does not hold as much carbon as a forest. In a forest, large trees hold carbon for many years in their trunks, roots, stems, and leaves, which are mainly composed of this element. Even after they die the dead trees will continue to hold carbon for quite a while. The wood frame of your house, the furniture in it, and even this book in your hands all serve as storage places for carbon. Contrast this with today's agriculture, where plants like corn and soybeans are removed from the field and used rapidly. The carbon within them is not stored for a significant period of time but instead finds its way quickly back into the environment, and usually into the air as carbon dioxide.

What all of this means is that with the advent of modern industry and transportation, we have been releasing lots of carbon dioxide into the environment, and we have been destroying the things that do the best job of sucking this carbon out of the air and holding onto it. We know that, in our atmosphere, carbon dioxide absorbs light and converts it into heat instead of letting it escape back into space. It all fits together nicely. We are slowly causing our world to heat, and this heating will cause some very damaging things to happen over time: rising oceans, the movement of species across continents, and an increase in tornadoes, hurricanes, and other extreme weather. The Intergovernmental Panel on Climate Change (IPCC), a group of very prominent scientists who study this phenomenon, confirms that all of this is happening and that trouble is coming. It seems like an open-and-shut case—so why can't everyone just agree and *do* something?

But the case against carbon dioxide is not ironclad.

The Dissenters

All of the facts just discussed do not necessarily make the case for controlling carbon dioxide emissions. There are significant weaknesses in these arguments. Since the world does not have an absolutely predictable climate, and since climates change over time, there is the possibility that what we are seeing is a natural warming that would happen with or without humans. Indeed, respected scientists have theorized that solar activity, volcanic eruptions, or El Niño patterns in the Pacific Ocean could play an important part in global warming. If we look at the history of the earth, we find that global warming seems to predate an increase in atmospheric concentrations of carbon dioxide, which wouldn't make any sense at all if carbon dioxide is supposed to be driving the change! In 2009, an article published by Kyle Swanson and Anastasios Tsonis pointed out that from 2001 until 2009, the earth's climate was stabilizing, and warming was not taking place. While the authors themselves seem to believe that global warming is a reality, others have used their data as an indication that the IPCC has no idea what it's talking about. These skeptics believe that the earth is simply going through a natural cycle and that there's nothing significant that can be done about it. They believe that if we did try to do something we might, in a worst-case scenario, damage civilization by destroying our economy, which is in many ways dependent upon fossil fuels.

Since the world does not have an absolutely predictable climate, and since climates change over time, there is the possibility that what we are seeing is a natural warming that would happen with or without humans.

Some scientists believe that the amount of radiation coming from our sun, which varies over time, has a significant effect on the earth's climate and could account for anywhere from as little as 14 percent to an overwhelming majority of the warming that we've already seen. A recent decrease in the size of the ice caps on Mars (which are actually made of carbon dioxide) seems to support this theory, at least to some degree.

From the public's perspective, the more important climate change dissenters may not be the climate scientists but local television weather forecasters, from whom the public gets much of their weather-related information. A 2010 survey of TV forecasters found that about half thought that global warming was occurring, and only one-third thought that climate change was "caused mostly by human activities." Further, half said they had discussed climate change issues on air, while 90 percent had done so in talks to community groups.

One reason that local forecasters are more likely to end up in the dissenter camp than climate scientists is that they use different forecasting models. Meteorologists, such as television forecasters, are concerned with predicting the weather in a particular location at a particular moment in time. They use weather prediction models that are intensely sensitive to small changes in the atmosphere but have little accuracy beyond a week. Because they are used to predictions with a short shelf life, they are skeptical about the accuracy of long-term climate predictions. Climate scientists, by contrast, use complex models of global weather and weather patterns to estimate the effects of climate trends decades into the future. Variations in local weather patterns cancel out when observing and predicting long-term trends, so despite the inaccuracy of meteorological predictions of next week's weather, climatologists remain confident in their ability to see unfolding trends.

There are also arguments that increasing the amount of carbon dioxide in the atmosphere would actually be a good thing, because plants would be able to carry out more photosynthesis, allowing our crops to grow faster. Carbon dioxide is frequently pumped into greenhouses to speed the growth of crops, and short-term studies in which carbon dioxide is pumped onto fields generally show that most plants grow more quickly.

Carbon Dioxide's Other Impacts

Whether or not it has a role in global warming, carbon dioxide affects the environment in other significant ways. All plants take up carbon dioxide and convert it into the building blocks that make up their bodies, but not all plants respond in the same way to carbon dioxide enrichment. Some plants respond very well, and some plants not so well. Much of this difference is dependent upon how the plant collects carbon dioxide from the air. Most trees (as well as many other plants) utilize what is called a C_3 pathway, while other plants, like corn and many other grasses, use a C_4 pathway. Plants that use the C_3 pathway keep their leaf pores open so that carbon dioxide flows into them much of the time. This leads to a rapid loss of moisture through the pores, but it also means that the plants can take up and use quite a bit of carbon dioxide. Plants that use the C_4 pathway are much more efficient. They take up a certain amount of carbon dioxide and are quickly satiated, so they only need to keep their pores open for a shorter time. Plants in desert situations often use the C_4 pathway (or the similar CAM pathway).

When carbon dioxide levels are increasing, C_3 plants may have an advantage over C_4 plants, which could create changing weed dynamics that might profoundly influence our crops. This is because C_3 plants (including weeds such as Canadian thistle) are able to take up and utilize more carbon dioxide than their C_4 relatives (including important crops such as corn).

An increase in carbon dioxide may also cause problems because it could result in a more rapid depletion of nutrients from the soil. Such an increase might stimulate plant growth at first, but it would also lead the plants to absorb more nutrients, such as nitrogen, from the earth than they normally would. This would lead to a decline in how quickly the plants grow after a few years because of the limited amount of nitrogen left in the ground. Some plants will tolerate higher carbon dioxide and lower nitrogen levels more readily than others, and in some cases, weeds may be able to handle these conditions better than our crops. Such is the case with barnyard grass, a weed that competes with rice crops and that could, eventually, cause a significant problem.

The problems caused by atmospheric carbon dioxide concentration go beyond the terrestrial. The oceans are affected as well. As carbon dioxide levels in the atmosphere increase, the oceans absorb more of this gas, which ultimately leads to a decrease in pH, meaning the oceans are more acidic. Under these conditions, the ability of the sea creatures that use calcium carbonate to make their homes—coral, oysters, clams, and mussels, among others—decreases and they grow more slowly. Seashells are composed of calcium carbonate and are formed more readily in alkaline seas. Although the full impact of a decrease in ocean pH is not yet fully understood, rest assured that it has the potential to significantly change the status quo of our ocean ecology.

Government Policy

Though policy options to deal with climate change have been under discussion in Washington since the late 1980s, it is fair to say that the U.S. government does not have a climate change policy. George H. W. Bush's administration signed the Rio de Janeiro "framework" in 1992, in which industrialized countries agreed to the goal of reducing greenhouse emissions to 1990 levels by 2000. These objectives were nearly impossible to achieve, and there were no consequences for failing to achieve them, so no country took the goals seriously. The Clinton administration agreed to the Kyoto Protocol in 1998, which set targets for industrialized nations to decrease their emissions of greenhouse gases. But it was never submitted for approval to the U.S. Senate because the Senate had voted 99–0 the previous year to urge the president not to sign any climate change agreements that did not include emissions standards for developing countries. Since Kyoto exempted developing countries (in order to get any agreement at all), the protocol would have faced certain defeat in the Senate.

George W. Bush's administration withdrew the United States from the Kyoto Protocol in 2001 because the administration's energy proposals, which emphasized increased exploration and development of fossil fuels, were incompatible with the agreement. The Bush administration's EPA also refused to classify carbon dioxide as a pollutant. Doing so would have allowed the EPA to regulate emissions of this gas under the Clean Air Act. The attorney generals of Connecticut, Maine, and Vermont challenged the EPA's decision in court in 2003, suing to force the EPA to regulate carbon dioxide and address climate change. The EPA also denied California's request for a waiver from federal air pollution laws so that the state could regulate greenhouse gases on its own.

In 2007, the U.S. Supreme Court ruled that carbon dioxide was a pollutant under the Clean Air Act, and that the EPA had the authority to regulate it. The court also ruled that the agency had the authority to grant California's waiver. In 2009, the EPA of the Obama administration started the process of developing regulations for carbon dioxide and the president made climate change one of his major priorities in terms of congressional legislation.

The EPA has the authority to move forward and regulate carbon dioxide emissions whether or not Congress enacts climate change legislation. To the extent that Congress might disagree with the EPA's approach, it would be pressured to pass climate change legislation that would then instruct the EPA on what policies Congress preferred it to implement. If the EPA's actions are not acceptable to Congress, the EPA risks a backlash. Congress could repeal the EPA's regulations and severely restrict the EPA's future authority on climate change (and even other environmental issues).

President Obama's economic stimulus package of 2009 allocated funds to develop renewable energy, promote hybrid cars, and make government buildings and private homes more energy efficient. Later that year, at the United Nations summit on climate change in Copenhagen, the leading industrial nations (the United States, China, India, the European Union, Brazil, South Africa, and Japan) set emissions reductions goals, established a system for reporting progress toward meeting those goals, and pledged to fund $100 billion a year by 2020

THE MAJOR congressional debates over climate change policy in the 2000s occurred in the U.S. Senate over proposals to institute a cap-and-trade system for carbon dioxide and greenhouse gases. Cap-and-trade systems were first used for sulfur dioxide in the Clean Air Act of 1990. They allow the government to sell (or give) permits to generators of pollution. Companies that are polluting more than their permits allow must buy more permits from the government or from other companies that have permits. This gives companies an economic incentive to decrease their emissions to avoid paying for more permits. And companies with low emissions can make money by selling their unused permits to the highest bidder.

to help poor countries cope with the effects of climate change. The agreement did not set legally binding emissions limits nor did it include a way to sanction those countries that did not meet their goals. Because it was not a legally binding agreement, it also did not risk rejection by any of the countries' legislatures.

***

Some state governments have stepped into the void created by the lack of a federal climate change policy. For the most part, states have not made a frontal assault on greenhouse gases, but they have passed energy policies to assist their own economic development, with climate change being a secondary benefit. The 1992 Energy Policy Act gave states the ability to create more competition in their electricity markets and to promote alternatives to fossil fuels. By 2009, thirty states had responded by establishing mandatory Renewable Portfolio Standards (RPS), which require utilities to offer certain percentages of power from renewable sources. Five other states had set goals for increases in renewable energy consumption. Likewise, the federal 1991 Intermodal Surface Transportation Efficiency Act gave money to states to develop long-term transportation plans that would include alternative transportation options that would reduce pollution and energy consumption.

While state politicians might be uncertain about or even downright hostile to the science of climate change and the cost it might impose on existing industry, many want to take advantage of opportunities to develop new "green" technologies. We would not expect Texas, for example, to be a leader in alternative energy, given its longstanding association with the oil industry—but it is, in part because it is one of the best places to generate wind power. Other states see alternative energy and green technologies as ways to emphasize quality of life considerations in their marketing to potential residents and "new economy" investors.

States have instituted their own emissions trading programs and empowered their public utility commissions to reward those utilities that increase their offerings of renewable or low-carbon fuels, or develop programs to reduce energy consumption. Six New England states have set regionwide standards with five Canadian provinces. Agricultural states have encouraged farmers to follow conservation tillage practices, which hold more carbon in the soil, thereby decreasing greenhouse gases. (States were promoting conservation tillage anyway, to reduce operating costs and soil erosion).

California has traditionally been a national leader in environmental policy and has continued this innovation in its climate change policy. It adopted regulations covering greenhouse emissions from cars in 2004, created a statewide cap on carbon emissions in 2006, and passed a green building code in 2008. The consequences of these actions are significant. California is the world's eighth largest economy and releases more greenhouse gases per year than many nations, as do other states as well. States that create effective policies to reduce emissions at acceptable cost to the economy also provide models for federal policies on climate change.

Local governments have set goals to reduce greenhouse gas emissions and promote carbon sequestration by setting more stringent building codes, planting trees, improving mass transportation, reducing energy use, and increasing the use of renewable energy sources. New York City Mayor Michael Bloomberg even proposed that drivers pay a "congestion fee" to drive in certain sections of Manhattan at certain times in order to increase the use of public transportation. Although this plan was rejected by the state legislature, Bloomberg did succeed in requiring cab drivers (as well as the city government) to purchase environmentally friendly vehicles.

The Political Dynamics

Global warming burst abruptly onto the political agenda in 1988 during an extremely hot summer. *Time* magazine capped off the year with a twist on its custom of naming the person of the year by instead naming the "Endangered Earth" as the "Planet of the Year." And the United Nations formed the Intergovernmental Panel on Climate Change (IPCC) to serve as a science "court" to evaluate scientific issues regarding climate change. In the late 1980s and early 1990s, scientists dominated the early discussions. Climate change was still a new issue and the question was, what is happening? Public officials and the public itself were still trying to understand the basics. But economics replaced science in the forefront of the debate once the question became, what do we do about it?

Even if politicians broadly accepted that warming is occurring and that humans are causing it, they can still disagree about whether the threat is dangerous enough to warrant spending money to tackle

THOUGH there may be, as political scientist Lamont Hempel describes it, a "tentative and fragile scientific consensus" on the cause and effect relationship between greenhouse gases and climate change, there is enough uncertainty and sufficient opposing scientific voices that policymakers have reason to be cautious as they make decisions. Beyond the divergence of scientific analyses, predicting the effects of climate change on our economy isn't easy, and neither is predicting exactly what will happen if we pass laws that control greenhouse gas emissions. Likewise, anticipating human adaptations to climate change is difficult. Policymakers want to be able to predict demographic, economic, technological, and social trends—and the interactions among all of them. Any analysis this complex is bound to be plagued with uncertainty, and small variations in how the predictions are made can produce substantial differences in the final result. With such divergent scientific and economic analyses available, politicians are free to pick and choose only those results that fit their ideological predispositions and the desires of their constituencies.

it. Policymakers are faced with a sticky situation. If they react, there is a good chance that they will overreact and impose substantial burdens on the economy but produce few measurable environmental impacts. On the other hand, if they don't react because there is no immediate crisis, then there is a chance that they will allow massive, long-term environmental damage and human displacement to occur. Policymakers must decide whether they prefer the risks of inaction or overreaction. In the end, the lack of scientific unanimity or an immediate and incontrovertible crisis makes it easier not to act, and to hope that we can adapt to whatever changes occur.

Greenhouse gases are emitted from many different sources, so regulating only factories and utilities would not have much of an effect (as with nonpoint source pollution, discussed in the chapter on fertilizers). Furthermore, technologies such as smokestack scrubbers, which the U.S. government has mandated factories install for other air pollutants, do not work for carbon dioxide, methane, and other prominent greenhouse gases. If imposing the costs of environmental cleanup on the easiest targets (various industries) is ineffective, policymakers must ask the rest of us to do our part. That's where the real political challenges appear.

Because greenhouse gases are invisible, often occur naturally, and do not produce incidents of clear-cut environmental disaster (like the Gulf of Mexico oil spill or Love Canal), it makes it hard to rally politicians and the public against the villains who emit them. The public sides with environmentalists when confronted with obvious environmental disasters, but it is harder to get the public to demand action on long-term trends like global climate change. Besides, *we* are the "villains"! Even straightforward and less expensive approaches to limiting greenhouse gas emissions, such as conserving energy, could force significant changes in our energy-intensive American lifestyle—from our love affair with cars to our overly heated and air-conditioned buildings. Politicians are loath to impose such costs directly on their constituents, particularly when any direct benefits of slowing global warming are hard to predict. This is especially true when Americans would pay a price, while newly industrializing countries would not face the same emissions cuts and consequent social costs (as would have occurred if the United States had approved the Kyoto Protocol).

It's also true that some of the environmental consequences from the emission of greenhouse gases and other pollutants fall outside a politician's home base, or even outside the country. In 2009 a report from CARE International, in conjunction with a number of other

INACTIVITY by politicians is also the result of a public that is ambivalent about climate change. On one hand, according to Gallup polls, a clear majority agrees that it is a serious problem. On the other hand, in a July 2009 Gallup poll, only 2 percent rated it as the most important issue for the government to address and the one-third of the public that "worries" about it has remained steady in Gallup polls since 1990. In fact, global warming ranked last out of eight environmental concerns, and environmental issues in general declined in their importance relative to economic growth during the 2000s. Without public pressure to act, politicians have every incentive to avoid taking any potentially costly risks to address climate change.

agencies, explained why, as the world gets warmer, poorer countries will be disproportionately affected. Many poorer nations are coastal and very close to sea level, and would be subject to flooding as the oceans rise; countries with large arid regions that are not able to farm as efficiently as others may be under more pressure as rains become even more scarce; and poorer countries have less of an ability to react to natural disasters.

In many ways, global warming exemplifies the fundamental challenge of environmental issues. It's hard to coordinate action among multiple players when each is trying to assure that everyone else is bearing at least as much of the cost as they are. Even if each player knows that they will benefit in the long run, each prefers to avoid paying any of the cost if they can stick someone else with the bill. The United States is worried that it will pay the greatest cost of an international treaty while letting competitors in developing countries (China, India, Brazil) off the hook. The problem, of course, is that it's hard to develop a method of distributing the cost that everyone will see as fair. Some countries—and some U.S. states—have economies that are more dependent on coal and heavy manufacturing than others. In their eyes, climate change proposals that restrict their industries place a disproportionate cost on them and give polluters an incentive to move to countries with fewer restrictions.

Similar dynamics were present in passing clean air and clean water laws in the United States, though it's easy to forget that history now that we take those laws for granted. Until the 1970s, state and local governments had most of the responsibility for developing environmental rules about land and water use. Unfortunately, they had a hard time addressing environmental problems because taking action usually meant confronting a major local employer who was also a major source of jobs, civic philanthropy, and political support. If a local government attempted to regulate the employer, it could threaten to move, shut down, or recruit and fund more supportive politicians. None of these options looked very good to politicians, and made local governments hesitate to do anything without extremely strong backing from the public and from an influential sector of the business community. It took intervention by the federal government in the form of the Clean Air Act and the Clean Water Act to ensure that everyone paid a share of the cost and received a share of the benefits. Now we hear the same concerns about dealing with the costs of climate change.

POLITICIANS are most likely to respond to their constituents who are most active on an issue and who write, call, and show up at town hall meetings to voice their opinions. Business owners and their employees will mobilize to fight for their jobs and will threaten to vote against politicians who help to pass legislation that risks their livelihoods. In the political fight over global warming, there are lots of states and congressional districts that produce coal and natural gas and don't want environmental restrictions. The people who might benefit from future green jobs don't have those jobs yet, so they won't mobilize to support legislation. And the people of less developed countries, who are likely to bear the brunt of the effects of global warming, obviously can't vote here. Even politicians who publicly support climate change legislation will usually leave themselves a critical caveat: they will vote for legislation *if* they are able to get provisions in the legislation that help to protect the particular industries in their states or districts that would be most negatively affected by the legislation. Thus, the climate change bill that passed the House of Representatives in 2009 gave free carbon emission permits to approximately 80 percent of businesses that would otherwise have had to buy them in the cap-and-trade system that the bill established. Such mass exemptions were necessary to gain enough votes to pass the bill, and even then, it passed by the narrowest of margins. While the climate change debate in Washington may appear to be about science, its passage was based on protecting economic interests (jobs) in a representative's or senator's own district or state.

The politics of the environment is polarized, and the attention given to global warming—and environmental issues generally—shifts dramatically depending on which party controls Congress and the presidency. Democrats tend to make environmental issues a priority; Republicans react more skeptically out of a concern over the cost to business and government. For example, Republicans in the House of Representatives never brought climate change legislation to the House floor for debate while they held the majority between 1995 and 2007. Similarly, the fate of environmental legislation in the U.S. Senate shifted dramatically in 2003, when Republicans regained majority control, and the chairmanship of the Environment and Public Works committee shifted from environmentalist Jim Jeffords, an Independent from Vermont, to climate change critic James Inhofe, an Oklahoma Republican. All of a sudden, environmental groups were invited to testify much less frequently on their views of the consequences of proposed legislation to control carbon dioxide emissions. Similar shifts have occurred in the executive branch. When Republican George W. Bush (2001–2009) succeeded Democrat Bill Clinton (1993–2001), for example, the number of published regulations fell by more than 50 percent at the FDA and by 57 percent at the EPA. The agencies also withdrew numerous regulations that had been proposed but not finalized during the Clinton administration. Not coincidently, climate change legislation first passed the House in 2009 after the Democrats had regained majority control of Congress, and a Democratic president, Barack Obama, made it a priority.

Policy Option One: Leave Things as They Are

The best reason to avoid controlling carbon emissions is that, economically, it would be too expensive. Estimates of how much it would cost our economy to implement Kyoto-like protocols to reduce carbon dioxide emissions vary greatly, but there is no question that it would hurt our economy to some extent and put a damper on energy availability. The result would be higher energy bills, and the cost of everything else would go up as well.

Currently, there is some state and local legislation that regulates carbon dioxide emissions (though the EPA could issue regulations, since carbon dioxide can now be considered a pollutant). We should leave it at that.

There is a strong possibility that the data supporting the catastrophic claims made by those who believe that global warming will irrevocably damage this planet has been misinterpreted or is simply false. The assumption that carbon dioxide is associated in a meaningful way with global warming is nothing more than an educated guess. And even if global warming is caused by humans and is altering the earth's climate, we should accept the cost and benefits of just letting it be, as compared to the cost and effort of trying to change it. Our use of fossil fuels will decrease over the years because it must—they're a finite resource. With global warming, there is the potential for some crops to grow better, and it may even be healthier for humans, since more people die every year from cold than from heat.

If there are positive consequences of climate change, we can take advantage of them. The best approach to any negative effects is to adapt to them, if and when it becomes necessary. If the seas start to rise, we can build sea walls to protect critical developed areas. We can use zoning in coastal areas and flood plains to prevent additional development in those risky areas. We can beef up our public health and emergency services planning and personnel. We can provide expertise, technologies, and aid to poor countries that are more severely affected.

Rather than spending money on hypothetical predictions or trying to prevent changes that we may or may not be able to prevent, our efforts are better spent on actual problems as they arise. It's entirely possible that controlling these problems may be cheaper, perhaps much cheaper, than trying to reduce our carbon emissions. Even if carbon dioxide is causing major problems, our efforts to control high levels of this gas now won't prevent problems in the near future. The most optimistic scientists think that it will take decades just to stabilize, let alone reduce, the amount of carbon dioxide in our atmosphere.

Right-Wing Rating ★★★★★ We don't need our industries competing with foreign countries on a playing field that isn't level, especially when we haven't even proven that carbon dioxide emissions can cause the catastrophes that environmental radicals claim. Once again, they are crying "wolf." We shouldn't damage our economy on the basis of highly uncertain computer projections of climate change fifty years or more from now.

Left-Wing Rating ★★ The evidence that climate change is already affecting humans and ecosystems is real. Every scientific objection raised by skeptics has been answered; they just ignore the results or discover a new objection. If we don't do something about climate change now, we'll all pay the price eventually. It's less expensive and less disruptive to act now than to wait until the effects of global warming are severe.

Policy Option Two: Pass Laws to Reduce Greenhouse Gas Emissions

Our federal government has the power to create laws requiring the EPA and other agencies to develop policies that would greatly increase control of greenhouse emissions. Since the courts decided that carbon dioxide can be considered a pollutant, the EPA can now act to restrict emissions. The IPCC has found that certain natural disasters may, in part, have been due to global warming, and there is evidence that global warming will cause worldwide hardships, particularly in less developed countries.

The best way for the government to control these carbon dioxide emissions is to tax them. This approach allows our industries to find the most cost-effective ways to decrease emissions in order to save money on taxes. It also would get businesses and consumers to conserve energy, which is good for our economy and our national security, since we'd be less reliant on oil-rich dictators in unstable parts of the world.

Even though the cost of carbon is going up as our resources become depleted, the government can speed this inflationary process by taxing people and/or industries based on the amount of carbon dioxide they release, or by fining them if they release more than a given amount, or even by shutting down industries that release more than the EPA (or, potentially, another regulatory agency) allows. By artificially making carbon more expensive through legislation, we will really just be accelerating something that would eventually happen anyway. Over time, we will need to find alternatives to fossil fuels, so why not do it sooner rather than later? Carbon dioxide affects more than global warming, it also has the potential to shift the balance in favor of weeds over crops, and decrease the pH of the world's oceans, both of which could have catastrophic effects.

It is important that efforts to reduce emissions are imposed nationally, or better yet, internationally, so that everyone is on a level playing field and businesses don't have an incentive to move to avoid pollution restrictions. The effects of greenhouse gases on the climate are the same, regardless of which state or country produces them.

Right-Wing Rating ★★ We can't increase taxes on U.S. businesses and expect them to be able to compete globally against competitors who play by different rules.

Left-Wing Rating ★★★★★ We need to control emissions, and taxing or capping them is the best way to do it. Taxing carbon allows companies to find the most economically efficient ways to reduce their pollution. We have experience with cap-and-trade methods to reduce sulfur dioxide; we know that it works and that it is not harmful to business.

Policy Option Three: Encourage Use of Technology to Control Greenhouse Gases

Though alternative fuels are usually given top billing (see the chapter on alternative energy), there are many other ways that technology may be able to control carbon dioxide. One radical suggestion is to use concrete to absorb and hold carbon dioxide. Carbon Sense Solutions, a company in Canada, has suggested a method of storing large amounts of carbon dioxide in concrete. Sixty tons of carbon dioxide could be stored per thousand tons of concrete, according to one estimate.

Though alternative fuels are usually given top billing there are many other ways that technology may be able to control carbon dioxide.

We may also be able to control carbon dioxide emissions by getting rid of the places from which these emissions originate. Recently, the concept of growing meat through in vitro methods—in other words in a test tube or petri dish without the use of an actual animal—has taken hold. Growing meat in this way would not only reduce carbon dioxide emissions by up to 80 percent, in large part because the land used for the crops (mostly corn) to feed livestock would no longer be needed, it is also likely to reduce the massive amount of methane produced by cow flatulence (and burping), which is also thought to have a significant effect on global warming. Between planting more trees, using concrete to store carbon dioxide, and doing away with our livestock, perhaps we could control greenhouse gas emissions enough that we wouldn't need to worry about fossil fuels. We could continue to use them as they dwindle and become more expensive than the alternative fuels they compete with.

There are also techniques we could use that wouldn't necessarily affect the amount of carbon dioxide in the atmosphere, but that would, instead, allow us to deal with the warming trend. They would be similar to taking an aspirin to control the pain from a headache without controlling the headache's cause. This is effective, as long as the headache isn't being caused by something terminal. It has been suggested that we release sulfur compounds, or release small reflective particles into the air, to reduce the amount of sunlight reaching the earth. This might work, though we would need to assess what would happen with all this sulfur—it might cause acid rain and other results that are worse than the original problem.

Right-Wing Rating ★★★★★ Technology is always a winner. It allows entrepreneurs to succeed, and it avoids putting restraints on our important industries. Allow science to produce the best solutions to scientific problems.

Left-Wing Rating ★★★ Relying on technology is overly optimistic. The science of technology won't necessarily produce solutions on a scale or timeline appropriate to preventing the effects of climate change. Reducing emissions is a more surefire method.

The Bottom Line

There are some legitimate reasons to question the extent to which global warming is occurring because of human activities. Yet, while there isn't absolute proof that we are causing this warming, carbon dioxide and other greenhouse gases do provide the most reasonable explanation. If we choose to reject these gases as the primary cause of global warming, then we are relegated to pointing to somewhat more inexact natural cycles that may have something to do with the sun, volcanoes, or something completely different. As of yet, these potential causes haven't clearly demonstrated themselves as capable of causing the changes we are now seeing. This doesn't mean that these natural cycles aren't the main reason why the earth is warming, but the science needs to be fleshed out quite a bit

It's hard to argue that the environment wouldn't benefit long term from a reduction in carbon dioxide, regardless of whether it is actually the most prevalent cause of global warming.

more before they are as good a suspect as carbon dioxide and other greenhouse gases.

Concerns about social disruption and the rising costs of energy are certainly reasons to avoid controlling carbon dioxide emissions, and it's hard to argue that controlling these emissions would help our economy in the short term. But, likewise, it's hard to argue that the environment wouldn't benefit long term from a reduction in carbon dioxide, regardless of whether it is actually the most prevalent cause of global warming.

While many point to global warming as *the* reason to regulate carbon emissions, the truth is that there are actually many other compelling reasons to cut these emissions. Carbon dioxide is produced largely from burning fossil fuels and fossil fuels come from sources that are finite. We must conserve them or lose them. They are also frequently found in regions of the world that are not politically stable, and the governments in a number of these regions are not the best allies of the United States. Additionally, the increase in carbon dioxide in our atmosphere has the potential to alter how crops grow and their interactions with weeds, and to change the acidity of our oceans. These are powerful reasons, in and of themselves, to try and regulate the amount of carbon dioxide in our air.

CHAPTER 12

Conclusions: Balancing Nature and Politics

P. J. O'ROURKE, the political satirist, once wrote: "The college idealists who fill the ranks of the environmental movement seem willing to do absolutely anything to save the biosphere, except take science courses and learn something about it." This may be the truest thing ever said about our environmental problems, but it doesn't just apply to college idealists. Many people claim to love the environment, yet few spend the serious amount of time needed to understand the issues or the various sides of any argument, including the side that they claim to support. If there's a unifying message in this book, it is this: don't be one of those people.

Our personal ideological perspectives, such as whether we identify ourselves as liberal or conservative, right wing or left wing, help us sort out the role we think government should play in society. But the flip side of this identification is that it ends up providing us with prejudgments about whether certain problems exist and the best way to solve them, rather than helping us to find and evaluate the evidence that we need to make informed decisions. Instead, seek out and evaluate evidence with an open mind. Don't take the easy way out by only looking for information and perspectives that confirm your preexisting assumptions.

You can't influence public policy just by being knowledgeable, however. Woody Allen once said that 90 percent of life is just showing up. Politics is similar: those who show up and attempt to make a difference can have an outsized influence. Sometimes, when public officials are intimidated by an uninformed sector of the public that is raising a ruckus, they decide it's not worth the effort to push back and oppose the loudmouths. Political action is more effective, however, when you know what you're talking about, and not only understand the merits of your own position, but know enough about the opposing perspective that you can intelligently refute it.

Government officials and scientists generally work hard to uncover as much relevant information as they can on issues they think are important. But science doesn't always produce results that provide clear evidence about which policies will work effectively; more often it raises questions and makes developing a political consensus more difficult. Often, the best government officials can do is gather knowledge, make predictions about what a certain policy will do, and then apply this knowledge to their value systems. Rarely does this result in easy answers that please everybody. A clear scientific consensus can sometimes rally the public and the politicians to make tough choices, but sometimes the scientific consensus gets ignored if the economic or value tradeoffs seem too steep.

The U.S. Constitution purposely makes change difficult, with or without scientific or public consensus. Through much of our nation's history, advocates of environmental protection were frustrated by these barriers to change. Before the 1960s and 1970s, businesses consistently won on environmental issues because they were organized and had the incentive to fight intensely to avoid paying for their pollution. The public wanted business to clean up, but since the costs of pollution were widely spread, few people felt strongly enough to do anything about it.

The numerous laws discussed in the preceding chapters show that change is possible, even if it is not at the pace or the scale that some would like. In most cases, the history of these environmental laws provides evidence that political leadership matters. Public policy usually changes in ways that benefit the general public and overturn the advantages of special interests when public figures, especially presidents, lead the charge. Leaders must take advantage of crisis events and the media spotlight on an issue in order to define for the public how current policies benefit the special interests, and how and why change would benefit the public. The alliance between the leader, the interest groups, and the temporarily engaged public is the key to overcoming the barriers to change inherent in our political system.

In the end, most of the answers to our environmental issues don't come from the left wing or the right wing, but rather from a compromise between the two. We are often better off trying to find a compromise that everyone can live with rather than trying to make the other side capitulate. Compromise is almost always necessary to move policy along in our political system. And, from the perspective of someone who wants to move things along, compromise is a good thing. But it is not an end in itself. Often, the key compromises that legislators seek in exchange for their votes are those that provide special protection, exemptions, or benefits to the industries in their states or districts. Pragmatists see this as a necessary evil: if you want to pass legislation, you do what you have to do to get the votes. Nevertheless, many citizens are turned off because they see this as a violation of principles. It's one thing to compromise between competing principles; it's another to just compromise your principles out of expediency. Likewise, compromise is not worthwhile if it leads to a policy that is so weak it doesn't achieve its goals and is not worth the investment of resources necessary to implement it. The question is whether the compromise is an improvement over the status quo. Knowledge about the issue and the policy alternatives will help you make that judgment.

All of us love to debate about where our environment is going, and why it's going there, but most of the information that we spew is superficial because, by and large, the information that is readily available to us comes from people who want to push us one way or the other. The authors of this information avoid trying to offer us the whole, complex picture, preferring to focus on the few bits that support their values. What we end up seeing is a terribly oversimplified picture of the situation.

We hope this book has helped you to see the other side of the equation. But maybe you don't trust some of the things we've said. Perhaps, despite our best efforts, you think we're biased! Well, we consider it healthy to be skeptical. This book wasn't written to help you reach definitive conclusions, it was written to encourage you to think about the possible benefits and drawbacks of different environmental policies that our government could adopt and to consider factors that you may not have considered before. Your authors have undoubtedly missed some important ideas for policy change. But science and government are dynamic forces. Between the time that we wrote this book and when you picked it up, more research and more politics have occurred that could apply to the topics we've covered. And more topics have arisen. Go find them. Think of other possibilities. Let this be a starting place, not an ending.

★★★

Notes

PAGE

Introduction

15. political party affiliation: Dunlap 2009.
16. 70-point gulf: Klyza and Sousa 2008, 22–23.
16. consistently voting conservative: Theriault 2008.
17. passed between 1991 and 2006: Klyza and Sousa 2008.

Chapter 1

21. "emotional hell-raising": Browne 2001, 143.
22. more important than documents: Whiteman 1995.
22. real people's lives: Stone 2002; West and Loomis 1998.
24 eleven Senate committees: Rosenbaum 2005, 72.
26. based on insufficient data: Rosenbaum 2005.
28. inappropriate studies: Mooney 2005.
28. delay or avoid government regulation: Mooney 2005.
30. the 1950s and 1960s: Bosso 1987, 91–94.
30. would react negatively: Richtel 2009.
31. evidence in their advertising: Libby 1998.
32. "passive consensus": Rosenbaum 2005, 54.
32. "the most important issue": Morales 2009.
33. sound public policy: Smith 2000.

Chapter 2

35. $23 billion in 2009: USDA 2009.
37. toxic to certain plants: Epstein and Bassein 2001.
38. greater environmental effect: Kovach et al. 1992.
38. organic pesticides have been found: Newsome and Shields 1980; Ryan, Pilon, and Leduc 1982.
38. significantly alter this percentage: Baker et al. 2002.

39. uncomposted manure: Kudva, Blanch, and Hovde 1998.
39. from nonorganic sources: Mukherjee et al. 2004.
39. evidence to support that: Worthington 2001.
39. which tend to be lower: Williams 2002; Rosen and Allen 2007; Asami et al. 2003; Carbonaro et al. 2002.
39. difference is not consistent: Rosen and Allan 2007.
39. provide any health benefits: Dangour et al. 2009; Rosen and Allen 2007; Magkos, Arvaniti, and Zampelas 2003.
40. they are grown organically: Caretto et al. 2008; Kopsell et al. 2004.
40. food was produced organically: Magkos, Arvaniti, and Zampelas 2003.
40. health problems in cattle: Dohoo et al. 2003.
40. milk from untreated cows: Juskevich and Guyer 1990.
40. some human cancers: Yu et al. 2002.
40. finds its way to the stomach: U.S. Food and Drug Administration 2009.
44. ran a story: Lavigne 2006a, b.
44. organic producers and processors: Neuman 2010.
45. "not prepared to do that": Cloud 1990, 1265.
51. with hot water: Holland et al. 1994.
51. organic food is elitist: DeGregori 2003.

Chapter 3

60. unblemished foods: Pimentel 2009.
62. non-Hodgkin's lymphoma: Buckley et al. 2000.
62. and pancreatic cancer: Andreotti et al. 2009.
62. over 100,000 participants: Ascherio et al. 2006.
62. around the home: Whyatt et al. 2004.
63. the population at large: Blair 2005.
63. decrease in colon cancer: Lee et al. 2007.
63. to become hermaphrodites: Hayes et al. 2002.
64. creatures will be killed: Relyea 2005.
65. close to an agricultural field: Hayes et al. 2010.
65. as they normally would: Relyea 2009.
66. affecting their lives: Tierney et al. 2008.
68. coming onto the market: Bosso 1987.
68. validity of the information: Bosso 1987.
71. "weight of scientific evidence": Bosso 1987, 161
75. to get skin cancer: Freedman et al. 1997.

Chapter 4

81. now phosphorus free: Struss 2007.
82. highly debatable theory: Smil 2001.
83. is applied worldwide: Raun and Johnson 1999.
84. double the number in 1990: Clemmitt 2005.
84. "in surface or groundwater": Gross, Angle, and Welterlen 1990.
85. phosphorus in runoff water: Dittrich et al. 2003.
85. enters a body of water: Schultz et al. 1995; Patty, Réal, and Gril 1997; Lee, Isenhart, and Schultz 2003.
85. becoming more popular: Wendt and Burwell 1985.
87. after the law had passed: Cooper 2000.
87. "pollution budget": Copeland 2008.
87. from the court to do it: U.S. EPA 2009.
88. during a given time: Hartman, Alcock, and Pettit 2008.
89. acted on since: Copeland 2008.
92. enforcement actions: Rabe 2004, 17.
92. from the state government: Klyza and Sousa 2008.
93. water many miles away: Pew Oceans Commission 2003.
94. phosphorus will start to dwindle: Cordell, Drangert, and White 2009.

Chapter 5

98. wind, solar, and biomass power: U.S. Department of Energy 2009.
99. current demand for gasoline: Hill et al. 2006.
100. would be generated: Hill et al. 2006.
100. and that's a problem: Andreoli and De Souza 2006–2007.
100. than any other crop: Pimentel 2003.
101. used to make it: Hill et al. 2006.
101. ethanol a more significant fuel source: Dias De Oliveira 2005.
102. between 15 and 28 percent: Rajagopal et al. 2009.
102. that amount of time: Kanellos 2009.
103. takes a lot of power: Schenk et al. 2008.
103. 3.5 cents for natural gas: Schilling and Esmundo 2009.
104. geothermal and wind: Schilling and Esmundo 2009.
104. using their own stills: Bettelheim 2006.
105. risen to 2.6 percent: U.S. Energy Information Administration 2009.

Chapter 6

114. "GM Bacteria Could Kill All Life": *Evening Post* (New Zealand) and *Christchurch Press*, 2 February 2001.
114. probably wouldn't survive: Walter et al. 2001.
114. "false claims about the ecological impact": Fletcher 2001.
116. in certain situations: Kunik et al. 2001.
116. eat the tomatoes: Roueche 1991.
117. 88 percent of the cotton: USDA 2009.
117. contain some GE material: Becker 2005.
118. China, Australia, and other countries: Head et al. 2005; Pray, Huang, and Qiao 2001; Fitt 2003.
118. modified to resist insects: Huang et al. 2005.
119. no human was ever affected: Nordlee et al. 1996.
119. psoralens that the plants contained: Ames and Gold 2000.
119. digestive system of rats: Ewen and Pusztai 1999.
119. dangerous in humans: Prescott et al. 2005.
119. some of their organs: Finamore et al. 2008; Malatesta et al. 2008; Velimirov, Binter, and Zentek 2008; Kilic and Aday 2008.
120. Roundup Ready gene: Quist and Chapela 2001.
120. identified in Oregon in 2006: Reichman et al. 2006.
120. from transgenic canola: Warwick et al. 2008.
120. exposure to this herbicide: Gunsolus 2008; Ulloa and Owen 2009.
120. use in transgenic cotton: Tabashnik et al. 2008.
121. it can kill them: Hansen and Obrycki 2000.
121. they wouldn't survive: Dunham et al. 1999.
122. an increase in pesticide use: Phipps and Park 2002.
122. changed its original stance: U.S. Regulatory Agencies 2009.
124. response to public pressure: Vogel 1995.
124. Europeans themselves admitted: Vogel 1995.
125. producers and distributors is minimal: Paarlberg 2010.
125. dominant political party: Vogel 1995.
125. the proregulation coalition: Libby 1998.
126. consumers will reject it: Libby 1998.
127. contaminated corn seed: Hosansky 2001a; Segarra and Rawson 2001.
133. "shortcomings in the studies": European Food and Safety Authority 2008.

Chapter 7

134. quality of reblooming: Cook 1931.
136. problems with White's patent: Huff 1999.
138. didn't warrant a patent: Wiser 1999.
138. distribute these beans: ETC Group 2009.
141. impact of this case: Pollack 2010.
142. to last the entire time: U.S. Patent and Trademark Office 2005.
142. R&D in 2006: Biotechnology Industry Organization 2008.
142. between 2003 and 2007: Biotechnology Industry Organization 2008.
143. people in the United States: Biotechnology Industry Organization 2008.
144. between 1983 and 2004: Jost 2006.
147. broken beyond repair: ETC Group 2009.

Chapter 8

152. arthropods (insects and mites): Pimentel et al. 2000.
152. that have been introduced: Westbrooks 2004.
153. a single species is present: Tilman 2000.
153. very rarely the case: Davis 2009.
153. His answer: "Zero": Breining 2010.
154. twice as fast as sugar maples: Kloeppel and Abrams 1995.
154. from native sugar maples: Webb, Pendergast, and Dwyer 2001.
154. built dams and mills: Walker and Merritts 2009.
154. more effectively than other plants: Ziska 2003; Ziska and George 2004.
155. "Brave New Ecology": Del Tredici 2006.
156. pests that are already here: Hosansky 2001b.
157. 5 percent of U.S. imports: Prah 2006.
157. other pests each year: Hosansky 2001b.
161. predation by invasive species: Cooper 1999.
162. that family causes problems: Hosansky 2001b.
165. beneficial to our health: Moerman 2009.
166. during 2003 and 2004: Connecticut Green Industries.

Chapter 9

170. died in 1998: Brown, A. 1998; Ostrom 1997.
170. ibogaine and noribogaine: Kubiliene et al. 2008.
170. making the user stoned: Iversen 2000.

171. mothers who smoke it: Zuckerman et al. 1989.
171. tasks like reading: Huestegge 2009.
171. car, train, or other vehicle: Ashton 2001.
171. damaging their brains: Yücel et al. 2008.
171. or even worse than, tobacco: Wu et al. 1988.
171. marijuana in 2004: Katel 2009.
171. even a heart attack: Spengos, Schwartz, and Hennerici 2000; Borowiak et al. 1998.
171. particularly the cerebellum: Xu et al. 2000.
171. it could just kill you: Violeta et al. 2006.
171. nausea (as for Ralph Seeley): Söderpalm, Schuster, and DeWitt 2001.
171. appetite of AIDS patients: Beal et al. 1995.
171. treatment of glaucoma: Tomida, Pertwee, and Azuara-Blanco 2004.
171. ability to help control pain: Russo 2008.
171. for migraine headaches: Russo 1998.
171. once a month or more: Schwartz, Voth, and Sheridan 1997.
171. control substance addictions: Maisonneuve and Glick 2003.
171. had done in their lives: Griffiths et al. 2008; Shiue 2010.
172. target for government restrictions: Musto 1999.
172. not vigorously enforced: Katel 2009.
174. a five-year sentence: Katel 2009.
174. on criminal records: NORML 2009b.
174. using marijuana as medicine: Katel 2009.
175. considered socially marginal: Musto 1999.
176. permit medical marijuana: NORML 2009b.
176. initiatives approved by voters: author's calculation based on data available from NORML 2009a.
177. scientific analysis of medical marijuana: Marshall 2005.
178. grounds for passage are not fertile: National Conference of State Legislatures 2009.
178. 36 percent in 2005: Carroll 2005.

Chapter 10

184. the slammer that Sunday: Sullivan 2008; Tillman 2008.
185. was so weak: Rappaport 1993.
185. the right-of-way: Brenneman 2009; Carlsson 2009.
186. aren't well landscaped: Wolf 2009.
186. nicely landscaped house: Stigarll and Elam 2009.

186. in the United States: U.S. Department of Commerce 2008, Table 414.
187. animals in urban yards: Jost 1995.
189. federal housing guidelines: Dilger 1992.
189. in the street during certain hours: Blakely and Snyder 1997; Dilger 1992; McKenzie 1994.
191. "misdeeds of one's neighbors": McKenzie 1994, 14.

Chapter 11

196. these synthetic gases: Andino and Rowland 1999.
197. glaciers in the Arctic: Josberger, March, and O'Neel 2009.
197. South America: Steitz et al. 2003.
197. the Himalayas: Ren et al. 2004.
197. and in Africa: Ansari 2009.
197. find cooler climates: Lenoir et al. 2008.
197. tropics are expanding: Lovett 2007.
197. do not seem to be warming: Doran et al. 2002; Turner et al. 2005.
199. as much carbon as a forest: Post and Kwon 2000.
200. concentrations of carbon dioxide: Soon 2007.
200. was not taking place: Swanson et al. 2009.
201. an overwhelming majority: Soon 2007.
201. we've already seen: Erlykin, Sloan, and Wolfendale 2009.
201. at least to some degree: Ravilious 2007.
201. "caused mostly by human activities": Kaufman 2010.
202. left in the ground: Reich et al. 2006.
202. a significant problem: Zhu et al. 2008.
203. in alkaline seas: Doney et al. 2009.
204. regulations for carbon dioxide: Broder 2009.
205. a secondary benefit: Rabe 2004.
205. renewable energy consumption: Pew Center on Global Climate Change 2009.
205. generate wind power: Rabe 2004.
205. reduce energy consumption: Rabe 2004; Pew Center on Global Climate Change 2009.
206. green building code in 2008: Greenblatt 2009.
206. as do other states as well: Rabe 2004, 5.
206. renewable energy sources: Greenblatt 2009.
207. "fragile scientific consensus": Hempel 2006.
208. a serious problem: Saad 2009a.

208. July 2009 Gallup poll: Morales 2009.
208. Gallup polls since 1990: Newport 2008.
208. eight environmental concerns: Saad 2009b.
208. during the 2000s: Newport 2009.
209. disproportionately affected: Warner et al. 2009.
211. control carbon dioxide emissions: Bosso 2005.
211. 57 percent at the EPA: Weeks 2009.
211. economy to some extent: Energy Information Administration 1998.
212. from cold than from heat: Lomborg 2007.
214. according to one estimate: Hamilton 2008.
214. up to 80 percent: Ford 2009.
215. might cause acid rain: Blackstock et al. 2009.

Chapter 12

218. lead the charge: Wilson 1980.

★★★

Bibliography

Ames, B. N., and L. S. Gold. 2000. Paracelsus to parascience: the environmental cancer distraction. *Mutation Research* 447: 3–13.

Andino, J. M., and F. S. Rowland. 1999. Chlorofluorocarbons (CFCs) are heavier than air, so how do scientists suppose that these chemicals reach the altitude of the ozone layer to adversely affect it? *Scientific American*, 21 October. http://www.scientificamerican.com/article.cfm?id=chlorofluorocarbons-cfcs#comments.

Andreoli, C., and S. De Souza. 2006–2007. Sugarcane: the best alternative for converting solar and fossil energy into ethanol. *Economy and Energy* 9:59. http://ecen.com/eee59/eee59e/sugarcane_the_best_alternative_for_converting_solar_and_fossil_energy_into_ethanol.htm.

Andreotti, G., L. E. Beane Freeman, L. Hou, J. Coble, J. Rusiecki, J. A. Hoppin, D. T. Silverman, and M. C. R. Alavanja. 2009. Agricultural pesticide use and pancreatic cancer risk in the Agricultural Health Study Cohort. *International Journal for Cancer* 124: 2495-2500.

Ansari, A. 2009. Glaciers disappearing from Kilimanjaro. CNN. http://www.cnn.com/2009/TECH/science/11/02/kilimanjaro.glaciers/index.html.

Archer, D. 2007. *Global Warming: Understanding the Forecast*. Malden, MA: Blackwell Publishing.

Asami, D. K., Y. J. Hong, D. M. Barrett, and A. E. Mitchell. 2003. Comparison of the total phenolic and ascorbic acid content of freeze-dried and air-dried marionberry, strawberry, and corn using conventional, organic, and sustainable agricultural practices. *Journal of Agricultural and Food Chemistry* 51(5): 1237–1241.

Ascherio, A., H. Chen, M. Weisskopf, E. O'Reilly, M. McCullough, E. Calle, M. Schwarzschild, and M. Thun. 2006. Pesticide exposure and risk for Parkinson's disease. *Annals of Neurology* 60(2): 197–203.

Ashton, C. 2001. Pharmacology and effects of cannabis: a brief review. *The British Journal of Psychiatry* 178: 101–106.

Baker, B. P., C. M. Benbrook, E. Groth III, and K. L. Benbrook. 2002. Pesticide residues in conventional, integrated pest management (IPM)-grown and organic foods: insights from three U.S. data sets. *Food Additives and Contaminants* 19(5): 427–446.

Beal J., R. Olson, L. Laubenstein, J. Morales, P. Bellman, B. Yangco, L. Lefkowitz, T. Plasse, and K. Shepard. 1995. Dronabinol as a treatment for anorexia associated with weight loss in patients with AIDS. *Journal of Pain Symptom Management* 10: 89–97.

Becker, G. S. 2005. Agricultural biotechnology: background and recent issues. Congressional Research Service, 7 March.

Bettelheim, A. 2006. Biofuels boom: can ethanol satisfy America's thirst for foreign oil? *CQ Researcher* 16(34).

Biotechnology Industry Organization (BIO). 2008. Guide to biotechnology 2008. http://bio.org/speeches/pubs/er/BiotechGuide2008.pdf.

Blackstock, J., D. Battisti, K. Caldeira, D. Eardley, J. Katz, D. Keith, A. Patrinos, D. Schrag, R. Socolow, and S. Koonin. 2009. Climate engineering responses to climate emergencies (Novim). http://arxiv.org/pdf/0907.5140.

Blair, A., D. Sandler, R. Tarone, J. Lubin, K. Thomas, J. Hoppin, C. Samanic, J. Coble, F. Kamel, and C. Knott. 2005. Mortality among participants in the agricultural health study. *Annals of Epidemiology* 15(4): 279–285.

Blakely, E. J., and M. G. Snyder. 1997. *Fortress America: Gated Communities in the United States*. Washington: Brookings Institution.

Borowiak, K., K. Ciechanowski, and P. Waloszczyk. 1998. Psilocybin mushroom (*Psilocybe semilanceata*) intoxication with myocardial infarction. *Journal of Toxicology and Clinical Toxicology* 36: 47–49.

Bosso, C. J. 1987. *Pesticides and Politics: The Life Cycle of a Public Issue*. Pittsburgh: University of Pittsburgh Press.

Bosso, C. J. 2005. *Environment, Inc.: From Grassroots to the Beltway*. Lawrence: University of Kansas Press.

Breining, G. 2010. The carp are coming. *Star Tribune*, 24 January.

Brenneman, R. 2009. Conflicting versions mark case of the errant victory gardens. *The Berkeley Daily Planet*, 25 June.

Broder, J. M. 2009. EPA moves to curtail greenhouse gas emissions. *New York Times*, 30 September. www.nytimes.com.

Brown, A. 1998. Comment: In memoriam: Ralph Seely: Obscured by smoke: Medicinal marijuana and the need for representation reinforcement review. *Seattle University Law Review* 176.

Browne, W. P. 2001. *The Failure of National Rural Policy*. Washington: Georgetown University Press.

Buckley, J. D., A. T. Meadows, M. E. Kadin, M. M. Le Beau, S. Siegel, and L. L. Robison. 2000. Pesticide exposures in children with non-Hodgkin lymphoma. *Cancer* 89(11): 2315–2321.

Carbonaro, M., M. Mattera, S. Nicoli, P. Bergamo, and M. Cappellone. 2002. Modulation of antioxidant compounds in organic vs. conventional fruit (peach, *Prunus persica* L., and pear, *Pyrus communis* L.). *Journal of Agricultural and Food Chemistry* 50: 5458–5462.

Caretto, S., A. Parente, F. Serio, and P. Santamaria. 2008. Influence of potassium and genotype on vitamin E content and reducing sugar of tomato fruits. *HortScience* 43(7): 2048–2051.

Carlsson, C. 2009. Food bad, lawns good? Berkeley bureaucrats target transition activist. sf.streetsblog.org. http://sf.streetsblog.org/2009/06/04/food-bad-lawns-good-berkeley-bureaucrats-target-transition-activist/.

Carroll, J. 2005. Who supports marijuana legislation? Gallop Polls. http://www.gallup.com/poll/19561/Who-Supports-Marijuana-Legalization.aspx.

Clemmitt, M. 2005. Saving the oceans: is more action needed to stem pollution and overfishing? *CQ Researcher* 15(39).

Clemmitt, M. 2009. Energy and climate: should carbon-based fuels be phased out? *CQ Researcher* 19(26).

Cloud, D. S. 1990. Agricultural semantics. *CQ Weekly Reports*, April 28.

Connecticut Green Industries. Economic impact of banning plants. http://www.flowersplantsinct.com/invasive_index.htm.

Cook, R. C. 1931. The first plant patent. *Journal of Heredity* 22: 313–319.

Cooper, M. H. 1999. Endangered Species Act: does it put an unfair burden on landowners? *CQ Researcher* 9(37).

Cooper, M. H. 2000. Water quality: are the government's new pollution rules fair? *CQ Researcher* 10(41).

Copeland, C. 2008. Clean Water Act and Total Maximum Daily Loads (TMDLs) of pollutants. Congressional Research Service, 25 August.

Cordell, D., J. Drangert, and S. White. 2009. The story of phosphorus: global food security and food for thought. *Global Environmental Change* 19(2): 292–305.

Dangour, A., S. Dodhia, A. Hayter, E. Allen, K. Lock, and R. Uauy. 2009. Nutritional quality of organic foods: a systematic review. *The American Journal of Clinical Nutrition* doi:10.3945/ajcn.2009.28041.

Davis, M. 2009. *Invasion Biology*. New York: Oxford University Press.

DeGregori, T. 2003. *The Origins of the Organic Agriculture Debate*. Ames, Iowa: Iowa State Press.

Del Tredici, P. 2006. Brave new ecology. *Landscape Architecture*. February.

Dessler, A. E., and E. A. Parson. 2006. *The Science and Politics of Global Climate Change: A Guide to the Debate*. New York: Cambridge University Press.

Dias De Oliveira, M., B. Vaughan,and E. Rykiel. 2005. Ethanol as fuel: energy, carbon dioxide balances, and ecological footprint. *BioScience* 55(7): 593–602.

Dilger, R. J. 1992. *Neighborhood Politics: Resident Community Associations in American Governance*. New York: New York University Press.

Dittrich, T., L. Geohring, M. Walter, and T. Steenhuis. 2003. Revisiting buffer strip design standards for remodeling dissolved and particulate phosphorus. Total Maximum Daily Load (TMDL) Environmental Regulations–II Proceedings: 527–534.

Dohoo, I. R., L. DesCôteaux, K. Leslie, A. Fredeen, P. Dowling, A. Preston, and W. Shewfelt. 2003. A meta-analysis review of the effects of recombinant bovine somatotropin. *Canadian Journal of Veterinary Research* 67(4): 241–251.

Doney, S., V. Fabry, R. Feely, and J. Kleypas. 2009. Ocean acidification: the other CO2 problem. *Annual Review of Marine Science* 1: 169–192.

Doran, P. T., J. C. Priscu, W. Berry Lyons, J. E. Walsh, A. G. Fountain, D. M. McKnight, D. L. Moorhead, R. A. Virginia, D. H. Wall, G. D. Clow, C. H. Fritsen, C. P. McKay, and A. N. Parsons. 2002. Antarctic climate cooling and terrestrial ecosystem response. *Nature* 415: 517–520.

Dunham R., C. Chitmanat, A. Nichols, B. Argue, D. Powers, and T. Chen. 1999. Predator avoidance of transgenic channel catfish containing salmonid growth hormone genes. *Marine Biotechnology* 1(6): 545–551.

Dunlap, R. E. 2009. Climate-change views: Republican-Democratic gaps expand. Gallup Polls, May 29. http://www.gallup.com/poll/107569/ClimateChange-Views-RepublicanDemocratic-Gaps-Expand.aspx.

Energy Information Administration, Department of Energy. 1998. What does the Kyoto Protocol mean to U.S. energy markets and the U.S. economy? A briefing paper on the energy information administration's analysis and report prepared for the committee on science, U.S. House of Representatives.

Epstein, L., and S. Bassein. 2001. Pesticide applications of copper on perennial crops in California, 1993 to 1998. *Journal of Environmental Quality* 30: 1844–1847.

Erlykin, A. D., T. Sloan, and A. W. Wolfendale. 2009. Solar activity and mean global temperature. *Environmental Research Letters* 4:014004.

ETC Group. 2009. Enola patent considered invalid: haven't we been here before? ETC Group News Release, 14 July.

European Food and Safety Authority. 2008. Safety and nutritional assessment of GM plants and derived food and feed: the role of animal feeding trials. *Food and Chemical Toxicology* 46: S2–S70.

Ewen, S. W. B., and A. Pusztai. 1999. Effects of diets containing genetically modified potatoes containing *Galanthus nivalis lectin* on rat small intestines. *Lancet* 354: 9187.

Finamore, A., M. Roselli, S. Britti, G. Monastra, R. Ambra, A. Turrini, and E. Mengheri. 2008. Intestinal and peripheral immune response to MON 810 maize ingestion in weaning and old mice. *Journal of Agricultural and Food Chemistry* 56(23): 11533–11539.

Fitt, G. P. 2003. Implementation and impact of transgenic Bt cottons in Australia. In *Cotton Production for the New Millennium*, Proceedings of the Third World Cotton Research Conference.

Fletcher, L. 2001. New Zealand GMO debacle undermines green lobby. *Nature Biotechnology* 19: 292.

Ford, M. 2009. In-vitro meat: would lab-burgers be better for us and the planet? CNN. http://www.cnn.com/2009/TECH/science/08/07/eco.invitro.meat/index.html.

Freedman, D. M., S. H. Zahm, and M. Dosemeci. 1997. Residential and occupational exposure to sunlight and mortality from non-Hodgkin's lymphoma: composite (threefold) case-control study. *Bio-Medical Journal* 314: 1451.

Greenblatt, A. 2009. Confronting warming: can states and localities prevent climate change? *CQ Researcher* 19(1).

Griffiths, R., W. Richards, M. Johnson, U. McCann, and R. Jesse. 2008. Mystical-type experiences occasioned by psilocybin mediate the attribution of personal meaning and spiritual significance 14 months later. *Journal of Psychopharmacology* 22(6): 621–632.

Gross, C. M., J. S. Angle, and M. S. Welterlen. 1990. Nutrient and sediment losses from turfgrass. *Journal of Environmental Quality* 19(4): 663–668.

Gunsolus, J. 2008. Glyphosate-resistant weeds in Minnesota. *The Farmer*. 9 May.

Hamilton, T. 2008. A Concrete Fix to Global Warming. *Technology Review*, 23 July 2008. http://www.technologyreview.com/energy/21117/?a=f.

Hansen, L., and J. Obrycki. 2000. Field deposition of Bt transgenic corn pollen: lethal effects on the monarch butterfly. *Oecologia* 125(2): 241–248.

Hartman, R., F. Alcock, and C. Pettit. 2008. The spread of fertilizer ordinances in Florida. *Sea Grant Law and Policy Journal* 1(1): 98–11

Hayes, T. B., A. Collins, M. Lee, M. Mendoza, N. Noriega, A. A. Stuart, and A. Vonk. 2002. Hermaphroditic, demasculinized frogs after exposure to the herbicide atrazine at low ecologically relevant doses. *Proceedings of the National Academy of Sciences of the United States of America* 99(8): 5476–5480.

Hayes, T. B., V. Khoury, A. Narayan, M. Nazir, A. Park, T. Brown, L. Adame, E. Chan, D. Buchholz, T. Stueve, and S. Gallipeau. 2010. Atrazine induces complete feminization and chemical castration in male African clawed frogs (*Xenopus laevis*). *Proceedings of the National Academy of Sciences of the United States of America* 107(10): 4612–4617.

Head, G., W. Moar, M. Eubanks, B. Freeman, J. Ruberson, A. Hagerty, and S. Turnipseed.2005. A multiyear, large-scale comparison of arthropod populations on commercially managed Bt and non-Bt cotton fields. *Environmental Entomology* 34(5): 1257–1266.

Hempel, L. C. 2006. Climate policy on the installment plan. In *Environmental Policy: New Directions for the Twenty-First Century*, 6th ed. Ed. Norman J. Vig and Michael E. Kraft. Washington: CQ Press.

Hill, J., E. Nelson, D. Tilman, S. Polasky, and D. Tiffany. 2006. Environmental, economic, and energetic costs and benefits of biodiesel and ethanol biofuels. *Proceedings of the National Academy of Sciences* 103: 11206–11210.

Holland, P. T., D. Hamilton, B. Ohlin, and M. W. Skidmore. 1994. Effects of storage and processing on pesticide residues in plant products. *Pure and Applied Chemistry* 66(2): 335–356.

Hosansky, D. 2001a. Biotech foods: should they be more strictly regulated? *CQ Researcher* 11(12).

Hosansky, D. 2001b. Invasive species: can harmful foreign plants and animals be stopped? *CQ Researcher* 11(34).

Huang, J., R. Hu, S. Rozelle, and C. Pray. 2005. Insect-resistant GM rice in farmers' fields: assessing productivity and health effects in China. *Science* 308(5722): 688–690.

Huestegge, L. 2009. Long-term effects of cannabis on oculomotor function in humans. *Journal of Psychopharmacology* 23(6): 714–722.

Huff, D. 1999. Regarding the public hearing being conducted by the United States Patent and Trademark Office regarding the issue of identification of prior art during the examination of a patent application. http://www.uspto.gov/web/offices/com/hearings/priorart/comments2.doc.

Iversen, L. 2000. *The Science of Marijuana*. New York: Oxford University Press.

Josberger, E., R. March, and S. O'Neel. 2009. Fifty-year record of glacier change reveals shifting climate in the Pacific Northwest and Alaska, USA. *USGS Fact Sheet 2009–3046*.

Jost, K. 1995. Property rights: do government regulations infringe on landowners' rights? *CQ Researcher* 5(22).

Jost, K. 2006. patent disputes: does the system help or hurt innovation? *CQ Researcher* 16(44).

Juskevich, J. C., and C. G. Guyer. 1990. Bovine growth hormone: human food safety evaluation. *Science* 249: 875–884.

Kanellos, M. 2009. Algae biodiesel: it's $33 a gallon. Greentechmedia. http://www.greentechmedia.com/articles/read/algae-biodiesel-its-33-a-gallon-5652.

Katel, P. 2009. Legalizing marijuana: should pot be treated like alcohol and taxed? *CQ Researcher* 19(22).

Kaufman, L. 2010. Among weathercasters, doubt on warming. *New York Times*, 29 March.

Kilic A., and M. Aday. 2008. A three generational study with genetically modified Bt corn in rats: biochemical and histopathological investigation. *Food Chemistry and Toxicology* 46(3): 1164–1170.

Kloeppel, B. D., and M. D. Abrams. 1995. Ecophysiological attributes of the native *Acer saccharum* and the exotic *Acer platanoides* in urban oak forests in Pennsylvania, USA. *Tree Physiology* 15: 739–746.

Klyza, C. M., and D. Sousa. 2008. *American Environmental Policy, 1990–2006: Beyond Gridlock*. Cambridge, Massachusetts: MIT Press.

Kopsell, D. A., D. E. Kopsell, M. G. Lefsrud, J. Curran-Celentano, and L. Dukach. 2004. Variation in lutein, beta-carotene, and chlorophyll concentrations among *Brassica oleracea* cultigens and seasons. *HortScience* 39(2): 361–364.

Kovach, J., C. Petzoldt, J. Degni, and J. Tette. 1992. A method to measure the environmental impact of pesticides. *New York's Food and Life Sciences Bulletin*. NYS Agricultural Experiment Station Cornell University, Geneva, New York. nysipm.cornell.edu/publications/eiq/default.asp.

Kubiliene, A., R. Marksiene, S. Kazlauskas, I. Sadauskiene, A. Razukas, and L. Ivanov. 2008. Acute toxicity of ibogaine and noribogaine. *Medicina (Kaunas)* 44(12): 984–987.

Kudva, I. T., K. Blanch, and C. J. Hovde. 1998. Analysis of *Escherichia coli* O157:H7 survival in ovine or bovine manure and manure slurry. *Applied and Environmental Microbiology* 64(9): 3166–3174.

Kunik T., T. Tzfira, Y. Kapulnik, Y. Gafni, C. Dingwall, and V. Citovsky. 2001. Genetic transformation of HeLa cells by agrobacterium. In *Proceedings of the National Academy for Science, U.S.A.* 98 (4): 1871–1876.

Lavigne, P. 2006a. The real deal? Is your organic milk really organic? *Dallas Morning News*, 16 July, 9A. Accessed via http://www.newbank.com.

Lavigne, P. 2006b. Organic certifier targeted: USDA seems set, for first time, to pull such a firm from program. *Dallas Morning News*, 22 July. Accessed via http://www.newbank.com.

Lee, K. H., T. M. Isenhart, and R. C. Schultz. 2003. Sediment and nutrient removal in an established multi-species riparian buffer. *Journal of Soil and Water Conservation* 58(1): 1–8.

Lee, W. J., D. P. Sandler, A. Blair, C. Samanic, A. J. Cross, and M. C. R. Alavanja. 2007. Pesticide use and colorectal cancer risk in the Agricultural Health Study. *International Journal of Cancer* 121: 339–346.

Lenoir, J., J. C. Gegout, P. A. Marquet, P. de Ruffray, and H. Brisse. 2008. A significant upward shift in plant species optimum elevation during the 20th century. *Science* 320 (5884): 1768–1771.

Libby, R. T. 1998. *Eco-Wars: Political Campaigns and Social Movements*. New York: Columbia University Press.

Lomborg, B. 2007. *Cool It*. New York: Alfred A. Knopf.

Lovett, R. A. 2007. Climate change pushing tropics farther, faster. *National Geographic News*, 3 December.

Magkos, F., F. Arvaniti, and A. Zampelas. 2003. Organic food: nutritious food or food for thought? A review of the evidence. *International Journal of Food Science and Nutrition* 54(5): 357–371.

Maisonneuve, I., and S. Glick. 2003. Anti-addictive actions of an iboga alkaloid congener: a novel mechanism for a novel treatment. *Pharmacology Biochemistry and Behavior* 75(3): 607–618.

Malatesta M., F. Boraldi, G. Annovi, B. Baldelli, S. Battistelli, M. Biggiogera, and D. Quaglino. 2008. A long-term study on female mice fed on a genetically modified soybean: effects on liver aging. *Histochemistry and Cell Biology* 130(5): 967–977.

Marshall, P. 2005. Marijuana laws: should state and federal marijuana laws be reformed? *CQ Researcher* 15(6).

McKenzie, E. 1994. *Privatopia: Homeowner Associations and the Rise of Residential Private Government*. New Haven, Connecticut: Yale University Press.

Moerman, D. 2009. *Native American Medicinal Plants*. Portland, Oregon: Timber Press.

Mooney, C. 2005. *The Republican War on Science*. New York: Basic Books.

Morales, L. 2009. Unemployment remains pressing issue for Americans. Gallup Polls, July 15. http://www.gallup.com/poll/121712/Unemployment-Remains-Pressing-Issue-Americans.aspx.

Mukherjee, A., D. Speh, E. Dyck, and F. Diez-Gonzalez. 2004. Preharvest Evaluation of coliforms, *Escherichia coli, Salmonella*, and *Escherichia coli* O157:H7 in organic and conventional produce grown by Minnesota farmers. *Journal of Food Protection* 67(5): 894–900.

Musto, D. F. 1999. *The American Disease: Origins of Narcotics Control*. New York: Oxford University Press.

National Conference of State Legislatures. 2009. Initiative and referendum states. http://www.ncsl.org/Default.aspx?TabId=16589.

Neuman, W. 2010. U.S. plans spot tests of organic products. *New York Times*, 19 March.

Newport, F. 2008. Little increase in Americans' global warming worries. Gallup Poll, April 21. http://www.gallup.com/poll/106660/Little-Increase-Americans-Global-Warming-Worries.aspx.

Newport, F. 2009. Americans: economy takes precedent over environment. Gallup Poll. http://www.gallup.com/poll/116962/Americans-Economy-Takes-Precedence-Environment.aspx.

Newsome, W. H., and J. B. Shields. 1980. Residues of rotenone and rotenolone on lettuce and tomato fruit after treatment in the field with rotenone formulations. *Journal of Agricultural and Food Chemistry* 28: 722–724.

Nordlee, J., S. Taylor, J. Townsend, B. Laurie, R. Thomas, and R. Bush. 1996. Identification of a Brazil-nut allergen in transgenic soybeans. *New England Journal of Medicine* 334(11): 688–692.

NORML (National Organization for the Reform of Marijuana Laws). 2009a. Active state medical marijuana programs. http://www.norml.org/index.cfm?Group_ID=3391.

NORML. 2009b. State-by-state laws. http://www.norml.org/index.cfm?Group_ID=4516.

Ostrom, C. 1997. He made the case for pot. *Seattle Times*, 9 April.

Paarlberg, R. 2010. *Food Politics: What Everyone Needs to Know*. New York: Oxford University Press.

Patty, L., B. Réal, and J. Gril. 1997. The use of grassed buffer strips to remove pesticides, nitrate and soluble phosphorus compounds from runoff water. *Pesticide Science* 49: 243–251.

Pew Center on Global Climate Change. 2009. Renewable and alternative energy portfolio standards. http://www.pewclimate.org/node/6917.

Pew Oceans Commission. 2003. America's living oceans: charting a course for sea change. http://www.pewtrusts.org/uploadedFiles/wwwpewtrustsorg/Reports/Protecting_ocean_life/env_pew_oceans_final_report.pdf.

Phipps, R. H., and J. R. Park. 2002. Environmental benefits of genetically modified crops: global and European perspectives on their ability to reduce pesticide use. *Journal of Animal and Feed Sciences* 11: 1–18.

Pimentel, D. 2003. Ethanol fuels: energy balance, economics, and environmental impacts are negative. *Natural Resources Research* 12(2): 127–134.

Pimentel, D. 2009. Pesticides and pest control. In *Integrated Pest Management: Innovation Development Process*. Ed. R. Peshin and A. K. Dhawan. New York: Springer Publishing Company.

Pimentel, D., L. Lach,R. Zuniga, and D. Morrison. 2000. Environmental and economic costs of nonindigenous species in the United States. *Bioscience* 50(1): 53–65.

Pollack, A. 2010. Taking stock after gene patents are invalidated. *New York Times*, 30 March.

Post, W., and K. Kwon. 2000. Soil carbon sequestration and land-use change: processes and potential. *Global Change Biology* 6: 317–328.

Prah, P. M. 2006. Are new anti-terrorism measures adequate? *CQ Researcher* 16(15).

Pray, C., D. Ma, J. Huang, and F. Qiao. 2001. Impact of Bt cotton in China. *World Development* 29(5): 813–825.

Prescott, V., P. Campbell, A. Moore, J. Mattes, M. E. Rothenberg, P. S. Foster, T. J. V. Higgins, and S. P. Hogan. 2005. Transgenic expression of bean r-amylase inhibitor in peas results in altered structure and immunogenicity. *Journal of Agriculture and Food Chemistry* 53(23): 9023–9030.

Quist, D., and I. H. Chapela. 2001. Transgenic DNA introgressed into traditional maize landraces in Oaxaca, Mexico. *Nature* 414: 541–543.

Rabe, B. G. 2004. *Statehouse and Greenhouse: The Emerging Politics of American Climate Change Policy*. Washington: Brookings Institution.

Rajagopal, D., S. Sexton, G. Hochman, D. Roland-Holst, and D. Zilberman. 2009. Model estimates food-versus-biofuel trade-off. *California Agriculture* 63(4): 199–201.

Rappaport, B. 1993. Green landscaping: Greenacres. *The John Marshall Law Review* 26(4). http://www.epa.gov/greenacres/weedlaws/index.html#BRETT.

Raun, W. R., and G. V. Johnson. 1999. Improving nitrogen use efficiency for cereal production. *Agronomy Journal* 91: 357–363.

Ravilious, K. 2007. Mars melt hints at solar, not human cause for warming, scientist says. *National Geographic News*, 28 February.

Reich, P. B., S. E. Hobbie, T. Lee, D. S. Ellsworth, J. B. West, D. Tilman, J. M. H. Knops, S. Naeem, and J. Trost. 2006. Nitrogen limitation constrains sustainability of ecosystem response to CO2. *Nature* 440: 922–925.

Reichman, J. R., L. S. Watrud, E. H. Lee, C. A. Burdick, M. A. Bollman, M. J. Storm, G. A. King, and C. Mallory-Smith. 2006. Establishment of transgenic herbicide-resistant creeping bentgrass (*Agrostis stolonifera* L.) in nonagronomic habitats. *Molecular Ecology* 15(13): 4243–4255.

Rejmanek, M., and M. Pitcairn. 2002. When is eradication of exotic plant pests a realistic goal? In *Turning the Tide: The Eradication of Invasive Species*. Ed. C. R. Veitch and M. N. Clout. IUCN, Gland, Switzerland. 249–253.

Relyea, R. A. 2005. The impact of insecticides and herbicides on the biodiversity and productivity of aquatic communities. *Ecological Applications* 15: 618–627.

Relyea, R. A. 2009. A cocktail of contaminants: how pesticide mixtures at low concentrations affect aquatic communities. *Oecologia* 159: 363–376.

Ren, J., D. Qin, S. Kang, S. Hou, J. Pu, and Z. Jing. 2004. Glacier variations and climate warming and drying in the central Himalayas. *Chinese Science Bulletin* 49(1): 65–69.

Richtel, M. 2009. U.S. withheld data on risks of distracted drivers. *New York Times*, 20 July.

Rosen, C. J., and D. L. Allan. 2007. Exploring the benefits of organic nutrient sources for crop production and soil quality. *HortTechnology* 17(4): 422–430.

Rosenbaum, W. A. 2005. *Environmental Politics and Policy*, 6th ed. Washington: CQ Press.

Roueche, B. 1991. *The Medical Detectives*. New York: Plume Publishing.

Russo, E. 1998. Cannabis for migraine treatment: the once and future prescription? An historic and scientific review. *Pain* 76(1–2): 3–8.

Russo, E. 2008. Cannabinoids in the management of difficult to treat pain. *Theraputics and Clinical Risk Management* 4(1): 245–259.

Ryan, J. J., J. C. Pilon, and R. Leduc. 1982. Composite sampling in the determination of pyrethrins in fruit samples. *Journal of the Association of Official Analytical Chemists* 65: 904–908.

Saad, L. 2009a. Increased number think global warming is "exaggerated." Gallup Poll, 11 March. http://www.gallup.com/poll/116590/Increased-Number-Think-Global-Warming-Exaggerated.aspx.

Saad, L. 2009b. Water pollution Americans' top green concern. Gallup Poll, March 25. http://www.gallup.com/poll/117079/Water-Pollution-Americans-Top-Green-Concern.aspx.

Schenk, P., S. Thomas-Hall, E. Stephens, U. Marx, J. Mussgnug, C. Posten, O. Kruse, and B. Hankamer. 2008. Second generation biofuels: high-efficiency microalgae for biodiesel production. *BioEnergy Research* 1: 20–43.

Schilling, M., and M. Esmundo. 2009. Technology S-curves in renewable energy alternatives: analysis and implications for industry and government. *Energy Policy* 37: 1767–1781.

Schultz, R., J. Collettil, T. Isenhart, W. Simpkins, C. Mize, and M. Thompson. 1995. Design and placement of a multi-species riparian buffer strip system. *Agroforestry Systems* 29(3): 201–226.

Schwartz, R., F. Voth, and M. Sheridan. 1997. Marijuana to prevent nausea and vomiting in cancer patients: a survey of clinical oncologists. *Southern Medical Journal* 90(2): 167–172.

Segarra, A. E., and J. M. Rawson. 2001. StarlinkTM corn controversy: background. Congressional Research Service, 10 January.

Shiue, L. 2010. Hallucinogens ("magic mushrooms") for medical use? *Open Salon*. 14 April. http://open.salon.com/blog/doctorandmama/2010/04/13/hallucinogens_magic_mushrooms_for_medical_use.

Smil, V. 2001. *Enriching the Earth: Fritz Haber, Carl Bosch, and the Transformation of World Food Production*. Cambridge, Massachusetts: MIT Press.

Smith, Mark A. 2000. *American Business and Political Power*. Chicago: University of Chicago Press.

Smith, R. A. 2007 (first printing 1872). *Air and Rain: The Beginnings of a Chemical Climatology*. Whitefish, Montana: Kessinger Publishing.

Söderpalm A., A. Schuster, and H. DeWitt. 2001. Antiemetic efficacy of smoked marijuana: subjective and behavioral effects on nausea induced by syrup of ipecac. *Pharmacology Biochemistry and Behavior* 69: 343–350.

Soon, W. 2007. Implications of the secondary role of carbon dioxide and methane forcing in climate change: past, present, and future. *Physical Geography* 28(2): 97–125.

Spengos, K., A. Schwartz, and M. Hennerici. 2000. Multifocal cerebral demyelination after magic mushroom abuse. *Journal of Neurology* 247: 224–225.

Steitz, D. E., A. Buis, and C. Adriasola. 2003. South American glaciers melting faster, changing sea level. NASA News Release 03–336. http://www.nasa.gov/home/hqnews/2003/oct/HQ_03336_So_Amer_glaciers.html.

Stigarll, A., and E. Elam. 2009. Impact of improved landscape quality and tree cover on the price of single-family homes. *Journal of Environmental Horticulture* 27(1): 24–30.

Stone, D. 2002. *Policy Paradox: The Art of Political Decision Making*, 3rd ed. New York: W.W. Norton.

Struss, R. 2007. Report to the Minnesota legislature: effectiveness of the Minnesota phosphorus lawn fertilizer law. Minnesota Department of Agriculture: Pesticide and Fertilizer Management Division.

Sullivan, E. 2008. Man jailed for brown lawn gets help from neighbors. *St. Petersburg Times*, 13 October.

Swanson, K. L., and A. A. Tsonis. 2009. Has the climate recently shifted? *Geophysical Research Letters* 36: L06711, doi:10.1029/2008GL037022.

Tabashnik, B. E., A. J. Gassmann, D. W. Crowder, and Y. Carrière. 2008. Insect resistance to Bt crops: evidence versus theory. *Nature Biotechnology* 26: 199–202.

Tallamy, D. 2007. *Bringing Nature Home*. Portland, Oregon: Timber Press.

Theriault, S. M. 2008. *Party Polarization in Congress*. New York: Cambridge University Press.

Tierney, K., J. Sampson, P. Ross, M. Sekela, and C. Kennedy. 2008. Salmon olfaction is impaired by an environmentally realistic pesticide mixture. *Environmental Science and Technology* 42(13): 4996–5001.

Tillman, J. 2008. Brown lawn means jail time. *St. Petersburg Times*, 11 October.

Tilman, D. Causes, consequences and ethics of biodiversity. 2000. *Nature* 405: 208–211.

Tomida, I., R. Pertwee, and A. Azuara-Blanco. 2004. Cannabinoids and glaucoma. *British Journal of Ophthalmology* 88(5): 708–713.

Turner, J., S. Colwell, G. Marshall, T. Lachlan-Cope, A. Carleton, P. Jones, V. Lagun, P. Reid, and S. Iagovkina. 2005. Antarctic climate change during the last 50 years. *International Journal of Climatology* 25: 279–294.

Ulloa, S., and M. Owen. 2009. Response of Asiatic dayflower (*Commelina communis*) to glyphosate and alternatives in soybean. *Weed Science* 57(1): 74–80.

U.S. Department of Agriculture. 2009. Organic agriculture: organic market overview. http://www.ers.usda.gov/Briefing/Organic/Demand.htm.

U.S. Department of Agriculture Economic Research Service. 2009. Adoption of Genetically Engineered Crops in the U.S.: Extent of Adoption. http://www.ers.usda.gov/Data/BiotechCrops/adoption.htm.

U.S. Department of Commerce. 2008. Statistical Abstract of the United States, 2008. Washington: U.S. Government Printing Office.

U.S. Department of Energy. 2009. Annual Energy Review DOE/EIA-0384(2008).

U.S. Energy Information Agency. 2009a. Estimated consumption of vehicle fuels in the United States, by fuel type. April. http://www.eia.doe.gov/cneaf/alternate/page/atftables/attf_c1.html.

U.S. Environmental Protection Agency. 2009. Litigation status: summary of litigation on status of TMDL establishment. March. http://www.epa.gov/owow/tmdl/lawsuit.html.

U.S. Food and Drug Administration. 2009 (updated). Report on the Food and Drug Administration's Review of the Safety of Recombinant Bovine Somatotropin. http://www.fda.gov/AnimalVeterinary/SafetyHealth/ProductSafetyInformation/ucm130321.htm.

U.S. Patent and Trademark Office. 2005. General information concerning patents. http://www.uspto.gov/web/offices/pac/doc/general/index.html#ptsc.

U.S. Regulatory Agencies Unified Biotechnology Website. 2009. Frequently asked questions. http://usbiotechreg.nbii.gov/FAQRecord.asp?qryGUID=2.

Velimirov, A., C. Binter, and J. Zentek. 2008. Biological effects of transgenic maize NK603xMON810 fed in long term reproduction studies in mice. Report-Federal Ministry of Health, Family and Youth (Austria).

Violeta, K., O. Mathieu, J. Mathieu-Daude, P. Vainauskas, T. Casper, E. Baccino, and F. Bressolle. 2006. Distribution of ibogaine and noribogaine in a man following a poisoning involving root bark of the *Tabernanthe iboga* shrub. *Journal of Analytical Toxicology* 30(7): 434–440.

Vogel, D. 1995. *Trading Up: Consumer and Environmental Regulation in a Global Economy*. Cambridge, Massachusetts: Harvard University Press.

Walker, R. C., and D. J. Merritts. 2009. Natural streams and the legacy of water-powered mills. *Science* 319(5861): 299–304.

Walter, C., M. Berridge, and D. Tribe. 2001. Genetically engineered *Klebsiella planticola*: A threat to terrestrial plant life? Presentation to the Royal Commission on Genetic Engineering, 1 February. www.biotech-info.net/ingham_rebuttal.pdf.

Warner, K., C. Ehrhart, C., A. deSherbinin, S. Adamo, and T. Chai-Onnand. 2009. In search of shelter, mapping the effects of climate change on human migration and displacement. Report for CARE international. U.N. University's Institute for Environment and Human, CARE International and Columbia University's Center for International Earth Science Information Network (CIESIN).

Warwick, S. I., A. Legere, M. J. Simard, and T. James. 2008. Do escaped transgenes persist in natre? The case of an herbicide resistance transgene in a weedy *Brassica rapa* population. *Molecular Ecology* 17(5): 1387–1395.

Webb, S. L., T. H. Pendergast, and M. E. Dwyer. 2001. Response of native and exotic maple seedling banks to removal of the exotic, invasive Norway maple (*Acer platanoides*). *Journal of the Torrey Botanical Society* 128(2): 141–149.

Weeks, J. 2009. Regulating toxic chemicals: do we know enough about chemical risks? *CQ Researcher* 19(3).

Wendt, R., and R. Burwell. 1985. Runoff and soil losses for conventional, reduced, and no-till corn. *Journal of Soil and Water Conservation* 40(5): 450–454.

West, D. M., and B. A. Loomis. 1998. *The Sound of Money: How Political Interests Get Want They Want*. New York: W.W. Norton.

Westbrooks, R. G. 2004. Invasive plants. Coming to America. Overview of the FICMNEW National Early Detection and Rapid Response System for Invasive Plants. USGS.

Whiteman, D. 1995. *Communication in Congress: Members, Staff, and the Search for Information*. Lawrence: University of Kansas Press.

Whyatt, R., V. Rauh, D. Barr, D. Camann, H. Andrews, R. Garfinkel, L. Hoepner, D. Diaz, J. Dietrich, A. Reyes, D. Tang, P. Kinney, and F. Perera. 2004. Prenatal insecticide exposures and birth weight and length among an urban minority cohort. *Environmental Health Perspectives* 112(10): 1125–1132.

Williams, C. 2002. Nutritional quality of organic food: shades of grey or shades of green? In *Proceedings of the Nutritional Society* 61: 19–24.

Wilson, J. Q. 1980. *The Politics of Regulation*. New York: Basic Books.

Wiser, G. M. 1999. PTO rejection of the "Ayahuasca" patent claim. The Center for International Environmental Law. http://www.ciel.org/Biodiversity/ptorejection.html.

Wolf, K. L. 2009. Strip malls, city trees, and community values. *Arboriculture & Urban Forestry* 35(1): 33–40.

Worthington, V. Nutritional quality of organic versus conventional fruits, vegetables and grains. *The Journal of Alternative and Complementary Medicine* 7(2): 161–173.

Wu, T., D. Tashkin, B. Djahed, and J. Rose. 1988. Pulmonary hazards of smoking marijuana as compared with tobacco. *The New England Journal of Medicine* 318(6): 347–351.

Xu, Z., L. Chang, W. Slikker, S. Ali, R. Rountree, and A. Scallet. 2000. A dose-response study of ibogaine-induced neuropathology in the rat cerebellum. *Toxicological Sciences* 57: 95–101.

Yu, H., F., Jin, X. Shu, B. D. L. Li, Q. Dai, J. Cheng, H. J. Berkel, and W. Zheng. 2002. Insulin-like growth factors and breast cancer risk in Chinese women. *Cancer Epidemiology, Biomarkers, and Prevention*, August, 705–712.

Yücel, M., N. Solowij, C. Respondek, S. Whittle, A. Fornito, C. Pantelis, and D. Lubman. 2008. Regional brain abnormalities associated with long-term heavy cannabis use. *Archives of General Psychiatry* 65(6): 694–701.

Zhu, C., Q. Zeng, L. H. Ziska, J. Zhu, Z. Xie, and G. Liu. 2008. Effect of nitrogen supply on carbon dioxide-induced changes in competition between rice and barnyardgrass (*Echinochloa crus-galli*). *Weed Science* 56: 66–71.

Ziska, L. H. 2003. Evaluation of the growth response of six invasive species to past, present and future atmospheric carbon dioxide. *Journal of Experimental Botany* 54(381): 395–404.

Ziska, L.H., and K. George. 2004. Rising carbon dioxide and invasive, noxious plants: potential threats and consequences. *World Resource Review* 16: 427–447.

Zuckerman, B., D. Frank, R. Hingson, H. Amaro, S. Levenson, H. Kayne, S. Parker, R. Vinci, K. Aboagye, L. Fried, H. Cabral, R. Timperi, and H. Bauchner. 1989. Effects of maternal marijuana and cocaine use on fetal growth. *New England Journal of Medicine* 320(12): 762–768.

★★★

Index

acid rain, 196
Agrobacterium, 116, 132
air pollution, 26, 92, 93, 96, 110, 203–204
Alar scare, 44, 68–69
algae for biodiesel, 102–103, 111
alternative energy, 98–113
  automobiles fueled by, 100, 106, 112, 204
  background on, 98–99
  biofuels for transportation, 99–103, 110
  bottom line, 113
  for electricity production, 103–104, 110
  geothermal power, 103, 104, 106, 112
  government policy, 104–106
  policy options/ratings, 110–113
  political dynamics, 106–109, 205
  solar power, 98, 103–104, 106, 109, 112
  subsidizing, 107–111, 113, 204
  tax breaks for, 104–105, 109
  tidal power, 98, 103, 112
  wind power, 98, 103, 104, 106, 112, 205
amphibians, 63–66
Animal and Plant Health Inspection Service (APHIS), 123, 156–159, 161–163
animals
  antibiotics in livestock, 35, 40, 41, 49
  effect of pesticides on, 58, 63–66
  genetic engineering and, 119, 123–125, 129
  growth hormones and, 40, 41, 49, 124–125, 126
  nonnative species impact, 152, 155
Anslinger, Harry J., 28, 172
antibiotics in livestock, 35, 40, 41, 49
Anti Drug Abuse Acts, 173–174
apple growing, 37–38, 40, 53, 60, 68–69
Asian longhorned beetle, 157–158
atrazine, 63, 65, 66, 118
automobile emissions, 26, 27, 107–108, 110, 206
automobiles, alternative fuels for, 100, 106, 112, 204

Beltway bandits, 29
Big Ag, 90, 125, 127, 131, 145, 146
biodiesel, 99–103, 104, 111
biodiversity, 153
biofuels, 99–103, 106, 111–113. *See also* ethanol
biopiracy, 137–138, 146, 148, 149

biotechnology. *See* genetic engineering (GE)
biotechnology firms, 127, 128, 142–145, 148, 149
bipartisan politics, 14–17, 19, 20–21, 218–219
bluegrass patent, 135–136
Bosenberg, Henry, 134, 135, 146–147
BP's 2010 Deep Horizon oil spill, 32
Brazilian ethanol, 99, 100
Brown, C. B., 84–85
Bt *(Bacillus thuringiensis),* 116, 120, 121, 132
BTU tax proposal, 108
buffer strips, 84–85, 87–88, 94, 95, 97
burden of proof, 25, 73
Bush, George H. W., 16, 203
Bush, George W., 89, 177, 203, 211
business
  cap-and-trade systems, 204, 210, 214
  greenhouse gas emissions, 207–208
  influence of Big Ag, 90, 125, 127, 131, 145, 146
  left-/right-wing views of, 17–18
  political advantages of, 30, 32–33, 218
  power of biotechnology firms, 127, 128, 142–145, 148, 149
  regulation of pesticide manufacturers, 66–67, 70–73, 76
  "sound science" movement, 28

California
  greenhouse gas regulations, 203–204, 206
  marijuana legislation, 174, 178
  Million Solar Roofs initiative, 109
  organic food industry, 42, 44, 45
campaign advertising, 31
Canadian pesticide ban, 56–57, 76
cancer, 27, 61–63, 67, 69–70, 74–75, 80
cap-and-trade systems, 204, 210, 214
carbon dioxide
  alternatives to managing, 214–215
  biofuels and, 101, 102–103
  classification and regulation, 203–204, 211, 212
  conservation to decrease, 108, 113
  effects beyond global warming, 202–203, 216
  global warming and, 197–201
  tax on, 213, 214
Carson, Rachel, 26, 36, 47, 58–59
castor bean, 173, 180, 181
cellulosic ethanol, 102, 106, 111
Certificates of Protection (plants), 139
Certified Naturally Grown program, 54
Chesapeake Bay compact, 88
Clean Air Acts, 16, 26, 105, 203–204, 209
Clean Water Act (CWA), 86–87, 89, 92, 209
climate change. *See also* global warming
  complexity/uncertainty of, 16–17, 207, 210, 212
  Copenhagen summit, 204–205
  farming and, 199, 201, 202, 205–206, 211–212, 216
  impact on oceans, 202–203, 212
  international dynamics around, 203, 204–205, 208–209, 213–214

invasive *vs.* native plants, 154, 155
poorer nations and, 205, 208–209, 212
social disruption potential, 208, 216
Clinton, Bill, 69, 89, 108, 159, 177, 203, 211
cocaine use, 173–174
"community standards," 18
composted manure, 36, 38–39, 41
compromise, 218–219
concrete, for decarbonization, 214
Congress. *See* U.S. Congress
conservation, 98, 108, 112–113
conservation tillage, 84, 85, 94, 95, 97, 205–206
Controlled Substances Act, 172–173
copper sulfate, 37, 52, 58, 64
corn
and carbon dioxide, 199, 202
chemicals to grow, 60, 65, 83
ethanol from, 99–102, 105, 106–107, 109–112
genetically modified, 117, 119, 120, 127, 135
subsidized, 97
cotton, transgenic, 117, 118, 121
crop subsidies, 89–91, 96–97

dairy farming, 40, 42, 49, 117
DDT, 58–59, 63, 68
dead zones, 83–84, 94
decarbonization, 214
deforestation, 101, 199
Delaney Amendment, 67, 69–70, 72
Democrats, 15–16, 20–21, 210–211
DNA patents, 137, 141
Dodsworth, Asa, 185
Drug Enforcement Agency (DEA), 173, 174

E. coli, 32, 38–39
electricity, alternative sources of, 99, 103–106, 110, 112, 205
emerald ash borer, 158, 164, 167
eminent domain, 187–188
Energy Policy Act, 205
energy tax, 108, 109
environmentalists
on fertilizer regulations, 88–89
on native/invasive species, 151, 158, 161–163
need to understand issues, 217
politics and, 15, 33
support of farm subsidies, 91
environmental policy, 14–19, 24, 32, 210–211
EPA. *See* U.S. Environmental Protection Agency (EPA)
ethanol
Brazil's success with, 99, 100
cellulosic ethanol, 102, 106, 111
corn-based, 99–102, 105, 106–107, 109–113
drawbacks of, 99–102, 105–106
policy and politics of, 104–108
removing tariffs on foreign, 109
from sugarcane, 100–101, 109, 111
European Union (EU) GMO bans, 123–125

farming. *See also* livestock; organic food; sustainable food production
Big Ag, 90, 125, 127, 131, 145, 146
buffer strips in, 84–85, 87–88, 94, 95, 97
climate change and, 199, 201, 202, 205–206, 211–212, 216
export bans on GMOs, 123–125

family farms, 41–42, 45, 47–48, 90, 97, 124–127
fertilizer dependency, 82–83
genetically engineered crops, 117–118, 125, 127, 129–130, 148
government subsidies, 89–91, 96–97
impact of plant patents on, 129–130, 144–145, 146, 148
invasive plants/pests and, 151, 162–163
pesticide use, 59, 60, 66–70
protecting image of conventional, 45, 47, 50, 54
reduced tilling/no-till practices, 84, 85, 94, 95, 97, 205–206
uncertified organic farming, 41–42
as unhealthy and dangerous, 34–35
use of fossil fuels, 51, 52–53, 101
water pollution from runoff, 83–84, 93
Federal Agriculture Improvement and Reform Act, 91
Federal Environmental Pesticide Control Act (FEPCA), 68
Federal Insecticide, Fungicide, and Rodenticide Act (FIFRA), 67, 71
fertilizers, 81–97
avoiding in organic farming, 35, 36, 37, 41, 49–50, 53
bottom line, 97
enforcing regulations, 87–89
fraudulent use of, 43–45
government policy, 86–87
harvesting/safety concerns, 38–39, 51, 52
history of, 81–82
mining for, 38, 82, 94
mitigating the damage from, 84–85
policy options/ratings, 93–97
political dynamics of, 89–93
science behind, 82–83
sewage sludge, 41, 47
flex-fuel vehicles, 106
Florida native vegetation legislation, 189
Florida water regulations, 87–88
Food, Drug, and Cosmetics Act, 66–67
food irradiation, 41, 47
food labeling, 41–42, 48, 122–123, 125–126, 130–131, 133
Food Quality Protection Act (FQPA), 70, 71–72
food safety, 34, 39, 119, 124–125, 129
food supply
advent of government inspections, 66
biofuel's impact on, 101–102, 111, 113
chemical residues in, 51, 54, 64–65, 67–73
ensuring adequate, 69, 89–90, 139
prevalence of GMOs, 117
reliance on nonnative foods, 150
foreign oil dependency, 105, 108, 110–111, 216
fossil fuels
biofuels *vs.*, 101, 110–111
and carbon dioxide emissions, 198–199, 216
dependency on, 98, 105, 108, 110
food production's use of, 51–53, 101
oil crisis (1970s), 104–105
rising cost, 103
Freedom to Farm Act, 91

free market adherents, 94, 96–97, 109, 110
frogs, 63–66
fruit growing, 37–38, 40, 53, 60, 64–65, 68–69
fungicides, 37, 52, 58, 59–60, 64, 67

gene guns, 115–116
General Agreement on Tariffs and Trade (GATT), 124
genetic engineering (GE), 114–133
  benefits of, 117–118
  bottom line, 132–133
  concerns about, 16–17, 117–122
  export bans, 123–125
  government policy, 47, 122–125
  lack of food labeling, 122–123, 125–126, 130–131, 133
  natural selection and, 120–121, 132
  pesticide use and, 118, 121–122, 128–129, 131, 132
  policy options/ratings, 127–131
  political dynamics, 14, 125–127
  prevalence in food supply, 117
  science behind, 114–117
  superweeds, 120–121, 123, 128
  "terminator" seeds, 127
  utility patents on plants, 135, 141, 146–149
geothermal power, 103, 104, 106, 112
global warming, 196–216
  bottom line, 215–216
  email hacking incident, 29
  government policy, 203–206
  policy options/ratings, 211–215
  political dynamics of, 15, 20–21, 206–211
  scientific debate on, 27, 196–201, 211–212, 215–216
  technology proposed to combat, 215
Gore, Al, 20
government, role of, 17–19
government subsidies, 19, 89–91, 96–97, 107–111, 113
grafted plants, 116
grass restrictions. *See* yard restrictions
greenhouse gas emissions. *See also* carbon dioxide
  biofuels and, 101
  and global warming debate, 198, 215–216
  government policy on, 203–207
  policy options to reduce, 213–215
  politics around, 207–209
growth hormones in livestock, 40, 41, 49, 117, 124–125, 126
guano harvesting, 38, 52, 82
Gulf of Mexico dead zone, 83–84
Gulf oil spill, 32

Hagar, Donald, 184–185
harm, evidence of, 25
herbicides
  control of noxious weeds, 75, 160, 185–186
  environmental effects, 63, 65–66
  GMO resistance to, 120–121, 132
  history of, 58
  link to cancer, 27, 62
  science of, 59, 60
home gardens, 86, 88, 185, 192–193
homeowners' association (HOA) restrictions, 18, 189–192
homeowner use of pesticides, 27, 56–57, 63, 64, 74–79
House Committee on Agriculture, 30, 45–46
Howard, Albert, 36, 38

Hudson Institute, 47
human health
GMOs and, 119, 124–125, 129, 130, 132–133
invasive species harming, 159
organic food nutrient content, 39–40, 50–51
pesticides and cancer, 27, 61–63, 67, 69–70, 74–75, 80
stress over pesticide concerns, 65, 80
hybrid vehicles, 106, 112

iboga, 170, 171
illegal drugs, 172–173, 174, 177, 179–183. *See also* marijuana
Ingham, Elaine, 114
insects
APHIS "pest lists," 156–157, 161–162
insecticides to control, 35, 58–61, 63–66
threat of invasive, 152, 157–158, 159, 164, 167
transgenic plants and, 121–122, 128–129, 132
Intergovernmental Panel on Climate Change (IPCC), 200, 206, 213
Intermodal Surface Transportation Efficiency Act, 205
international dynamics
climate change issues, 203, 204–205, 208–209, 213–214
foreign oil dependency, 105, 108, 110–111, 216
GMOs, 123–125
invasive species, 157–159, 161–165, 167
invasive plants, 150–168
background of debate, 150–152
bottom line, 167–168
definition of, 151
and foreign trade, 157–159, 161–165, 167
government policy, 156–160
and native species protection, 151, 155, 164–166, 168
noxious weed lists, 150, 157, 160
policy options/ratings, 163–167
political dynamics of, 160–163
scientific viewpoint on, 152–156
Invasive Species Act, 159, 162
in vitro meat production, 214

Japanese trade, 123, 125
Jefferson, Thomas, 150, 156

Kac, Eduardo, 129
Kyoto Protocol, 203, 208, 211

land use laws, 187–188, 190, 209
lawns. *See* yard maintenance; yard restrictions
LD50 (lethal dose/50 percent), 60–61
left-wing ideology, 17–18, 76, 217
legal and illegal drugs
alcohol use, 175, 176, 180–183
legal and illegal plants, 169–183. *See also* marijuana
bottom line, 182–183
government policy, 172–175
list of illegal plants, 170, 180
peyote, 175, 179, 182
policy options/ratings, 179–183
political dynamics, 175–179
politicians, drug use by, 176–177
Schedule I drugs, 172–173, 174, 177, 179–183
science of, 171–172
social/racial biases and, 173–174, 175, 180
taxes and, 172, 178, 181

livestock
antibiotics/growth hormones in, 35, 40, 41, 49, 124–125, 126
dairy farming, 40, 42, 49, 117
technological methods to replace, 214
lobbyists, 30–31, 32
local government. *See* state and local government
locally produced foods, 52–53, 54

magic mushrooms, 170, 171, 181
maple trees, 154, 163
marijuana
benefits of, 169, 171
general legalization of, 177, 178
health problems from chronic use, 170–171
left-/right-wing view of, 18
legislation outlawing, 28, 172–173, 174
medical marijuana, 169–170, 174–180, 182, 183
research curtailed on, 177
as Schedule I drug, 172–173, 174, 177, 183
social biases against, 175, 180
THC in, 169, 181
Marijuana Tax Act, 172
meat exports, 123–125
Meat Inspection Act, 66
milk production, 40, 42, 117
Miller, Loren, 137–138
Million Solar Roofs initiative, 109
mining for fertilizer, 38, 82, 94
Minnesota water pollution laws, 81, 87–88
Mississippi River runoff, 83
Monsanto, 127, 145

National Invasive Species Council (NISC), 159, 162
National Organic Program (NOP), 40, 41, 44, 48–49
National Organic Standards Board (NOSB), 40–41, 46–47
native species promotion, 151, 155, 164–166, 168, 189
natural selection, 120–121, 132
nitrogen
carbon dioxide's effect on, 202
natural sources of, 38, 82, 186, 193
synthetic, 37, 82, 94
Nixon, Richard, 16, 26
NOEL (No Observed Effect Level), 62
Non-GMO Project, 131
nonnative species, 137–138, 146, 147, 148, 150, 152
nonpoint source pollution, 86, 91–93, 95
Norway maple, 154, 163
no-till practices, 84, 85, 94, 95, 97, 205–206
noxious weeds, 150–151, 157, 160

Obama, Barack, 50, 179, 204, 211
Occupational Safety and Health Administration (OSHA), 68
oceans and climate change, 202–203, 212, 216
oil crisis (1970s), 104–105
Oregon land use laws, 188
organic food, 34–55. *See also* fertilizers in organic farming; pesticides in organic farming
background of, 34–36
bottom line, 53–55
certification standards, 35–36, 40–44, 46–50, 52–53
cheating and the consequences, 42–44
as elitist, 51, 54

fertilizer and pesticide overview, 37–39
government policy, 40–42
labeling of, 41–42, 48, 133
locally produced, 52–53, 54
nutrient content of, 39–40, 50–51
organic livestock, 35, 40, 41, 49
policy options/ratings, 49–53
political dynamics, 44–49
science behind concept, 36
and sustainability, 35, 49–54
Organic Foods Production Act (OFPA), 40, 45–46
organic livestock, 35, 40, 41, 49
Organic System Plan (OSP), 43
Organic Trade Association, 49
ozone thinning, 196

Palin, Sarah, 20
Pasteur, Louis, 140
Patent Acts, 138, 139, 141
patents. *See also* plant patents
high-/low-quality, 144
importance of, 143
legislation, 138, 139, 141
politics of biotechnology, 142–145
requirements for, 139–142
patent "trolls," 144
personal freedoms, 18, 57, 74, 75, 77, 190–193
pesticides, 56–80. *See also* herbicides
acute toxicity, 60–61
the Alar scare, 44
avoiding use in organic farming, 35, 36, 37, 41, 49–50, 53
banned in Canada, 56–57, 76
bottom line, 79–80
cancer and, 27, 61–63, 67, 69–70, 74–75, 80
chronic toxicity, 61–63
environmental effects, 63–66
genetic engineering and, 118, 121–122, 131, 132
government policy, 66–70, 86
history and dangers of, 57–59
home and yard use, 27, 56–57, 63, 64, 74–79
low dose effects, 64–66, 70, 76
policy options/ratings, 74–79
political dynamics of, 70–73
residues on food, 51, 54, 64–65, 68–73
science of, 59–60
pesticides in organic farming
call to ban all, 55
fraudulent use of, 43–45
residues on food, 38, 51, 54, 64, 77
varied/frequent use, 37–38
peyote, 175, 179, 182
phosphate mining, 38, 52, 82, 94
phosphorus, regulating use of, 81, 84, 87, 88, 95
Pickins, T. Boone, 98
Plant Patent Act, 138–139, 146
plant patents, 134–149
background on, 134–136
biopiracy, 137–138, 146, 148, 149
bottom line, 149
and Certificates of Protection, 139
government policy, 138–139
impact on farmers, 129–130, 144–145, 146, 148
policy options/ratings, 145–149
political dynamics around, 142–145
requirements for, 139–142
science and, 137–138
transgenic organisms, 135, 141
utility patents, 135–136, 137, 139–141, 145–149
Plant Quarantine Act, 156

plants. *See also* genetic engineering (GE); invasive plants; legal and illegal plants; plant patents; weeds
  biopiracy, 137–138, 146, 148, 149
  breeding of, 135–136, 147
  grafted, 116
  native species protection, 151, 155, 164–166, 168
Plant Variety Protection Act, 135, 137, 139, 146, 148–149
point source pollution, 92–93
polarized politics, 14–17, 19, 210–211
policy institutes, 29
policy-making process, 21–33
  abuse of scientific information, 21, 27–29
  burden of proof in, 25
  business in, 32–33, 218
  compromise in, 218–219
  environmental policies incompatible with, 24
  inherent difficulties in, 17, 19
  and the limitations of science, 23–27, 33
  lobbyists role in, 30–31, 32
  oral culture in, 22, 31
  politics continuing after, 46
  public role in, 14, 21–22, 31–33, 46, 210, 217–218
  sources of information, 29–33
  use of scientific information, 21–23, 24, 218
policy options rating system key, 17
political campaign advertising, 31
political dynamics, bipartisan, 14–17, 19, 210–211
pollution. *See also* water pollution
  air pollution, 26, 92, 93, 96, 110, 203–204
  nonpoint source pollution, 86, 91–93, 95
  regulations on, 33, 96, 204
poppies, 170, 171, 181
precautionary principle, 18, 76, 79
prescription for pesticides use, 78–79
Proctor, Larry, 138
Product Verification Program (PVP), 131
property rights movement, 188
property values, 188, 190, 191, 194, 195
Prudente, Joseph, 184
psilocybin mushrooms, 170, 171, 181
public relations campaigns, 28–29
"public use," 187–188
purple loosestrife, 155–156

racial biases, drug use and, 174, 180
R&D investments, 142–144
Reagan, Ronald and Nancy, 173
reduced tilling practices, 84, 85, 94, 95, 97, 205–206
religious use of drugs, 175, 179, 182
Renewable Portfolio Standards (RPS), 105, 205
Republicans, 15–16, 20–21, 210–211
research funding, 29–30, 45, 50
restorationists, 155
ricin, 180, 181
right-wing ideology, 18, 217
rock phosphate mining, 38, 52, 94
Rodale, J. I., 26, 36, 50
Roosevelt, Theodore, 15, 66
Roundup (glyphosate), 63–64, 66, 116, 118, 120–121
runoff, 83–85, 87–88, 94–97

salmon, 66, 117
Salmonella outbreak, 39

Saving the Planet with Pesticides and Plastic (Hudson Institute), 47
Schedule I drugs, 172–173, 174, 177, 179–183
science
 applying a standard of harm, 25
 factors motivating scientists, 23, 28–29
 limitations of, 23–27
 in policy-making process, 21–23, 24, 218
 political abuse of, 21, 23, 27–29
 research funding, 29–30
 scope of, 23, 25–26
 uncertainty in, 23–24
 value judgments outside realm of, 27, 33
seed propagation protection, 135, 139
Seeley, Ralph, 169–170, 171
September 11 attacks, 105, 158
sewage sludge fertilizers, 41, 47
ship transport, invasive species from, 157–159
Silent Spring (Carson), 26, 36, 58–59, 68
small farms, 41–42, 45, 47–48, 90, 97, 124–127
social bias, drug use and, 175, 180
solar power, 98, 103–104, 106, 109, 112
"sound science" movement, 28
soybeans, 100, 102, 119, 123, 129
special interest groups, 22, 30, 46
StarLink, 127
state and local government
 air quality standard incentives, 93
 climate change policy, 203–206
 drug laws and, 172, 175–179
 invasive species control, 159–160, 163, 166
 land use laws, 187–188, 190, 209
 left-/right-wing view of, 18
 organic food certification and, 42–45
 pesticide regulation, 70, 74, 76–77, 78
 Renewable Portfolio Standards (RPS), 105, 205
 TMDL enforcement, 87, 88–89, 91–92
 water regulations, 81, 87–88, 92, 96, 97, 209
 yard restrictions, 184–188, 194
subsidies, 19, 89–91, 96–97, 107–111, 113, 204
sugarcane ethanol, 100–101, 109, 111
superweeds, 120–121, 123, 128
sustainable food production
 current organic practices as, 14, 35, 38, 49, 51, 52
 locally produced foods, 52–53, 54
 "sustainably harvested" claims, 41–42, 45

Tallamy, Douglas, 151
taxes
 breaks for alternative energy, 104–105, 109
 BTU, 108
 carbon tax, 213, 214
 illegal drugs and, 172, 178, 181
 neighborhood restrictions and, 190, 191
 right-wing favoring, 19
"terminator" seeds, 127
terrorist threat, 86, 105, 110, 158
THC, 169, 181
think tanks, 29
tidal power, 98, 103, 112
tobacco industry, 24, 28, 175, 180, 183

total maximum daily load (TMDL) calculations, 87, 88–89, 91–92
trade agreements, 124, 161
transgenic plants. *See* genetic engineering (GE)
transportation biofuels, 99–103, 106, 111–113. *See also* ethanol
turf breeding, 135–136
2, 4-D (dichlorophenoxyacetic acid), 27, 58, 61, 63, 66, 75, 185–186

underdeveloped countries, 118, 205, 208–209, 210, 212
U.S. Congress
  and alternative energy, 104, 106, 107–108
  climate change legislation, 203, 204, 210–211
  departing from bipartisan cooperation, 16–17
  environmental policies/committees of, 24, 30
  fighting invasive species, 156, 158–159, 162
  marijuana debate, 174, 177
  oral culture of, 22
  and organic foods, 40, 45–47, 49
  and patent law, 143
  regulating hazardous chemicals, 69, 70–73, 92
U.S. Department of Agriculture (USDA)
  advent of food inspections, 66
  Animal and Plant Health Inspection Service (APHIS), 123, 156–159, 161–163
  and organic food, 14, 35–38, 40–44, 46–51, 53, 54, 133
  plant certificate protections and, 139
  politics of pesticides, 71, 74
  protection/support of farming interests, 47, 50, 69, 125, 127
U.S. Environmental Protection Agency (EPA)
  carbon dioxide classification/regulation, 203–204, 211, 213
  and the Clean Air Act, 26
  creation and perspective of, 68, 69
  pesticide policy enforcement, 69–74, 77–78
  water pollution regulation/enforcement, 87, 88–89, 91–92, 95
U.S. Food and Drug Administration (FDA), 66–69, 122–123, 126, 128, 173–175, 181–182
U.S. House of Representatives Committee on Agriculture, 30, 45–46
U.S. Patent and Trademark Office (PTO), 139, 144
U.S. Supreme Court, 72, 89, 140–141, 174, 175, 204
utility company emissions, 205
utility patents, 135–136, 137, 139–141, 145–149

value judgments, in politics, 27, 33
values, personal, 14, 18
vegetable gardens, 86, 88, 185, 192–193

water pollution
  causes/extent of, 83–84
  policies to fight, 81, 86–89, 92, 94–97, 209
  politics of, 91–93
  techniques to prevent, 84–85, 87–88, 94, 95, 97
  total maximum daily load (TMDL) reporting, 87, 88–89

Water Quality Act, 86–87, 91
weeds. *See also* invasive plants
  carbon dioxide and, 202, 216
  noxious, 150–151, 157, 160
  ordinances on, 160, 184–185
  superweeds, 120–121, 123, 128
West Nile virus, 159
White, Donald, 135–136, 140
wildlife, pesticide dangers to, 58, 63–66
wind power, 98, 103, 104, 106, 112, 205
World War II chemicals, 58, 185–186

yard maintenance
  control of noxious weeds, 160
  fertilized lawns, 81, 82, 84, 94–97
  pesticide use in, 27, 56–57, 63, 64, 74–79
yard restrictions, 184–195
  bottom line, 194–195
  conflicts over, 184–185
  government, 186–188
  homeowners' associations, 189–192
  policy options/ratings, 191–194
  political dynamics, 190–191
  and property values, 188, 190, 191, 194, 195
  scientific point of view, 184–186, 193

zebra mussels, 152, 158, 159, 162

WITHDRAWN

Mechanics' Institute Library
3 1750 03382 7588